THE ULTIMATE
4
INGREDIENT
COOKBOOK

OVER 700 RECIPES FROM
BRUNCH TO COCKTAILS, MENUS,
COOKING FOR FRIENDS

JO RICHARDSON

CONVERSION CHART

Conversions from Cups to Imperial and Metric

Solid Measures:

American	Imperial and Metric
2 cups butter or margarine	1 lb/500g
4 cups flour	1 lb/500g
2 cups granulated or caster sugar	1 lb/500g
3 cups icing sugar	1 lb/500g
1 cup rice	8oz/250g

Liquid Measures:

American	Imperial and Metric
⅔ cup	¼ pint/150ml
1¼ cups	½ pint/300ml
2 cups	¾ pint/450ml
2½ cups	1 pint/600ml
3¾ cups	1½ pints/900ml
5 cups	2 pints/1200ml

Oven Temperatures
Recommended Equivalents

°C	°F	Gas Mark
110	225	¼
120	250	½
140	275	1
150	300	2
160	325	3
180	350	4
190	375	5
200	400	6
220	425	7
230	450	8
240	475	9

THE ULTIMATE
4
INGREDIENT
COOKBOOK

Notes:

Nuts and nut derivatives
This book includes dishes made with nuts and nut derivatives. It is advisable for customers with known allergic reactions to nuts and nut derivatives and those who may be potentially vulnerable to these allergies, such as pregnant and nursing mothers, invalids, the elderly, babies and children, to avoid dishes made with nuts and nut oils. It is also prudent to check the labels of pre-prepared ingredients for the possible inclusion of nut derivatives.

Do not refreeze a dish that has been frozen previously.

Eggs should be medium to large unless otherwise stated.

It is advised that eggs should not be consumed raw. This book contains dishes made with raw or lightly cooked eggs. It is prudent for more vulnerable people such as pregnant and nursing mothers, invalids, the elderly, babies and young children to avoid uncooked or lightly cooked dishes made with eggs. Once prepared, these dishes should be kept refrigerated and used promptly.

Milk should be full fat unless otherwise stated.

Poultry should be cooked thoroughly. To test if poultry is cooked, pierce the flesh through the thickest part with a skewer or fork – the juices should run clear, never pink or red.

Fresh herbs should be used, unless otherwise stated. If unavailable, use dried herbs as an alternative but halve the quantities stated.

THE ULTIMATE

4

INGREDIENT
COOKBOOK

OVER 700 RECIPES FROM
BRUNCH TO COCKTAILS, MENUS,
COOKING FOR FRIENDS

CHANCELLOR
PRESS

First published in Great Britain in 2001
by Chancellor Press, an imprint of
Bounty Books, a division of
Octopus Publishing Group Limited,
2-4 Heron Quays, London, England, E14 4JP

Compiled by Jo Richardson

Reprinted 2002, 2003
Text and image copyright © Octopus Publishing Group Limited 2001

ISBN 0 7537 0458 7

A catalogue record for this book is available from the British Library.

Produced by Tien Wah Press
Printed in Malaysia

CONTENTS

INTRODUCTION

The 4-Ingredient Cookbook offers more than 700 recipes, each containing just four ingredients. You will find a wide variety of options for every meal type, taste, and occasion. The majority of recipes serve four people, but there are also plenty of meal choices for two, as well as dishes to cater for larger numbers.

EASE AND SPEED; QUALITY AND VARIETY

Despite having the same number of ingredients, the recipes are wide-ranging in style and content. Almost all are easy to make, and with a limited amount of ingredients, preparation is often minimal. Many are quick both to prepare and cook, and those that take longer to cook invariably need little effort and attention. But fast food doesn't mean junk food in this case. Some recipes are based on convenience foods for ease and speed, but these are products of reasonable quality in terms of taste and nutritional content. Many other convenience foods are not only high in cost but high in fat, salt, and additives, at the same time as being relatively low in nutritional value. The majority of recipes are based on fresh everyday, inexpensive ingredients, while a proportion feature high-quality, luxury ingredients for those special occasions.

ADDED BONUSES

These 4-ingredient recipes offer add-on benefits. Limited preparation means less cleanup time and effort, which in turns means more time to enjoy eating and relaxing! Another "hidden" extra is a lack of waste. For example, the oils and juices of canned and bottled ingredients are used, rather than being thrown away and extra ingredients required, with the added bonus of being ready-flavored. A related benefit is that in many instances the fat content is kept to a minimum—the natural fats contained in meat, for example, are often utilized to cook both the meat itself and other ingredients in the dish, without using additional cooking fats.

STORECUPBOARD STARS

Canned cooked beans and lentils are invaluable storecupboard items; they save all the time and effort of soaking and cooking the dried ingredients. Highly nutritious, they can be used in so many different ways, either whole in soups, casseroles, fillings, or in bakes, or whizzed in a food processor or blender to make dips or pâtés, sauces, and smooth soups. Some have salt and sugar added, so rinse well before use if you are watching your salt and sugar intakes. Canned tomatoes in their various forms are indispensable. Other canned vegetables, while often poor substitutes for their fresh equivalents, can be handy to have in store. Canned corn, including the creamed and Mexican-style kernels as well as whole baby corn, and pimientos are flavorsome and versatile ingredients, while peas, asparagus, and potatoes are good puréed for soups. Canned or bottled olives, including the pimiento-stuffed variety, and capers are not to be missed for adding piquancy to many kinds of dishes. Condensed cream soups offer a traditional and useful shortcut to creating a sauce, particularly for bakes.

Canned fish are another storecupboard essential. Oily fish, such as tuna, sardines, salmon, and anchovies, are especially beneficial nutritionally and are delicious in their own right. Flaked in salads and pasta sauces or mashed and mixed with other ingredients to make dips, pâtés, and patties, they are ultra easy to prepare and versatile. Canned shrimp and crabmeat may pale before the fresh items but have flavor in their own way and are highly convenient. Always make sure you have a store of good-quality bouillion cubes or bouillon powder in a range of flavors for making broth and for pepping up soups, sauces, and grains in an instant.

Canned fruits also have their uses when fresh fruits are not to hand or simply to save time—particularly useful for whizzing up to make smoothies or shakes, or whipped desserts. Use the varieties canned in natural fruit juices. Ready-to-eat dried apricots are great energy- and flavor-boosters for both savory and sweet dishes and drinks.

Bottled sauces and seasonings are another essential element of the smart cook's armory. Worcestershire sauce, hot pepper and/or chili sauce, soy and Hoisin sauce, teriyaki marinade, horseradish sauce, tomato catsup, tomato paste (bottled or in a tube), and good-quality mayonnaise and mustard; these are all vital, classic flavor-enhancers for all manner of savory dishes. Bottled pesto sauce (green and red), salsa, and tahini (sesame seed paste) offer extra pizazz. On the sweet side, good-quality clear honey and fruit preserves can complement savory and sweet ingredients alike, while maple and corn or golden syrup are staples in baking and for toppings and desserts.

Used for cooking or for dressings, olive oil makes a major flavor contribution. Herb- and spice-flavored oils are used extensively in the book to bring an instant extra taste dimension in both roles. These oils can be bought ready prepared but couldn't be easier to make yourself at home—see pages 102-03. Flavored vinegars are also useful for packing flavor into dressings. Again, they can be store-bought, but why not make your own? See pages 104-5.

Dried pasta, noodles, and rice and other grains, in their endless variety of shapes, sizes, and colors, are the ultimate convenience foods, having so many diverse uses and being quick to prepare. Always keep a good stock.

FREEZER STAPLES

Some frozen foods are hard to beat on cost, convenience, and even nutritional value—the vitamin content of some vegetables and fruits is preserved at the optimum level when commercially frozen, whereas in fresh produce it can be depleted during the packaging, transportation, and selling processes. Frozen peas and corn kernels can add color and bite to a wide variety of dishes, and are always popular served as vegetable side-dishes. Cooked frozen peas can also be puréed to make an alternative colorful vegetable accompaniment. Frozen fava beans are also commendable, packs of frozen Chinese-style stir-fry vegetables are useful standbys for knocking up super-fast wok dishes, and frozen spinach is excellent for fillings and sauces. Frozen berries—raspberries, strawberries, and blueberrries- are great for puréeing and creating easy desserts and homemade drinks. Ready-made frozen pastry dough—shortcrust, puff, and phyllo—is another freezer staple, for both sweet and savory pies.

SPICE AND FRAGRANCE

The ingredients list for each recipe excludes the standard seasonings of salt and pepper, although where appropriate the method indicates when to season to taste and on occasions specifies one or the other, for example where the ingredients are salty enough in themselves but could benefit from the addition of pepper. When to season and how much should be a matter of individual taste, and those looking to control or reduce their salt intake can choose to avoid adding salt altogether. Otherwise, it is worth investing in quality sea salt flakes. Pepper should be freshly ground black pepper for maximum flavor.

Spices in general are best bought whole, then ground when required. Cumin and coriander, for example, are at their most fragrant when the seeds are briefly toasted in a dry skillet until their aroma is released, allowed to cool, then ground in a coffee grinder. You may feel this is too much effort, but the difference in flavor is spectacular and is well worth doing if the spice is the central seasoning of the dish. However, ready-ground spice mixes offer instant access to a particular blend of flavors and so are valuable. When you have the time and inclination, consider making up your own spice mixes in a large enough batch to keep you supplied for up to sixth months, although no longer. You really will notice the difference. Otherwise, buy ground spices or spice mixes in small amounts, keep in airtight containers in cool, dry conditions out of sunlight, and use quickly before they lose their pungency.

"Must-have" spices include cumin, coriander, chili powder and/or whole dried chilies and dried chili flakes, cayenne, paprika, cardamom, mustard, fennel seeds, caraway seeds (great for sprinkling over cabbage or zucchini when boiling or steaming), sesame seeds, green peppercorns, ginger, nutmeg, cinnamon, and allspice; and spice mixes—curry powder, garam masala, five-spice powder, Cajun and Creole seasoning, Jamaican jerk seasoning, and apple pie spice.

There is no substitute for fresh herbs. They contribute a unique fresh, fragrant flavor as well as form and texture. Just a few leaves can transform a simple dish into a wonderful taste experience, so it is worth finding and using them as often as you can. Those with maximum impact include basil, cilantro, tarragon, mint, dill, chives, lemongrass, and parsley. Some herbs are excellent dried—their flavor may be different from the fresh herb but it has almost as much, and in some cases more, value. These include oregano, rosemary, bayleaves, thyme, and sage. But again, be ruthless about checking and throwing out ageing dried herbs. Garlic is a vital seasoning, and also has health-promoting qualities. Fresh garlic is without equal, but if you object to the lingering smell on your fingertips, or for convenience or as a standby, there are many other forms that can be used—garlic powder, salt, granules, paste, or bottled minced garlic.

BREAKFASTS
AND
BRUNCHES

FRUITFUL BEGINNINGS

BANANA AND APRICOT CRUNCH

2 bananas
$^1/_2$ cup dried apricots, cut into small pieces
$^1/_2$ cup oats
$^1/_2$ tablespoons maple syrup

Peel and slice bananas. Combine with apricots and divide between 2 serving dishes. Toast oats in a dry heavy-bottomed skillet. Scatter over fruits and drizzle over syrup.

2 servings

SUNSHINE COCKTAIL

2 papayas
2 bananas
14 ounce can pineapple chunks in natural juice
2 tablespoons sunflower seeds, toasted

Halve papayas and scoop out seeds. Peel and slice. Peel and slice bananas. Combine with pineapple and some of juice. Divide between 4 serving dishes. Sprinkle with sunflower seeds.

4 servings

MINTED STRAWBERRIES AND AVOCADO

1 cup strawberries
1 ripe avocado
$^1/_4$ cup orange juice
mint leaves

Hull and halve strawberries. Halve, stone, and pit avocado (see opposite). Dice or slice and gently combine with orange juice and mint.

2 servings

MANGO AND MELON MELANGE

1 mango
$^1/_2$ melon, deseeded
1 cup chopped almonds or pecans
$^1/_2$ cup dry unsweeetened shredded coconut or coconut chips

Working over a bowl to catch juice, slice mango either side of pit. Peel and slice flesh. Peel and slice melon. Combine with nuts and divide between 2 serving dishes. Toast coconut in a dry heavy-bottomed skillet. Scatter over fruits.

2-3 servings

SPICED DRIED FRUIT CUP

2 cups mixed dried fruits
2 cups orange juice
1 teaspoon cinnamon
plain or vanilla yogurt, to serve

In a pan, bring orange juice and cinnamon to a boil. Pour over dried fruits in a heatproof bowl. Let stand. When cool, cover and chill overnight. Spoon into serving dishes and serve with a swirl of yogurt.

4 servings

COOK'S KNOW-HOW

The quickest, cleanest way to pit an avocado is to cut it in half lengthwise, twist the two halves in opposite directions to separate, then stab the pit with a sharp knife and lift out. Always serve avocados soon after preparing to avoid discoloration. Sprinkling with lemon juice helps to prevent this.

EGGS OVER EASY

ASPARAGUS OMELET

1 pound fresh asparagus spears, trimmed
5 eggs
2 tablespoons olive oil
2 tablespoons shredded Parmesan cheese

Cook asparagus in salted boiling water for 10 minutes. Drain, then cut into ¹/₂ inch lengths. In a bowl, beat eggs with seasoning to taste. Stir in asparagus. Heat oil in a large nonstick or heavy-bottomed skillet. Pour in egg mixture, allow to settle, then cover and cook over low heat for about 10 minutes, until almost set. Sprinkle with Parmesan, then broil for 2-3 minutes until set and browned. Serve warm or cold.

4 servings

HAM AND CHEESE OMELET

5 eggs
¹/₂ pound cooked lean ham, finely chopped
2 tablespoons/¹/₄ stick butter
1 cup shredded Swiss cheese

In a bowl, beat eggs with seasoning to taste. Stir in ham. Melt butter in an 8 inch nonstick or heavy-bottomed skillet, pour in egg mixture, and cook, drawing mixture into the middle, until almost set on top. Sprinkle cheese over half the omelet. Fold over and serve.

4 servings

FRESH HERB OMELET

5 eggs
1 tablespoon chopped parsley
1 tablespoon scissored chives
2 tablespoons/¹/₄ stick butter

In a bowl, beat eggs with seasoning to taste. Stir in herbs. Melt butter in an 8 inch nonstick or heavy-bottomed skillet, pour in egg mixture, and cook, drawing mixture into the middle, until set but still creamy on top. Fold over and serve.

2-3 servings

PEPPERONI AND MUSHROOM OMELET

2 tablespoons/¹/₄ stick butter
2 cups mushrooms, sliced
2 ounces pepperoni, thinly sliced
5 eggs

Melt butter in a large nonstick or heavy-bottomed skillet and sauté mushrooms over low heat for 3-4 minutes, until any liquid has evaporated. Increase heat and cook pepperoni for 2 minutes, until lightly browned. In a bowl, beat eggs with seasoning to taste. Pour in eggs and cook, drawing mixture into the middle, until set. Broil for about 2 minutes, until set on top. Serve in wedges.

4 servings

COOK'S KNOW-HOW
Don't add milk to the eggs when making omelets—it makes them heavy. A teaspoon or so of water can lighten the mixture. When cooking, use sweet butter rather than salted, which can cause the eggs to stick to the pan. Use any kind of vegetable or nut oil in place of olive oil.

PESTO OMELET

5 eggs
2 tablespoons olive oil
2 tablespoons ready-made pesto sauce (or use Pistou, see page 85)
2 tablespoons shredded Parmesan cheese

In a bowl, beat eggs with seasoning to taste. Heat oil in an 8 inch
nonstick or heavy-bottomed skillet, pour in eggs, and cook, drawing
mixture into the middle, until set on bottom. Spread pesto over half the
omelet. Fold over and cook for a few seconds more. Sprinkle with
Parmesan. Broil for 1-2 minutes until melted.

2-3 servings

SHRIMP AND CHILI SOUFFLÉ OMELET

3 eggs, separated
2 tablespoons olive oil
1 cup peeled cooked shrimp
1 green chili, deseeded and finely chopped

In a bowl, beat egg yolks with seasoning to taste. In a separate bowl,
beat whites until stiff peaks form, then fold into yolks. Heat half the oil in
a small pan and sauté shrimp and chili for 2 minutes. Heat remaining oil
in a nonstick skillet, pour in mixture, and cook over low heat for 2-3
minutes. Spoon shrimp and chili over half the omelet and broil for about
2 minutes, until set and lightly browned.

2 servings

COOK'S KNOW-HOW
Soufflé omelets are much thicker than ordinary omelets, with a very
light, slightly drier texture. Because the mixture is so thick, it is difficult to
cook it quickly enough from the bottom, so it needs finishing off under a
broiler or in the oven.

ONION FRITTATA

3 tablespoons vegetable oil
1 pound red onions, very finely sliced
5 eggs, beaten
$^2/_3$ cup shredded Parmesan cheese

Heat oil in a heavy-bottomed skillet with a heatproof handle and sauté onions over very low heat, until soft and golden brown. Season well. Increase heat and pour in eggs. Cook for 3 minutes. Sprinkle with Parmesan. Put pan in a preheated oven, 400°F, for 15 minutes, until set and golden. Loosen with a spatula and slide onto a plate. Serve in wedges.
4 servings

SPINACH FRITTATA

6 eggs
1 pound fresh spinach, cooked and drained, or 10 ounce package frozen spinach, thawed and drained
$^1/_2$ teaspoon nutmeg
2 tablespooons/$^1/_4$ stick butter

In a bowl, lightly beat eggs. Stir in spinach, nutmeg, and seasoning to taste. Melt butter in a 12 inch nonstick skillet. Pour in eggs and cook over low heat for about 15 minutes, until almost cooked through. Broil for about 1-2 minutes, until top is set. Serve in wedges.
4 servings

SPANISH TORTILLA

$^2/_3$ cup olive oil
$1^1/_2$ pounds potatoes, thinly sliced
1 large onion, sliced
5 large eggs, beaten

Heat all but 2 tablespoons oil in an 8 inch nonstick skillet, add the potato and onions, and sauté for 15 minutes, stirring frequently, until golden and tender. Stir potato mixture into beaten eggs and season to taste. Let stand for 15 minutes. Clean skillet, then heat remaining oil. Add mixture and cook over low heat for 10 minutes, until almost cooked through. Slide onto a large plate, invert pan over tortilla, then flip back into pan. Cook for 5 minutes. Allow to cool, cut into wedges, and serve.

4-6 servings

SCRAMBLED EGGS WITH SMOKED SALMON

6 large eggs
2 tablespoons cream
2 tablespoons/$^1/_4$ stick butter
3 ounces smoked salmon, cut into thin strips

In a bowl, beat eggs, cream, and seasoning to taste. Melt butter in a pan until foaming. Pour in egg mixture and cook, stirring constantly with a wooden spoon, until thickened but still creamy. Remove from heat and stir in smoked salmon.

2 servings

BAKED EGGS AND HAM

$^1/_4$ pound cooked lean ham
$1^1/_4$ cups evaporated milk or heavy cream
2 tablespoons/$^1/_4$ stick butter
4 eggs

Finely chop ham and mix with milk or cream. Season to taste. Lightly grease 4 small individual ovenproof dishes. Spread sides and bottom with ham mixture. Break eggs one by one into a cup and slide one in each dish. Dot with butter and bake in a preheated oven, 375°F, for about 12 minutes, until set.

4 servings

MEDITERRANEAN EGGS

2 tablespoons Chili Oil (see page 102)
1 red bell pepper, cored, deseeded, and finely chopped
2 ripe beefsteak tomatoes, skinned and chopped
4 eggs

Heat oil in a skillet, add bell pepper and tomatoes, and cook over medium heat for 6-7 minutes. Season to taste. Beat eggs with seasoning to taste. Lower heat and stir in eggs. Cook, stirring gently, until set but still creamy.

2 servings

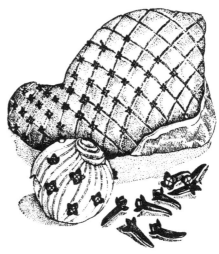

TOAST TOPPERS

CRAB MELT

6¹/₂ ounce can crabmeat, drained
1 cup shredded cheddar cheese
1 teaspoon Dijon mustard
4 thick slices whole-wheat bread

Flake crabmeat. Combine with cheese, mustard, and seasoning to taste.
Lightly toast one side of bread. Spread mixture onto untoasted sides.
Broil until melting.
4 servings

CRISPY BACON AND CHEESE BITES

6 thin slices bacon
4 slices white bread, crusts removed
1¹/₂ cups shredded Monterey Jack cheese
1 teaspoon Worcestershire sauce

Broil bacon until crisp. Allow to cool. Lightly toast one side of bread.
Crumble bacon over untoasted sides and top with cheese. Sprinkle over
Worcestershire Sauce. Broil until cheese is bubbling. Cut into fingers
4 servings

PROSCUITTO AND MOZZARELLA SLICES

1 clove garlic
8 slices French bread
¹/₄ pound thinly sliced proscuitto or cooked lean ham
¹/₄ pound mozzarella, sliced

Cut garlic clove in half and rub cut sides over bread. Lay proscuitto or
ham on each bread slice. Top with mozzarella. Bake in a preheated oven,

425°F, for about 10 minutes, until cheese is bubbling and lightly browned.

4 servings

SOUFFLÉD HAM RAREBITS

4 slices bread, crusts removed
$^1/_4$ pound Monterey Jack jalapeño cheese, thinly sliced
4 thin slices cooked lean ham
4 eggs, separated

Toast one side of bread. Arrange toasted side down on a cookie sheet. Top each slice with one cheese and one ham slice. In a bowl, beat egg yolks with seasoning to taste. In a separate bowl, beat egg whites until stiff peaks form, then fold into yolks. Spoon over each rarebit. Bake in a preheated oven, 350°F, for 15-20 minutes, until soufflé topping is set and golden brown. Serve immediately.

4 servings

SARDINE FINGERS

4 ounce can sardines in olive oil
1-2 tablespoons tomato relish
lemon juice, to taste
4 slices bread, crusts removed

Drain sardines, reserving oil. Mash with a little reserved oil. Combine with relish, lemon juice, and seasoning to taste. Toast one side of bread. Spread mixture onto untoasted sides. Broil until piping hot. Cut into fingers.

2–4 servings

TUNA AND ANCHOVY TOASTS

6 $1/2$ ounce can tuna in olive oil
4 canned or bottled anchovy fillets
10 pimiento-stuffed green olives, finely chopped
4 thick slices whole-wheat bread

Drain tuna, reserving oil. Flake tuna. Pound anchovies with a little reserved oil. Combine anchovy paste with tuna and chopped olives, and season with pepper to taste (don't add salt). Toast one side of bread. Spread mixture onto untoasted sides. Broil until piping hot. Cut into triangles.
4 servings

POTATO HEAVEN

POTATO AND BACON PATTIES

2 cups mashed potatoes
$1/2$ onion, finely chopped
1 tablespoon chopped parsley
4 thin slices bacon

Combine mashed potatoes with onion and parsley. Cook bacon in a nonstick skillet until fat runs and turns crisp. Allow to cool, then crumble and mix with mashed potato mixture. Form into patties and cook in bacon drippings until well browned on both sides.
2 servings

POTATO AND BLUE CHEESE PATTIES

2 cups mashed potatoes
6 scallions, finely chopped
1 cup crumbled blue cheese
2 tablespoons/$1/4$ stick butter

Combine mashed potatoes with scallions and blue cheese. Form into patties. Melt butter in a nonstick skillet. Cook patties until well browned and crisp on both sides.

2 servings

CORNED BEEF HASH

12 ounce can corned beef
1 cup mashed potatoes
1 egg, beaten
2 tablespoons vegetable oil

Flake corned beef. Combine with mashed potatoes, egg, and seasoning to taste. Heat oil in a heavy-bottomed skillet. Spread mixture evenly. Cook over low heat until underside is browned and mixture is thoroughly hot. Fold as an omelet and turn onto a warmed serving plate.

2 servings

HASH BROWN CAKE

2 pounds potatoes, halved, or quartered if large
1 large onion, grated
1 egg, beaten
4 tablespoons/^{1}/$_2$ stick/^{1}/$_4$ cup butter.

Put potatoes in a large pan of salted water. Bring to a boil, cover, and simmer for 5 minutes. Drain, then allow to cool. Grate into a bowl and add onion. Stir in egg and seasoning to taste. Heat butter in a heavy-bottomed skillet. Spread mixture evenly. Cook over medium heat for about 15 minutes, until lightly browned on both sides, turning one section over at a time. Press mixture together with a spatula to form a large pancake. Cook for 2-3 minutes until underside is browned and crisp. Invert cake onto a plate, slide back into pan, and cook other side. Cut into wedges to serve.

4-6 servings

BUBBLE AND SQUEAK

2 cups mashed potatoes
2 cups cooked greens, e.g. cabbage, collard greens, spinach, or leeks
1 onion, finely chopped
4 tablespoons/$^1/_2$ stick/$^1/_4$ cup drippings or butter

Combine potatoes with greens. Heat drippings or butter in a heavy-bottomed skillet. Spread mixture evenly. Cook over low heat until underside is browned and mixture is thoroughly hot. Invert onto a plate, slide back into pan, and cook other side.

4 servings

CRISPY POTATO SKINS

6 large potatoes with unblemished skins
$^1/_4$ cup olive oil

Cut each potato into six pieces. Peel thickly, leaving some of flesh on skins. Use remaining potato flesh in any of mashed potato dishes on pages 24-6. Toss skins in oil to coat thoroughly. Spread on a cookie sheet and season well. Bake in a preheated oven, 400°F, turning occasionally, for 20-25 minutes. Serve with any of the dips opposite.

6–8 servings with a dip

SPICY SWEET POTATO WEDGES

2 large sweet potatoes
2 tablespoons olive oil
1 tablespoon cajun spice

Cut potatoes into wedges. Toss in oil to coat, then sprinkle over spice. Toss again. Bake in a preheated oven, 400°F, for 20-25 minutes, turning occasionally. Serve with any of the dips opposite.

4-6 servings with a dip

CREAM CHEESE AND CHIVES

8 ounce package cream cheese
3 tablespoons scissored chives

Beat together with seasoning to taste.

AVOCADO AND CHILI

2 ripe avocados, halved, pitted, and peeled (see page 15)
2 teaspoons chili sauce, or to taste

Mash avocado with sauce and seasoning to taste.

CILANTRO AND YOGURT

8 ounce carton plain yogurt
2 tablespoons finely chopped cilantro

Combine with seasoning to taste.

BAKED POTATO FILLINGS

4 baking potatoes

Prick potatoes all over with a fork. Bake in a preheated oven, 400°F, for 1-1$^{1}/_{2}$ hours. Serve with one of the fillings on page 28.

4 servings with a filling

HAM, CHEESE, AND CORN

$^1/_2$ x 16 ounce can creamed corn
$^1/_2$ cup diced cooked lean ham
1 cup shredded sharp cheddar cheese

Cut a large cross in each potato. Carefully squeeze and scoop out flesh into a bowl, taking care not to piece skins. Mash potato with corn. Combine with ham and cheese. Season to taste. Spoon mixture back into skins and pile on top. Return to oven for 15 minutes.

TUNA AND BEAN

$6^1/_2$ ounce can tuna in olive oil
$^1/_2$ x 15 ounce can red kidney beans
1 red onion, roughly chopped

Drain tuna, reserving oil. Drain beans, reserving a little liquid. Whizz in a food processor or blender, adding a little reserved oil, bean liquid, and seasoning to taste, until blended but still chunky. Cut a large cross in each baked potato. Spoon over filling and serve immediately.

EGG AND PARMESAN

4 eggs
3 tablespoons grated Parmesan cheese

Slice off top of each baked potato. Scoop out some of flesh (use potato in any recipes on pages 24-6). Break eggs one at a time into a cup. Pour an egg into each potato. Broil until just set. Sprinkle over Parmesan and broil until lightly browned.

TORTILLA TEMPTATION

MUSHROOM AND SOUR CREAM

4 x 6 ounce cans whole mushrooms
2 teaspoons paprika
1 cup sour cream
8 flour tortillas, warmed

Halve or slice mushrooms. Put into a pan with a little of can liquid.
Blend in paprika. Heat through over medium heat. Stir in sour cream.
Heat gently, stirring, for 1-2 minutes. Spoon onto tortillas and roll up.
4 servings

CHICKEN AND CHARBROILED BELL PEPPERS

2 red bell peppers
1 pound boneless, skinless chicken breasts
$^2/_3$ cup mayonnaise
8 flour tortillas, warmed

Broil bell peppers under medium heat, turning frequently, for 8–10
minutes, until blistered and charred. Wrap in aluminum foil and let stand
for a few minutes. Meanwhile, broil chicken under medium heat for
about 6 minutes on each side. Peel away skin from bell peppers. Halve,
deseed, and slice flesh. Slice chicken. Combine chicken and bell peppers
with mayonnaise. Season to taste. Spoon onto tortillas and roll up.
4 servings

CHILI BEAN AND CHEESE

15 ounce can chili beans or beans in a spicy sauce
4 scallions, thinly sliced
$^1/_2$ cup shredded sharp cheddar cheese

4 flour tortillas, warmed

Drain beans, reserving sauce and about 2 tablespoons beans. Put remainder in a food processor or blender with a little sauce and process until blended but still chunky. Heat in a heavy-bottomed skillet with whole beans, adding a little more sauce. Stir in cheese, and cook until melted. Spoon onto tortillas and roll up.

2 servings

HOT SALSA SHRIMP

3 cups chunky salsa
$2^1/_2$ cups peeled cooked shrimp
$^2/_3$ cup sour cream
8 flour tortillas, warmed

Put salsa and shrimp into a pan and heat until thoroughly hot. Spoon onto tortillas. Top with sour cream. Roll up and serve immediately.

4 servings

EGGPLANT AND MOZZARELLA

$^1/_2$ cup Garlic Oil (see page 102)
3 large eggplants, thickly sliced
6 ounces mozzarella or smoked mozzarella cheese, thinly sliced
8 flour tortillas, warmed

Brush a cookie sheet with oil. Lay eggplant slices on top and brush generously with oil. Bake in a preheated oven, 400°F, for 15-20 minutes, until tender. Cover with cheese and return to oven for a few minutes until melting. Transfer to tortillas, drizzle with oil, and roll up.

4 servings

SERIOUS SANDWICHES

SALAMI STACK

$^1/_2$ cup garlic and herbs soft spreadable cheese
6 slices crusty white or brown bread
12 thin slices salami, rind removed
1 cup cole slaw

Spread cheese onto 2 bread slices. Top each with 3 salami slices and cole slaw. Spread cheese onto 2 more bread slices and put spread side down on each sandwich. Spread uppermost sides of bread with more cheese. Top each with 3 salami slices and cole slaw. Spread remaining bread slices with remainder of cheese. Invert on each sandwich, press down, then cut stack into quarters. Pin layers together with a toothpick if necessary.

2 servings

CHILI BEAN STACK

15 ounce can chili beans or beans in a spicy sauce
1 red onion, finely chopped
12 thin slices bacon
9 thick slices white crusty bread

Drain off sauce from beans and reserve. Whizz beans in a food processor or blender, adding a little sauce to make a thick mixture, or mash with a fork. Heat with the onion in a pan over medium heat. Meanwhile, broil bacon until crisp. Toast bread on one side. Spread bean mixture onto untoasted sides of 3 bread slices. Top each with 2 bacon slices. Add 1 bread slice to each sandwich, untoasted side down. Spread with remaining bean mixture, then top each with 2 bacon slices and 1 bread slice, untoasted side down. Cut in half diagonally, or into quarters.

3-4 servings

CHUNKY PAN-FRIED SANDWICH

8 medium-thick slices white or whole-wheat bread, crusts removed
4 slices cooked lean ham
$^{1}/_{4}$ pound Monterey Jack or cheddar cheese, thinly sliced
4 tablespoons/$^{1}/_{2}$ stick/$^{1}/_{4}$ cup butter

Top each of 4 bread slices with a ham slice and cheese slices. Top with remaining bread slices and press down lightly. Spread a little butter on top of each sandwich. Heat a large, dry skillet over medium heat. Fry two sandwiches, buttered sides down, over low heat for 2-3 minutes, until golden brown. Butter top of sandwiches, carefully turn over, and fry for a further 3-4 minutes, pressing sandwiches down with a spatula until golden brown on both sides. Keep warm while frying remaining sandwiches. Cut each sandwich into 4 triangles.

4 servings

EGG-FRIED SWISS CHEESE SANDWICH

4 slices white bread, crusts removed
$^{1}/_{2}$ pound Swiss cheese, thinly sliced
4 tablespoons/$^{1}/_{2}$ stick/$^{1}/_{4}$ cup butter
2 eggs, beaten

Top 2 bread slices with cheese, then remaining bread slices. Press around the edges to seal. Melt butter in a large skillet. Dip one sandwich at a time in egg and add to pan. Fry for 2-3 minutes on each side, until lightly browned. Serve immediately.

2 servings

APPETIZERS AND SOUPS

FRUITY COCKTAILS

CUCUMBER AND STRAWBERRY SALAD

1 small cucumber, peeled and very thinly sliced
1-2 tablespoons bottled French vinaigrette dressing
1³/₄ cups strawberries, hulled and thinly sliced
handful of mint leaves

In a bowl, toss cucumber slices with dressing. Season to taste. Arrange cucumber and strawberry slices on a serving platter or individual plates. Scatter over mint. Chill for at least 30 minutes before serving.

4 servings

PROSCUITTO AND MELON

1 large Cantaloupe or Honeydew melon
6–8 thin slices proscuitto
cayenne pepper

Cut melon in half and scoop out seeds. Using a melon baller, scoop out balls of melon. Broil proscuitto until crisp. Cut or break into bite-size pieces. Pile melon balls into individual dishes and scatter over proscuitto. Sprinkle over a little cayenne.

4 servings

FIGS WITH PARMA HAM

4 ripe figs
2 tablespoons lemon juice
¹/₄ cup olive oil
12 paper-thin slices Parma ham

Cut figs into quarters and remove stems. Put in a nonmetallic dish with lemon juice and oil. Season to taste and toss gently. Let stand for 5 minutes. Arrange Parma ham on a serving dish and spoon over figs and dressing. Serve at room temperature.

4 servings

COOK'S KNOW-HOW

To segment citrus fruits, remove all white pith and outer skin. Working around the fruit (and over a bowl to catch juice), cut between the skin and flesh of each segment and gently push out the segments.

PEAR AND BLUE CHEESE SALAD

4 pears, peeled, cut into eighths, and cored
$1/2$ pound fresh baby spinach or lettuce
4 walnuts, chopped
2 cups crumbled blue cheese

Heat a griddle pan or nonstick skillet and cook pear slices on each side for 1 minute. Pile spinach or lettuce onto a serving platter and arrange pears on top. Sprinkle with walnuts and blue cheese. Serve immediately.

4 servings

PINK GRAPEFRUIT AND AVOCADO COCKTAIL

1 pink grapefruit
1 ripe avocado
$2/3$ cup peeled cooked shrimp
2 tablespoons mayonnaise

Remove peel and pith from grapefruit. Working over a bowl to catch juice, remove fruit segments. Reserve a few segments for garnish. Cut remainder into small pieces and put into a bowl. Halve avocado, pit, and slice (see page 15). Mix with grapefruit pieces, shrimp, and mayonnaise. Spoon into individual dishes. Garnish with reserved grapefruit segments.

2 servings

VEGETABLE TASTERS

ROASTED ASPARAGUS WITH CILANTRO AND LIME

1^1/$_2$ pounds fresh asparagus spears
^{1}/$_2$ cup olive oil
3 tablespoons lime juice
handful of cilantro leaves, torn

Trim tough part of asparagus stalks. Peel skin from about 2 inches of base of each stalk. Arrange asparagus in a single layer in a shallow roasting pan. Spoon over half the oil and shake lightly to coat. Roast in a preheated oven, 400°F, for about 20 minutes, until just tender, turning once during cooking. Allow to cool. Transfer to a shallow serving dish. Spoon over remaining oil and lime juice. Season to taste and toss gently. Garnish with cilantro.

4-6 servings

CHARBROILED BELL PEPPERS

6 red, yellow, or orange bell peppers
handful of basil leaves, torn
2 tablespoons Garlic Oil (see page 102)
1 tablespoon red wine vinegar

Broil bell peppers under medium heat, turning frequently, for 8-10 minutes, until blistered and charred all over. Wrap in aluminum foil or a clean damp dish towel. Let stand for a few minutes. Peel away skins. Halve bell peppers, and remove cores and seeds. Slice into strips and put into a serving dish with any juices. Scatter over basil. Whisk oil and vinegar together, with seasoning to taste, until blended. Pour over bell peppers and toss to coat. Cover and let stand at room temperature for 1 hour.

4 servings

BELL PEPPER AND TUNA ROLLS

4 red bell peppers
3 tablespoons bottled Italian dressing
6½ ounce can tuna, drained
1-2 tablespoons capers

Broil bell peppers under medium heat, turning frequently, for 8-10 minutes, until blistered and charred all over. Wrap in aluminum foil or a clean damp dish towel. Let stand for a few minutes. Peel away skins. Cut each bell pepper lengthwise into 3 strips, discarding stems, cores, and seeds. Put into a bowl with any juices. Pour over dressing and toss to coat. Cover and let stand at room temperature for 30 minutes. Flake tuna and combine with capers. Spoon mixture onto each bell pepper strip and roll up. Arrange in a shallow serving dish and spoon over dressing.

4 servings

GARLIC MUSHROOMS

3 tablespoons olive oil
2 cloves garlic, finely chopped
1 pound fresh button mushrooms
½ cup pine nuts

Heat oil in a large, heavy-bottomed skillet over medium-high heat. Sauté garlic for about 3 minutes until just beginning to brown. Sauté mushrooms with pine nuts and seasoning to taste for about 10 minutes, until tender.

4 servings

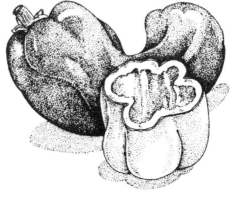

STUFFED TOMATOES WITH RICOTTA AND HERBS

4 beefsteak tomatoes
1 cup ricotta cheese
1 clove garlic, minced
2 tablespoons chopped oregano or basil

Make sure tomatoes stand upright; if not, cut a small slice from base. Slice top off each tomato. Carefully scoop out tomato pulp, finely chop, and put into a bowl. Upturn tomato shells and let drain. Combine ricotta, garlic, herb, and seasoning to taste. Spoon back into tomato shells.

4 servings

SAVORY DIPS

TZATSIKI

1 cucumber, peeled and shredded
2 cups plain yogurt
3 garlic cloves, minced
1 tablespoon chopped mint

Drain cucumber and put into a bowl. Add yogurt, garlic, and seasoning to taste. Mix well. Chill for 2 hours. Turn into a serving bowl and sprinkle with mint. Serve with Pita Chips (see page 45).

6 servings

FAVA BEAN AND MINT DIP

1 pound fresh or frozen fava beans
large handful of mint leaves
3-4 tablespoons olive oil
2 tablespoons lemon juice

Cook beans in boiling salted water until tender. Drain, reserving cooking liquid. Rinse beans under cold running water. Put beans into a

food processor or blender with mint, oil, and lemon juice. Purée, adding enough cooking liquid to give a soft consistency. Season to taste and adjust amount of lemon juice and oil, if necessary. Serve at room temperature with Crudités, or Pita or Bread Fingers (see pages 44-5).
4-6 servings

HUMMUS

14 ounce can chickpeas (garbanzo beans)
2 tablespoons tahini (sesame seed paste)
2 garlic cloves, minced
1 tablespoon lemon juice, or to taste

Drain chickpeas, reserving liquid. Put into a food processor or blender with tahini, garlic, and lemon juice. Blend until smooth, adding the reserved liquid to make a creamy consistency. Serve with Pita Chips or Fingers, or Crudités (see pages 44-5).
4 servings

GUACAMOLE

2 large ripe avocados
1 tablespoon lemon or lime juice
1 clove garlic, minced
1-2 teaspoons Tabasco sauce, to taste

Halve, pit, and peel avocados (see page 15). Roughly chop and put into a food processor or blender with remaining ingredients. Whizz until blended but still a little chunky. Serve with Pita or Bread Fingers or Crudités (see pages 44-5).
4 servings

ROASTED EGGPLANT DIP

3 eggplants
2 tablespoons Garlic Oil (see page 102)
juice of 1 lemon
1 fresh green chili, deseeded and chopped

Prick the eggplants all over with a fork. Brush with a little oil. Put directly on oven shelf in a preheated oven, 400°F, for 50 minutes–1 hour, until soft. Remove from oven and let cool. Cut off stems. Peel, then put flesh into a food processor or blender with the remainder of the oil, lemon juice, chili, and seasoning to taste. Blend until smooth. Chill for an hour or so before serving. Serve with Pita Chips or Fingers, or Bread Fingers (see page 45).

4-6 servings

GARLIC AND ANCHOVY DIP

6 cloves garlic, minced
6 canned or bottled anchovy fillets, mashed
$^1/_3$ cup olive oil
6 tablespoons/$^3/_4$ stick butter

Pound garlic with anchovies to form a paste. Gradually stir in oil. Put into a pan with butter. Cook over low heat for about 10 minutes, stirring occasionally. Serve hot with Crudités or Bread Fingers (see pages 44-5).

4 servings

CARROT AND CILANTRO DIP

1 pound carrots, grated
$^3/_4$ cup orange juice
$^1/_4$ cup cream cheese
3 tablespoons cilantro leaves

Put carrot into a pan with orange juice and 1^1/$_4$ cups water. Cover and simmer for 40 minutes, until very tender. Drain, reserving cooking liquid, and allow to cool. Transfer to a food processor or blender. Add cheese, cilantro, and a little cooking liquid. Blend until smooth. Add seasoning to taste and a little more liquid, if needed. Blend again. Chill for 30 minutes before serving with Pita Chips or Fingers, Bread Fingers, or Crudités (see pages 44-5).

4 servings

COTTAGE CHEESE AND CRABMEAT DIP

1 cup cottage cheese
5 tablespoons sour cream
2 x 1^1/$_2$ ounce cans dressed crabmeat
2-3 tablespoons finely chopped cucumber

Sieve cottage cheese into a bowl. Combine with the remaining ingredients and season to taste. Serve with Crudités, or Pita or Bread Fingers (see pages 44-5).

4–6 servings

BLUE CHEESE DIP

1 cup cottage cheese
2 cups crumbled blue cheese
^{2}/$_3$ cup sour cream
2-3 tablespoons mayonnaise

Sieve cottage cheese into a bowl. Combine with remaining ingredients and seasoning to taste. Serve with Crudités, Pita Fingers or Chips, or Bread Fingers (see pages 44-5).

4-6 servings

TUNA AND PINEAPPLE

6$^1/_2$ ounce can tuna, drained
$^2/_3$ cup mayonnaise
$^3/_4$ cup canned pineapple chunks in natural juice, drained
1 tablespoon garam masala or curry powder

Whizz ingredients in a food processor or blender with seasoning to
taste until blended. Chill for at least 30 minutes before serving. Serve with
Pita Chips (see page 45).   4 servings

SALMON AND GHERKIN

15 ounce can pink salmon, drained and bones removed
$^2/_3$ cup sour cream
2-3 tablespoons mayonnaise
4 cocktail gherkins, roughly chopped

Whizz ingredients in a food processor or blender, with seasoning to
taste, until blended. Chill for at least 30 minutes before serving. Serve
with Pita Chips or Crudités (see pages 44-5).
4-6 servings

SPEEDY PÂTÉS

LIVER PÂTÉ

$^1/_2$ cup liver paté or liver sausage
$^1/_4$ cup thick cream
1-2 tablespoons finely chopped olives
3 tablespoons finely chopped parsley

Whizz the first three ingredients in a food processor or blender until
blended. Form into 12 rolls. Roll in parsley and chill for 30 minutes.
Serve with hot Bread Fingers (see page 45) or toast. 4 servings

CHICKEN LIVER PÂTÉ

4 tablespoons/$^1/_4$ cup/$^1/_2$ stick butter
8 fresh chicken livers, or frozen and defrosted
1 clove garlic, chopped
$^1/_4$ cup heavy cream

Melt butter in a skillet and cook livers for about 3-4 minutes, until just tender. Add garlic and cook for another minute or so. Transfer to a food processor or blender, add cream and seasoning to taste, and blend until smooth. Serve with hot buttered toast, or hot Bread Fingers or Melba Toast (see page 45).   4 servings

SMOKED SALMON MOUSSE

6 ounces smoked salmon pieces
$^1/_4$ cup cream cheese
$^2/_3$ cup sour cream
1 tablespoon lemon juice

Put smoked salmon in a food processor or blender and process or a few seconds. Add remaining ingredients with seasoning to taste and blend until smooth. Chill for 30 minutes. Serve with Melba Toast (see page 45).
6 servings

POTTED TUNA AND CAPERS

$6^1/_2$ ounce can tuna, drained
$^1/_2$ cup mayonnaise
2-3 teaspoons chopped capers
1 tablespoon chopped parsley

Whizz the ingredients together in a food processor or blender until well blended. Serve with hot toast and butter or Melba Toast (see page 45).
4 servings

MACKEREL PÂTÉ

$^1/_2$ pound peppered mackerel fillets
$^3/_4$ cup sour cream
4 tablespoons/$^1/_2$ stick/$^1/_4$ cup butter, melted
grated zest of 1 lemon

Remove skin and bones from mackerel. Put into a food processor or blender with sour cream. With the motor running, gradually add melted butter and zest. Chill for 30 minutes. Serve with hot whole-wheat toast, or hot Bread Fingers or Melba Toast (see page 45).

6 servings

SMOKED TROUT CREAM

$^1/_2$ pound smoked trout fillets
$^1/_2$ cup cream cheese
1 tablespoon chopped parsley
2 teaspoons creamed horseradish

Whizz ingredients in a food processor or blender until smooth. Serve with hot whole-wheat toast, or hot Bread Fingers or Melba Toast (see page 45).

6 servings

DIP DUNKERS

CRUDITÉS

carrots, bell pepper, cucumber, celery

Peel carrots and cut into matchsticks. Cut bell pepper (green, red, yellow, or orange, or a mixture) into strips or rings. Cut cucumber into matchsticks, cutting off seeds, or cut into thick slices. Cut celery into matchsticks or cut stalks into 2 inch lengths, to use as scoops.

PITA CHIPS

brown or white pita pockets

Split pita pockets down one side and open out. Using kitchen scissors, cut into triangles. Broil under medium heat until crisp.

PITA FINGERS

4 white or brown pita pockets
3 tablespoons Chili or Garlic Oil (see page 102)
chili powder or onion salt

Brush pita pockets with oil. Sprinkle with chili powder or onion salt. Broil each side for about 3-4 minutes, until puffed up. Cut into fingers. Wrap in a clean dish towel or aluminum foil to keep warm.

BREAD FINGERS

thick slices white bread, crusts removed
corn or sunflower oil, for frying
garlic or celery salt

Cut bread into $1^1/_2$ inch wide fingers. Heat oil in a pan until almost smoking. Fry for about 1 minute on each side, until golden brown. Drain on paper towels. Sprinkle with garlic or celery salt. Serve hot with pâtés (see pages 42-4) or cold with dips (see pages 38-42).

MELBA TOAST

thin slices white bread, crusts removed

Toast bread on both sides, then split through the middle. Bake in a slow oven until crisp and browned. Serve with pâtés (see pages 42–4).

HOT SEAFOOD

BAKED SCALLOPS WITH BUTTER AND BREADCRUMBS

8-10 scallops in their shells, prepared
8 tablespoons/1 stick/^{1}/$_2$ cup butter
4 tablespoons fresh bread crumbs
2 tablespoons chopped parsley

Remove scallops from their shells, reserving 4 rounded shell halves. Chop white flesh coarsely, leaving orange coral whole. Divide chopped scallops and coral evenly between 4 shells. Season to taste and dot with half the butter. Sprinkle bread crumbs equally between shells and use remaining butter to dot over tops. Cook in center of a preheated oven, 350°F, for about 30 minutes, until top is crisp and bubbly. Sprinkle with parsley and serve immediately.

4 servings

PAN-FRIED SCALLOPS WITH BACON

12 scallops, shelled and prepared
4 slices smoked bacon
1-2 tablespoons chopped parsley
squeeze of lemon juice

Cut each scallop in half. Cut bacon into small pieces. Heat a heavy-bottomed skillet and fry bacon until beginning to brown. Reduce heat to medium-low. Cook scallops for a minute either side—be careful not to overcook. Add parsley and lemon juice, and heat through for 1 minute. Serve immediately.

4 servings

GRIDDLED SHRIMP WITH MINT AND LEMON

1¹/₂ pounds large shrimp, peeled and deveined (see page 173)
1 large bunch mint, chopped
2 cloves garlic, minced
¹/₂ cup lemon juice

Put shrimp into a glass bowl. Add mint (reserve a few leaves for
garnish), garlic, lemon juice, and seasoning to taste. Mix well. Cover and
chill in the refrigerator for at least 30 minutes, preferably overnight. Heat
a griddle pan or nonstick skillet. Cook shrimp with marinade for 2-3
minutes on each side. Serve garnished with mint.

6 servings

BAKED EGGS WITH SMOKED SALMON

butter, for greasing
2 ounces smoked salmon, cut into small pieces
4 eggs
4 tablespoons heavy cream

Grease 4 ramekin dishes and divide smoked salmon between them.
Break one egg into each dish, on top of smoked salmon. Season to taste
and top with 1 tablespoon cream. Put dishes in a roasting pan with water
to reach halfway up dishes. Cook in a preheated oven, 350°F, for 10-15
minutes, until set. Serve immediately.

4 servings

HOT CRAB CUPS

6¹/₂ ounce can crabmeat, drained
¹/₂ cup thick heavy cream
1 cup finely shredded cheddar cheese
3 tablespoons fresh bread crumbs

Flake crabmeat and combine with cream and all but 2 tablespoons cheese. Spoon into 4 ramekin dishes. Mix remaining cheese with bread crumbs and sprinkle over top of each. Transfer to a cookie sheet and bake in a preheated oven, 425°F, for 15–20 minutes, until golden brown on top.
4 servings

COLD SEAFOOD

TUNA AND BEANS

$6^{1}/_{2}$ ounce can tuna, drained
15 ounce can cannellini beans, drained
$^{1}/_{2}$ onion, finely sliced
2-3 tablespoons olive oil

Break tuna into chunks with a fork. Separate onion into rings. Toss tuna, beans, and onion rings with oil. Season to taste.
3-4 servings

SALMON ROLLS

8 thin slices smoked salmon
6 ounce carton garlic and herbs soft spreadable cheese
$^{1}/_{4}$ cup chopped walnuts
squeeze of lemon juice

Trim smoked salmon to strips 8–10 inches long, 2–3 inches wide. Finely chop any trimmings and blend with cheese, walnuts, and lemon juice. Spread each slice with mixture and roll up. Cover and chill for 30 minutes before serving.
4 servings

SHRIMP AND AVOCADO COCKTAIL

2 ripe avocados
1$^1/_2$ cups peeled cooked shrimp
$^1/_2$ cup mayonnaise
1 tablespoon lemon juice

Halve and pit avocados (see page 15). Peel, then dice flesh. Gently combine with shrimp, mayonnaise, and lemon juice. Cover and chill for 30 minutes before serving.

4 servings

CRABMEAT AND PAPAYA COCKTAIL

1 papaya
6$^1/_2$ ounce can crabmeat, or fresh crabmeat
2-3 tablespoons mayonnaise
1 teaspoon paprika

Halve papaya and scoop out seeds. Put one half on each of 2 serving dishes. Combine crabmeat with mayonnaise and pile into papaya halves. Sprinkle with paprika.

2 servings

EGG AND SHRIMP MAYONNAISE

2 hard-cooked eggs
2 x 4$^1/_2$ ounce cans shrimp, drained
2 tablespoons mayonnaise
$^1/_2$ small red bell pepper, diced

Shell and halve eggs. Divide between 2 serving dishes. Combine shrimp and mayonnaise. Spoon over egg halves. Scatter diced bell pepper around eggs.

2 servings

EASY CHEESEY

MOZZARELLA, AVOCADO, AND TOMATO SALAD

1 large ripe avocado, pitted, peeled, and sliced (see page 15)
$^1/_2$ pound mozzarella, sliced
2 beefsteak tomatoes, sliced
2-3 tablespoons bottled French vinaigrette or Italian dressing

Arrange overlapping slices of avocado, mozzarella, and tomatoes on a serving platter. Drizzle over dressing and season to taste.

4 servings

FETA, CUCUMBER, AND MINT SALAD

1 large cucumber, peeled and cut into chunks
$2^1/_2$-3 cups crumbled feta cheese
2 tablespoons chopped mint
2-3 tablespoons bottled French vinaigrette dressing

Put cucumber and feta into a bowl. Add mint and drizzle over dressing. Season to taste and toss gently. Chill for 30 minutes before serving.

4 servings

SWISS CHEESE AND APPLE COCKTAIL

$^2/_3$ cup plain yogurt
1 tablespoon lemon juice, or to taste
2 red-skinned dessert apples, diced or sliced
6 ounces Swiss or Gruyère cheese, cut into 1 inch cubes

Combine yogurt with lemon juice and season to taste. Toss apples and cheese in dressing. Serve immediately.

2 servings

GORGONZOLA AND GRAPE

$^2/_3$ cup sour cream
1-2 tablespoons mayonnaise
12 ounces seedless black grapes, halved
$2^1/_2$–3 cups crumbled Gorgonzola (or another blue cheese)

Combine sour cream with mayonnaise and season to taste. Toss grapes
and cheese in dressing. Cover and chill for 30 minutes before serving.
4 servings

BROILED HALOUMI CHEESE AND BEEFSTEAK TOMATOES

2 beefsteak tomatoes, sliced
6 ounces haloumi cheese, thickly sliced
a few torn basil leaves
1-2 tablespoons Garlic Oil (see page 102)

Arrange tomato slices on 2 serving plates. Cover broiler rack with
aluminum foil. Put cheese slices on top and broil until bubbling and
lightly browned. Top tomato slices with cheese, scatter with basil, and
drizzle over oil.
2 servings

CHILLED SOUPS

CUCUMBER AND GARLIC

1 large cucumber, peeled and roughly chopped
1 clove garlic, minced
1^1/$_4$ cups light cream
about 2 cups creamy milk

Put cucumber, garlic, and cream into a food processor or blender.
Whizz until smooth. Thin to the right consistency with milk and season
to taste. Chill for at least 1 hour before serving.
3–4 servings

AVOCADO AND LIME

4 ripe avocados
4 scallions, chopped
4 cups cold chicken broth
juice of 1 lime

Halve and pit avocados (see page 15). Peel and chop flesh. Put into a
food processor or blender with remaining ingredients and whizz until
blended. Chill for at least 1 hour before serving.
4 servings

ZUCCHINI AND PIMIENTO

1 pound young zucchini, sliced
2 x 4 ounce jars pimientos, drained and chopped
3 cups cold chicken broth
1^1/$_4$ cups plain yogurt

Whizz ingredients in a food processor or blender until smooth. Chill
for at least 1 hour before serving.   4 servings

QUICK GAZPACHO

14^{1}/$_{2}$ ounce can seasoned tomatoes
1 large red bell pepper, cored, deseeded, and chopped
1 clove garlic, minced
2 tablespoons bottled Italian dressing

Whizz ingredients in a food processor or blender until blended. Add seasoning to taste. Cover and chill for at least 1 hour before serving.
2-3 servings

BEETS AND SOUR CREAM

2 pounds cooked beets
3^{1}/$_{2}$ cups cold beef broth
^{1}/$_{2}$-1 teaspoon garlic salt
1^{1}/$_{4}$ cups sour cream

Peel beets, if necessary, and roughly chop. Put into a food processor or blender, add a little stock, and whizz until blended. Add remainder of stock and garlic salt, and process until well blended. Chill for at least 1 hour. Pour into chilled serving bowls and swirl sour cream on top.
4 servings

CELERY AND TOMATO

14^{1}/$_{2}$ ounce can seasoned tomatoes
1 small onion, finely chopped
14 ounce can cream of celery soup
1 tablespoon tomato paste

Put tomatoes and onion in a food processor or blender and whizz to blend. Add celery soup and tomato purée, and whizz again to blend. Chill for at least 1 hour before serving.
4 servings

HOT SOUPS

PEA AND HAM

16 ounce can processed peas
4 slices cooked lean ham, chopped
$2^1/_2$ cups ham or vegetable broth
$1^1/_4$ cups creamy milk

Put peas and liquid from can with ham into a food processor or blender. Process until blended. Add broth and whizz until smooth. Transfer to a pan. Stir in milk and season to taste. Gently heat, stirring, until hot but not boiling.

4 servings

BLACK-EYE PEA AND BACON

4 slices bacon
2 x 14 ounce can black-eye peas
$2^1/_2$ cups ham or vegetable broth
$1^1/_4$ cups creamy milk

Broil bacon. Allow to cool, then chop. Put 1 can of peas and liquid from can with broth into a food processor or blender. Process until smooth. Transfer to a pan. Drain second can and add beans to pan with bacon. Bring to a boil. Reduce heat and stir in milk. Season to taste. Gently heat, stirring, until hot but not boiling.

4–6 servings

CHORIZO AND BEANS

$3^1/_2$ cups pork or vegetable broth
6 ounces chorizo, skinned and thickly sliced
15 ounce can lima beans (or any other canned beans), drained
$14^1/_2$ ounce can seasoned tomatoes

Bring broth to a boil in a large pan. Crumble in chorizo. Add beans, tomatoes, and seasoning to taste. Cover and simmer for about 15 minutes.
4 servings

ASPARAGUS

2 tablespoons/$^1/_4$ stick butter
1 small onion, chopped
15 ounce can asparagus pieces
3$^1/_2$ cups chicken broth

Melt butter in a large pan and sauté onion for 5 minutes, until soft and golden. Add asparagus with liquid from can and broth. Bring to a boil, stirring, then reduce heat and simmer for 5 minutes. Add seasoning to taste. Transfer to a food processor or blender and purée until smooth. (Blend in 2 batches if necessary). Return soup to pan and reheat until hot but not boiling.
4 servings

LEEK AND POTATO

2 tablespoons/$^1/_4$ stick butter
2 leeks, trimmed and finely sliced
16 ounce can potatoes, drained and chopped
3$^1/_2$ cups chicken broth

Melt butter in a large pan and sauté leeks for about 10 minutes, until soft. Add potatoes and broth. Bring to a boil, stirring, then reduce heat and simmer for 5 minutes. Add seasoning to taste. Transfer to a food processor or blender and purée until smooth. (Purée in 2 batches if necessary). Return soup to pan and reheat until hot but not boiling.
4 servings

BLUE CHEESE AND CELERY

4 celery stalks, chopped
$3^1/_2$ cups chicken broth
1 cup crumbled blue cheese
2-3 tablespoons light cream

In a large pan, cook celery in simmering broth for about 20 minutes, until soft. Transfer to food processor or blender and purée until smooth. Return to pan and add cheese. Heat gently, stirring, until cheese melts. Season with pepper to taste. Divide soup between 4 serving bowls. Swirl a little cream into each.

4 servings

CRABMEAT WITH GINGER

2 cups fish broth
$^1/_2$-1 inch piece fresh gingerroot, peeled and chopped
2 teaspoons rice wine or dry sherry
$6^1/_2$ ounce can crabmeat, or fresh crabmeat

Bring broth to a boil in a large pan. Add ginger, wine or sherry, and crabmeat with any liquid from can, if using. Simmer for about 10 minutes. Serve very hot.   2 servings

CHICKEN AND CORN

$3^1/_2$ cups chicken broth
16 ounce can creamed corn
$1^1/_4$ cups diced cooked chicken
2 teaspoons light soy sauce

Bring broth to a boil in a large pan. Add creamed corn, chicken, and soy sauce. Taste and add seasoning if needed. Reduce heat and simmer for about 10 minutes.   4 servings

PEA AND ARTICHOKE

14 ounce can artichoke hearts, drained and chopped
10 ounce package frozen peas
3^1/$_2$ cups chicken broth
^{1}/$_3$ cup light cream

Bring broth to a boil in a large pan. Add peas, artichoke hearts, and seasoning to taste. Reduce heat and simmer for 15 minutes. Transfer to food processor or blender and purée until smooth. Return to pan and reheat until hot but not boiling. Stir in cream and adjust seasoning if necessary.

4 servings

SHRIMP GUMBO

5 cups fish broth
14^1/$_2$ ounce can seasoned tomatoes
^{1}/$_3$ cup long-grain rice
2 cups peeled cooked shrimp

Bring broth, tomatoes, and rice to a boil in a large pan, stirring. Reduce heat, cover, and simmer for about 15 minutes. Add shrimp and simmer for another 5 minutes.

4 servings

FRENCH ONION

4 tablespoons/^{1}/$_2$ stick/^{1}/$_4$ cup butter
1^1/$_2$ pounds onions, thinly sliced
2 teaspoons all-purpose flour
4^1/$_4$ cups beef broth

Melt butter in a large, heavy-bottomed pan. Cook onions over very low heat, stirring occasionally, for 20-30 minutes, until soft and deep golden brown. Stir in flour and cook over very low heat, stirring constantly, for about 5 minutes. Add broth and bring to a boil, stirring. Reduce heat, season to taste, and simmer, covered, for 15-20 minutes. Serve with Swiss Cheese Toasts (see page 60).

4 servings

CORN CHOWDER

$^1/_4$ pound bacon, diced
$^1/_2$ x 16 ounce can potatoes, drained and diced
16 ounce can creamed corn
$3^1/_2$ cups vegetable or chicken broth

Heat a large, heavy-bottomed pan. Cook bacon until the fat runs and bacon starts to crisp. Add potatoes and cook for a couple of minutes, stirring. Add corn and broth, and bring to a boil, stirring. Reduce heat, cover, and simmer for about 10 minutes.

4 servings

SOUP PLUS

PARMESAN CROUTONS

vegetable oil, for frying
3 thick slices white bread, crusts removed, cut into $^1/_2$ inch squares
1 tablespoon grated Parmesan cheese

Heat oil in a skillet until almost smoking. Fry bread cubes, turning constantly, for about 5 minutes. Drain on paper towels and toss in Parmesan while still hot. Add to soup just before serving.

6 servings as a soup garnish

GARLIC AND HERB CROUTONS

vegetable oil, for frying
3 thick slices white bread, crusts removed, cut into $^1/_2$ inch squares
2 garlic cloves, minced
2 teaspoons dried mixed herbs or dried oregano

Heat oil in a skillet until almost smoking. Fry bread cubes, turning constantly, for about 4 minutes. Add garlic and fry for a further minute, turning constantly. Drain on paper towels and toss in herbs while still hot. Add to soup just before serving.

6 servings as a soup garnish

SESAME SEED SLICES

3 ounces/$^3/_8$ cup butter
1 egg yolk
2 tablespoons sesame seeds
8 thick slices French bread

Using a wooden spoon, cream butter in a bowl and blend with egg yolk and sesame seeds. Spread generously onto both sides of bread slices. Broil both sides until sizzling and beginning to brown.

4-6 servings as a soup accompaniment

CHEESY GARLIC BREAD

1 baguette
8 tablespoons/1 stick/$^1/_2$ cup butter
1 clove garlic, minced
1 cup finely grated cheddar cheese

Cut baguette into 1 inch thick slices, cutting almost through to bottom crust but keeping slices together at base. Using a wooden spoon, cream butter in a bowl with garlic and cheese. Spread on either side of each slice and over top of loaf. Wrap loaf tightly in aluminum foil. Put onto a cookie sheet and bake in a preheated oven, 375°F, for 15 minutes. Carefully open up foil and fold back to expose top of baguette. Bake for 5 minutes more. Cut into slices and serve hot.

6-8 servings as a soup accompaniment

SWISS CHEESE TOASTS

4 thick slices French bread
2 teaspoons Dijon mustard
$^1/_2$ cup grated Swiss cheese

Lightly toast French bread on both sides. Spread mustard on top of toasted slices, then sprinkle with cheese. Put one toast in the bottom of each serving bowl. Ladle hot soup over the top. The toast will rise to the top; it can then be browned in the oven. The classic topping for French Onion Soup (see page 57), but try with other vegetable soups.

4 servings as a soup garnish

BREAD ROLL SOUP BOWLS

Bake large, crusty, round bread rolls on a preheated cookie sheet in a moderate oven for a few minutes to crisp outside. Slice off tops and scoop out middle of rolls (use bread to make bread crumbs). Ladle hot soup into rolls and serve immediately.

TWO-TONERS

Heat two contrastingly colored cans of soup—choose thick, smooth vegetable soups, for example cream soups. Pour half of one soup into shallow serving bowls, then spoon or pour the other soup into one half only of the bowl. Use a toothpick to create a swirling pattern. Cream of tomato and celery make a good combination.

PESTO PUNCH

Stir a spoonful of ready-made pesto sauce (or use Pistou, see page 85) into a bowl of hot soup, to give it extra flavor and body.

FLAVOR BOOSTERS

To bring an extra taste dimension—and style—to thick puréed or chunky soups, swirl a little herb- or chili-flavored oil (see pages 102–3) onto the surface of the soup after ladling into serving bowls.

BODY BUILDERS

Extend or pep-up canned soups by adding leftover cooked rice. Alternatively, to thicken soups, add a handful of uncooked rice or small pasta shapes and simmer for 10-15 minutes, until tender.

GREAT GARNISH

scissored chives
sprinkling of paprika or chili powder/cayenne pepper
toasted slivered almonds or sunflower seeds

Add instant color and interest to any soup by garnishing with any one of the above just before serving.

FOOD
ALFRESCO

IT'S A WRAP

CHICKEN, AVOCADO, AND BACON WRAP

1 large avocado, halved, pitted, and peeled (see page 15)
4 flour tortillas
$^1/_2$ pound cold cooked chicken breast, thinly sliced
4 thin slices bacon, cooked and crumbled

Mash avocado roughly with a fork or thinly slice. Spread over tortillas. Top with chicken and bacon. Season to taste. Roll up and slice crosswise in half.

4 servings

HAM, PINEAPPLE, AND MAYONNAISE WRAP

4 flour tortillas
4 tablespoons mayonnaise
8 thin slices cooked lean ham
8 ounce can pineapple chunks in natural juice, drained

Spread tortillas with mayonnaise. Top with ham and pineapple. Roll up and slice crosswise in half.

4 servings

TUNA AND GREEN BELL PEPPER WRAP

$6^1/_2$ can tuna in mayonnaise with corn
2 teaspoons horseradish sauce or creamed horseradish, or to taste
4 flour tortillas
2 green bell peppers, cut into thin strips

Combine tuna with horseradish. Spread mixture over tortillas. Top with bell pepper strips. Roll up and slice crosswise in half.

4 servings

SALMON AND CREAM CHEESE WRAP

4 flour tortillas
$^3/_4$ cup cream cheese
6$^1/_2$ ounce can pink salmon, drained, bones removed, and flaked
6 scallions, finely sliced

Spread tortillas with cheese. Top with salmon and scatter over scallions.
Roll up and slice crosswise in half.

4 servings

PESTO, CHEDDAR, AND PIMIENTO WRAP

4 flour tortillas
3–4 tablespoons pesto sauce (or use Pistou, see page 85)
5 ounces sharp cheddar cheese, thinly sliced
2 x 4 ounce jars pimientos, drained and chopped

Spread tortillas with pesto (or pistou). Top with cheese and pimientos.
Roll up and slice crosswise in half.

4 servings

PEANUT BUTTER AND BANANA WRAP

4 flour tortillas
4 tablespoons chunky peanut butter
3-4 ripe bananas, mashed
2 tablespoons clear honey or maple syrup

Spread tortillas with peanut butter. Top with mashed banana and
drizzle over honey or maple syrup. Roll up and slice crosswise in half.

4 servings

BAGUETTE SLICES

MOZZARELLA AND TOMATO

1 short baguette
3 tablespoons bottled Italian salad dressing
5 large ripe tomatoes, sliced
6 ounces mozzarella, sliced

Cut baguette in half horizontally and scoop out and discard most of middle, leaving a good $1/2$ inch thick edge. Leave to dry out slightly. Drizzle insides of baguette generously with dressing. Arrange a layer of tomato, then a layer of mozzarella on bottom half of baguette. Season to taste and drizzle with remaining dressing. Wrap tightly in plastic wrap or aluminum foil. Chill overnight. Return to "room" temperature and cut into 1 inch thick slices to serve.

2 servings

AVOCADO AND BROILED BELL PEPPERS

2 red bell peppers
1 short baguette
2 small ripe avocados (or $1/2$ cup store-bought guacamole)
2-3 tablespoons Lemon and Thyme Oil (see page 102)

Broil bell peppers under medium heat, turning frequently, for 8-10 minutes, until blistered and charred. Wrap in aluminum foil until cool. Cut baguette in half horizontally and scoop out and discard most of middle, leaving a good $1/2$ inch thick edge. Leave to dry out slightly. Peel, core, and deseed bell peppers. Cut flesh into quarters. Halve, pit, and peel avocados (see page 15), then thinly slice. Drizzle insides of baguette with oil. Arrange a layer of bell peppers, then avocado (or guacamole) on bottom half of baguette. Season to taste and drizzle with remaining oil. Wrap tightly in plastic wrap or aluminum foil. Chill overnight. Return to "room" temperature and cut into 1 inch thick slices to serve.

2 servings

SMOKED HAM, CHEESE, AND SALSA

1 short baguette
$^1/_2$ cup chunky salsa, or to taste
3–4 thin slices cooked lean smoked ham
$^1/_4$ pound Monterey Jack or cheddar cheese, thinly sliced

Cut baguette in half horizontally and scoop out and discard most of middle, leaving a good $^1/_2$ inch thick edge. Leave to dry out slightly. Spread bottom half of baguette with salsa. Top with a layer of ham, then a layer of cheese. Season to taste and top with remaining salsa. Wrap tightly in plastic wrap or aluminum foil. Chill overnight. Return to "room" temperature and cut into 1 inch thick slices to serve.
2 servings

ANCHOVY AND PARMESAN

1 short baguette
3 tablespoons bottled caesar salad dressing
$^1/_4$ pound Parmesan cheese
6 canned or bottled anchovy fillets

Cut baguette in half horizontally and scoop out and discard most of middle, leaving a good $^1/_2$ inch thick edge. Leave to dry out slightly. Drizzle insides of baguette generously with dressing. Shave Parmesan with a vegetable peeler. Arrange a layer of Parmesan on bottom half of baguette. Top with anchovies. Season to taste and drizzle with remaining dressing. Wrap tightly in plastic wrap or aluminum foil. Chill overnight. Return to "room" temperature and cut into 1 inch thick slices to serve.
2 servings

TUNA AND OLIVES

1 short baguette
3 tablespoons bottled Italian vinaigrette dressing
6$^1/_2$ ounce can tuna in olive oil, drained and flaked
about 12 pimiento-stuffed olives, sliced

Cut baguette in half horizontally and scoop out and discard most of middle, leaving a good $^1/_2$ inch thick edge. Leave to dry out slightly. Drizzle insides of baguette generously with dressing. Spread a layer of tuna on bottom half of baguette. Top with olives. Season to taste and drizzle with remaining dressing. Wrap tightly in plastic wrap or aluminum foil. Chill overnight. Return to "room" temperature and cut into 1 inch thick slices to serve.

2 servings

COOK'S KNOW-HOW
These filled baguettes are ideal for picnics.
Transport them whole in their wrappings, then unwrap and
cut into thick slices at the picnic site.

FILLED PITA POCKETS

SALAMI AND CREAM CHEESE

about $^1/_2$ cup cream cheese with herbs or garlic
16 large slices salami
4 white or brown pita pockets
crisp salad leaves

In a bowl, soften cream cheese and season with black pepper. Spread over one side of each salami slice. Split pita pockets open down one side. Put a few salad leaves in each, then add salami slices, loosely rolled up.

4 servings

TURKEY AND SWISS CHEESE

4 white or brown pita pockets
3–4 tablespoons cranberry sauce
6 ounces cooked turkey breast, thinly sliced
1 cup shredded Swiss cheese

Split pita pockets open down one side. Spread one inside half of each with cranberry sauce. Add turkey slices and cheese, and season to taste.
4 servings

MINTED LAMB AND YOGURT

4 white or brown pita pockets
2–3 tablespoons mint jelly
8-10 ounces cold cooked lamb, thinly sliced
3-4 tablespoons thick plain yogurt

Split pita pockets open down one side. Spread one inside half of each with mint jelly. Add lamb slices, then spoon over yogurt. Season to taste
4 servings

SAUSAGE AND RELISH

4 white or brown pita pockets
3–4 tablespoons tomato relish
8 cold cooked link sausages, sliced
4 dill pickles, sliced

Split pita pockets open down one side. Spread one inside half of each with tomato relish. Add sausage and dill pickle slices. Season to taste.
4 servings

PESTO, SMOKED MOZZARELLA, AND TOMATO

4 white or brown pita pockets
3–4 tablespoons pesto sauce (or use Pistou, see page 85)
about $1/2$ pound smoked mozzarella, thinly sliced
4 large ripe tomatoes, sliced

Split pita pockets open down one side. Spread one inside half of each
with pesto (or pistou). Add the cheese and tomato slices. Season to taste.
4 servings

SHRIMP AND EGG MAYONNAISE

4 white or brown pita pockets
about $1/3$ cup mayonnaise
4 hard-cooked eggs, sliced
2 cups peeled cooked shrimp

Split pita pockets down one side. Spread one inside half of each with
mayonnaise. Add the egg slices and shrimp. Season to taste.
4 servings

SALADS TO GO

TUNA, POTATO, AND OLIVE SALAD

3 large potatoes, boiled, cooled, and diced
2 x $6^{1}/_2$ ounce cans tuna in olive oil, drained and flaked, oil reserved
$1/3$ cup pitted and halved black olives
2 tablespoons Basil Vinegar (see page 104) or white wine vinegar

Put potatoes, tuna, and olives into a container. Put the reserved oil and
vinegar into a screw-top jar and season to taste. Replace lid and shake
well to combine. Pour dressing over salad. Cover container with lid or
plastic wrap.   4 servings

CHICKEN AND PARMESAN SALAD

2 boneless, skinless chicken breasts
1 head romaine lettuce
$^{1}/_{4}$ pound Parmesan cheese
4 tablespoons bottled caesar salad dressing

Broil chicken under high heat for about 5 minutes on each side, until cooked through. Leave to cool. Tear lettuce into bite-size pieces and put into a container. Slice chicken into strips and add to container. Shave Parmesan over chicken with a vegetable peeler. Cover container with lid or plastic wrap. Pack dressing separately and toss with salad just before serving.

4 servings

CHICKPEA AND RED ONION SALAD

1 red onion, finely sliced into rings
15 ounce can chickpeas (garbanzo beans), drained
2 tablespoons chopped parsley, thyme, or oregano
4 tablespoons bottled French vinaigrette dressing or Lemon and Oil Dressing (see page 99)

Separate onion rings. Put into a container with the chickpeas and herb. Pour over dressing and toss to combine. Cover container with lid or plastic wrap.

2 servings

LAYERED BEAN SALAD

$^{3}/_{4}$ pound green beans, trimmed
15 ounce can cannellini beans, drained
15 ounce can red kidney beans, drained
5-6 tablespoons bottled Italian vinaigrette dressing or Lemon and Oil Dressing (see page 99)

Cook green beans in boiling salted water until just tender. Drain, refresh under cold running water, and drain again. Put the cooled beans in a layer in the bottom of a round container. Top with a layer of cannellini beans, then red kidney beans. Pour over dressing. Cover container with plastic wrap. To serve, remove wrap and invert onto a serving platter.
6 servings

MIXED VEGETABLE RICE SALAD

generous 1 cup long-grain rice
1 red bell pepper
1 pound frozen mixed peas and corn
5-6 tablespoons bottled Italian vinaigrette dressing

Cook rice in boiling salted water until just tender. Drain and leave to cool. Broil bell peppers under medium heat, turning frequently, for 8-10 minutes, until blistered and charred all over. Wrap in aluminum foil or a clean damp dish towel. Leave for a few minutes. Cook the peas and corn according to the package instructions. Drain and leave to cool. Peel, core, and deseed bell peppers. Cut flesh into strips. Put rice into a container with bell peppers, peas, and corn. Pour over dressing and toss to combine. Cover container with lid or plastic wrap.
4-6 servings

PORTABLE SWEET TREATS

STRAWBERRIES IN RASPBERRY SAUCE

1 pound strawberries
$^1/_2$ pound raspberries
$^1/_4$ cup orange juice
confectioner's sugar, to taste

Wipe and hull strawberries. Put in a container, cover with lid or plastic wrap, and refrigerate. Put raspberries, orange juice, and sugar in a food processor or blender and blend until smooth. Strain purée through a nylon strainer. Place in an airtight container and chill well. Pour sauce over strawberries to serve, or spear fruit on toothpicks to dip into sauce.

4-6 servings

MANGO AND PINEAPPLE WITH CHOCOLATE SAUCE

2 ripe mangos
1 ripe pineapple
$^{1}/_{2}$ cup golden or corn syrup
6 ounces unsweetened or bitter chocolate, broken into small pieces

Slice mangos either side of narrow stone. Peel and slice flesh. Peel, slice, and core pineapple. Cut into chunks. Put fruit in a container, cover with lid or plastic wrap, and refrigerate. Put syrup, chocolate, and scant 1 cup water in a pan and melt over low heat. Bring to a boil and simmer for 5 minutes. Allow to cool, then pour into a wide-topped container and cover. Refrigerate until required. Spear fruit on toothpicks to dip into sauce.

6 servings

STRAWBERRY TARTLETS

6 ounces shortcrust pastry dough (store-bought or use recipe on page 294), defrosted if frozen
4 tablespoons redcurrant jelly
$^{1}/_{2}$ pound strawberries, hulled

Roll out pastry very thinly and use to line 12 patty pans. Press a piece of aluminum foil into each. Bake in a preheated oven, 375°F, for 10 minutes, until golden. Leave to cool, then remove foil and turn out shells. Heat jelly with 1 tablespoon water in a small pan. Bring to a boil, strain, and reheat. Brush shells with some of glaze. Arrange strawberries in shells, then brush with remaining glaze.

makes 12

WALNUT FLAPJACKS

12 tablespoons/1^1/$_2$ sticks/^{3}/$_4$ cup butter or margarine
1 cup demerara sugar
generous 2^1/$_4$ cups quick-cooking rolled oats
^{1}/$_2$ cup chopped walnuts

Melt butter or margarine in a pan over very low heat. Stir in sugar, oats, walnuts, and a pinch of salt. Stir well and turn mixture into a well-greased jelly roll pan. Press lightly together. Smooth surface with a knife. Bake in center of a preheated oven, 375°F, for 30-35 minutes, until golden brown. Leave in pan for a few minutes, then mark into 16 squares or fingers. Leave in pan until completely cold, then remove and store in an airtight container.
Makes 16

CHOCOLATE CRISPIES

2 tablespoons/^{1}/$_4$ stick butter or margarine
2 tablespoons golden or corn syrup
3 ounces semisweet chocolate
1^1/$_2$ cups cornflakes or other crisp breakfast cereal

Melt butter or margarine with syrup in a pan over low heat. Add chocolate and heat until melted and hot. Remove from heat and stir in cereal with a metal spoon, until combined. Spoon into 10 paper shells and leave to cool and set. Cover and refrigerate until required.
Makes 10

BAR-B-QUE!

LAMB CUTLETS WITH ROSEMARY AND LEMON

1 sprig rosemary, finely chopped
1 tablespoon olive oil
finely grated zest and juice of 1 lemon
8 lamb cutlets

Combine rosemary, oil, and lemon zest and juice in a shallow nonmetallic dish. Season to taste. Add lamb cutlets and coat with marinade. Set aside for 10 minutes, to marinate. Cook on a prepared outside barbecue over high heat for 5 minutes on each side, basting frequently with marinade.

4 servings

SKEWERED LAMB KOFTAS

$1^1/_2$ pounds lean ground lamb
1 large onion, finely chopped
finely grated zest and juice of 1 lemon, plus extra lemon juice for basting
2-3 tablespoons curry powder, garam masala, or ground cumin

Combine ingredients in a nonmetallic bowl, cover, and refrigerate for 30 minutes. Divide mixture into 18 equal-sized portions. Knead each portion to bind together, then form into a sausage shape. Thread onto greased metal skewers. Cook on a prepared outside barbecue over high heat, turning frequently and squeezing over lemon juice, for about 15 minutes, until well cooked.

4-6 servings

LEMON AND OREGANO LAMB KABOBS

$1/3$ cup olive oil
2 tablespoons lemon juice
2 teaspoons dried oregano
$1^1/_2$ pounds boned leg of lamb, cut into $1^1/_2$ inch cubes

Mix together oil, lemon juice, and oregano in a shallow nonmetallic dish. Season with black pepper. Toss lamb in oil mixture, cover, and refrigerate for 2 hours, turning occasionally. Thread lamb onto small skewers. Cook on a prepared outside barbecue over hot coals, turning frequently and basting with marinade, for about 10 minutes, until well browned on the outside but still a little pink inside. Season with salt before serving.

4-6 servings

STEAKS WRAPPED IN PARMA HAM

2 cloves garlic, finely chopped
4 x 6 ounce filet mignon steaks
8 slices Parma ham
$1/4$ pound buffalo mozzarella, cut into 4 slices

Press garlic into both sides of steaks and season to taste. Wrap in Parma ham to cover completely. Cook on a prepared outside barbecue on a well-greased rack over high heat. Cook on each side for 2-3 minutes for rare, or longer according to taste. Put slices of mozzarella onto steaks, return to barbecue, and cook until melting. Rest steaks for 5 minutes before serving.

4 servings

PORK CHOPS WITH ORANGE

2 tablespoons clear honey
finely grated zest and juice of 1 large orange
2 cloves garlic, minced
4 boneless thick loin pork chops

Mix together honey, orange zest and juice, and garlic in a dish. Add chops and turn to coat in marinade. Cover and refrigerate for 2 hours or overnight, turning occasionally. Cook on a prepared outside barbecue over high heat for 5-7 minutes on each side, basting with marinade, until well cooked.

4 servings

COOK'S KNOW-HOW
To test whether poultry or meat is cooked through, pierce the thickest part with the point of a sharp knife. If properly cooked, the juices should run clear rather than pink.

DEVILLED CHICKEN

2 Rock Cornish Hens
$^1/_2$ cup olive oil
$^1/_3$ cup lemon juice
2 tablespoons mixed peppercorns, coarsely crushed with a pestle and mortar

To "spatchcock" birds, place 1 breast side down on a work surface and cut along each side of backbone with poultry shears. Disard backbone or use it for making broth. Put bird, breast side up, on a board and press hard with your hand on breastbone to break it. To keep bird flat during cooking, push 2 metal skewers through bird, 1 through wings with breast in between, the other through thighs. Repeat with second bird. Put birds in a nonmetallic dish and slash all over with the point of a small, sharp knife. Beat together oil, lemon juice, and peppercorns, and brush all over birds, working marinade into cuts. Cover and refrigerate for 4 hours or

overnight. Season birds with salt and cook, skin side down, on a prepared barbecue over medium heat, for 15 minutes. Turn over and cook for 10 minutes more. Cut each bird in half lengthwise with poultry shears.
2-4 servings

CHICKEN AND PINEAPPLE KABOBS

14 ounce can pineapple slices in natural juice, drained, juice reserved
$^1/_4$ cup packed light brown sugar
3 tablespoons soy sauce
4 skinless, boneless chicken breasts

Put $^1/_3$ cup reserved pineapple juice in a pan with sugar and soy sauce. Bring to a boil and simmer for about 5 minutes. Leave to cool, then pour into a bowl. Cut chicken into $1^1/_2$ inch cubes and add to bowl, turning to coat. Cover and refrigerate for 2 hours. Cut pineapple into large chunks. Thread chicken and pineapple alternately onto 4 metal skewers. Cook on a prepared outside barbecue over high heat, turning frequently and basting with the marinade, for 15-20 minutes, until well cooked.
4 servings

THAI-STYLE BARBECUED CHICKEN

4 chicken breasts, on the bone with skin
$^2/_3$ cup canned coconut milk
finely grated zest and juice of 1 lime
3 tablespoons cilantro, leaves and stems, finely chopped

Slash chicken all over with the point of a small, sharp knife and put in a dish large enough to hold chicken in a single layer. Combine coconut milk, lime zest and juice, cilantro, and seasoning to taste. Add to dish and turn chicken to coat, working marinade into cuts. Cover and refrigerate for 2 hours. Cook on a prepared outside barbecue over medium heat, turning occasionally and brushing with marinade, for about 25 minutes, until well cooked.   4 servings

TURKEY AND SMOKED HAM KABOBS

1 pound turkey fillet, cut into $1^1/_2$ inch cubes
1 tablespoon pesto sauce (or use Pistou, see page 85)
3 tablespoons Lemon and Thyme Oil (see page 102) or olive oil
$^1/_4$ pound smoked ham, cut into strips

Put turkey into a shallow dish. Combine pesto (or pistou) with oil and season to taste. Add to dish and toss with turkey to coat. Cover and refrigerate for 2-4 hours, turning occasionally. Lift turkey from marinade and wrap each piece in a strip of ham. Thread onto 4 greased metal skewers. Cook on a prepared outside barbecue over high heat, turning frequently and basting with marinade, for 15-20 minutes, until cooked.
4 servings

BARBECUED SWEET AND SOUR DUCK

4 boneless, skinless duck breasts
2 tablespoons light brown sugar
4 tablespoons light soy sauce
1 tablespoon sesame oil

Cut each duck breast into 8 even-sized pieces. Combine remaining ingredients in a large bowl and add duck. Turn to coat, cover, and refrigerate for 3-4 hours or overnight, turning occasionally. Thread duck onto 8 bamboo skewers or 4 large metal skewers. Cook on a prepared barbecue over medium heat for 8-10 minutes for small skewers, 10-12 minutes for larger ones. Turn frequently during cooking, basting with marinade. Serve hot or cold, either on or off skewers.
4 servings

TROUT WITH GINGER

4 medium trout, cleaned
3 tablespoons clear honey

1 tablespoon finely chopped fresh gingerroot
1¹/₄ cups rice wine or dry sherry

Cut 3 or 4 slashes in both sides of each fish and put in a large shallow dish in a single layer. Combine honey, gingerroot, and rice wine or sherry, and season to taste. Add to dish and turn fish to coat, working marinade into cuts. Cover and refrigerate for 2 hours. Cook on a prepared outside barbecue over medium heat for 15-20 minutes, until flesh flakes when tested with a knife.

4 servings

CAJUN SWORDFISH

4 thick swordfish steaks, cut into 1¹/₂ inch cubes
¹/₄ cup peanut oil
2 tablespoons cajun seasoning
2 green bell peppers

Put fish in a shallow dish. Combine oil and spice mix, and add to dish. Toss with fish to coat. Cover and refrigerate for 2 hours, turning occasionally. Halve, core, and deseed bell peppers. Cut into bite-size chunks. Thread fish onto skewers, alternating with chunks of bell pepper. Cook on a prepared outdoor barbecue over high heat for 8-10 minutes, turning once and basting frequently with marinade.

4 servings

ANGLER FISH AND BACON KABOBS

1 pound skinned angler fish, cut into 1¹/₂ inch cubes
3 tablespoons olive oil
finely grated zest and juice of 1 lemon
4 thin slices bacon

Put fish into a shallow nonmetallic dish. Combine oil with lemon zest and juice, and season to taste. Add to dish and toss with fish to coat.

Cover and refrigerate for 2 hours, turning occasionally. Roll up bacon slices. Thread fish onto skewers, alternating with bacon rolls. Cook on a prepared outdoor barbecue over medium heat for about 8 minutes, turning once and basting frequently with marinade.

4 servings

SPICED SKEWERED SHRIMP

1$^1/_2$ pounds large green shrimp in their shells
$^1/_4$ cup Chili Oil (see page 102)
2 tablespoons whole-grain mustard
3 cloves garlic, minced

Put shrimp into a large shallow dish. Combine oil, mustard, and garlic, and add to dish. Toss with shrimp to coat. Cover and refrigerate for 2 hours, turning occasionally. Thread shrimp onto skewers. Cook over a prepared outside barbecue over high heat, turning once and basting frequently with marinade, for about 8 minutes, until cooked through. Serve immediately.

4-6 servings

COOK'S KNOW-HOW
Grease metal skewers before using. Soak wooden skewers in water for 30 minutes before using to prevent them from burning. They are best used for shorter barbecuing times.

CORN WITH PROSCUITTO

3 tablespoons olive oil
2 tablespoons finely chopped oregano
4 ears of corn, cut in half crosswise
4 slices proscuitto

Combine oil with oregano in a shallow dish. Add corn and turn to coat. Cut proscuitto slices in half lengthwise. Wrap around corn and secure with small wooden skewers. Cook on a prepared outdoor barbecue over medium heat for about 8 minutes, turning at intervals and brushing with oil and herb mixture, until corn is tender.

4 servings

SWEET POTATO AND MUSHROOM KABOBS

2 large sweet potatoes
1 teaspoon coriander seeds
4 tablespoons/$^1/_2$ stick/$^1/_4$ cup sweet butter
$^1/_4$ pound closed cup mushrooms

Cook potatoes whole in their skins in boiling water for 15-20 minutes, until just tender. Peel and cut into chunks. Meanwhile, toast coriander seeds in a dry skillet. Cool, then grind with a pestle and mortar or in a coffee grinder. Melt butter and blend in ground coriander. Thread potato chunks interspersed with mushrooms onto skewers. Brush with melted butter. Cook on a prepared outdoor barbecue over medium heat for about 5 minutes, turning frequently and brushing with melted butter, until browned and tender.   6 servings

BARBECUED BANANAS

6 bananas in their skins
$^2/_3$ cup thick cream
3 tablespoons maple syrup

Cook bananas in their skins on a prepared barbecue directly on the rack over medium heat for about 8 minutes, turning once. Cool a little, split open, and serve with thick cream drizzled with maple syrup.

6 servings

PINEAPPLE AND LIME KABOBS

finely grated zest and juice of 2 limes
3 tablespoons dark brown sugar
2 teaspoons apple pie spice, ground ginger, or cinnamon
1 large ripe pineapple

Put lime zest and juice, sugar, and spice into a pan. Bring to a boil and simmer for 5 minutes. Leave to cool. Peel, slice, and core pineapple. Cut into large chunks or wedges. Put into a shallow dish and pour over lime juice mixture. Toss to coat. Thread onto skewers. Cook on a prepared outdoor barbecue over medium heat for 5-8 minutes, turning once and basting frequently with mixture.

4 servings

PEACHES WITH GINGERSNAPS

3 large ripe peaches, halved and pitted
melted butter, for brushing
$^2/_3$ cup mascarpone cheese
6 gingersnaps, crumbled

Brush peaches with a little melted butter. Cook on a prepared outdoor barbecue over medium heat for about 10 minutes, turning at intervals and brushing with a little more butter. Top with mascarpone and crumbled gingersnaps to serve.

6 servings

SALSAS AND SAUCES

SWEET AND SOUR ONION SALSA

2 red onions, sliced
1 tablespoon olive oil
3 tablespoons balsamic vinegar
2 tablespoons light brown sugar

Put ingredients into a pan and season to taste. Simmer over low heat for 20 minutes, until soft and caramelized. Leave to cool. Serve with any barbecued meat, poultry, or game. Also good with mackerel.

4 servings

TOMATO AND CILANTRO SALSA

$^1/_2$ pound well-flavored tomatoes, skinned, deseeded, and chopped
$^1/_2$-1 dried red chili, deseeded and finely chopped
3 tablespoons finely chopped cilantro leaves
2 tablespoons lime juice

Mix ingredients together in a serving bowl. Let stand for 1 hour for flavors to develop. Serve with barbecued fish, shellfish, and poultry.

4 servings

APRICOT SALSA

$^1/_2$ pound fresh apricots, pitted and chopped
grated zest and juice of 1 lime
2 teaspoons clear honey
1 tablespoon finely diced fresh gingerroot

Put ingredients into a food processor or blender. Whizz briefly until combined but still chunky. Serve with barbecued gammon, pork, link sausages, poultry, and game.   4 servings

EASY TOMATO SAUCE

2 x 14$^1/_2$ ounce cans chopped tomatoes
2 tablespoons olive oil, or Chili or Garlic Oil (see page 102)
4 parsley sprigs
1 tablespoon sugar

Put ingredients into a pan. Bring to a boil, stirring. Simmer, uncovered, for about 20 minutes, until thick. Serve with any barbecued foods.
6-8 servings

PISTOU

3-4 cloves garlic
20 large basil leaves
1$^1/_4$ cups shredded Parmesan cheese
$^1/_2$ cup olive oil

Put garlic and basil with a pinch of salt into a food processor or blender. Whizz to a paste. Add Parmesan and, with the motor running, pour in oil in a thin trickle through feed tube, until a thick green paste forms. Use as a marinade for barbecuing poultry or fish, or serve as a sauce with barbecued poultry, fish, and vegetables. It can also be used as a substitute for pesto sauce in other recipes in this book.
4-6 servings

BASTING SAUCE

$^1/_2$ cup light brown sugar
2 tablespoons lime juice
3 tablespoons rum
1 teaspoon ground ginger or allspice

Blend ingredients together and use to baste barbecued pork, gammon, poultry, game, and fruits.   6 servings

SALADS AND VEGETABLES

QUICK CLASSIC SALADS

WALDORF SALAD

5 dessert apples, unpeeled, cored, and diced
1 head celery, finely diced, some leaves reserved for garnish (optional)
1 cup coarsely chopped walnuts or pecan nuts
scant 2 cups mayonnaise (store-bought or use recipe on page 101)

Combine apples, celery, and nuts with mayonnaise, reserving some nuts for garnish. Spoon into a serving bowl, arrange a few celery leaves around edge (if using), and top with remaining nuts.
4 servings

SPINACH, BACON, AND AVOCADO SALAD

$1^1/_2$ pounds young spinach
2 ripe avocados
$^1/_3$ cup bottled French vinaigrette dressing or Lemon and Oil Dressing (see page 99)
$^1/_4$ pound thickly sliced bacon, diced

Put spinach into a large salad bowl. Halve, pit, and peel avocados (see page 15). Slice and add to bowl. Add dressing and toss gently to combine. Heat a dry nonstick skillet over medium heat. Add bacon and cook, stirring, until fat runs and bacon is brown and crisp. Drain on paper towels. Scatter bacon over salad and pour over hot pan drippings.
4 servings

POTATO SALAD

$1^1/_2$ pounds waxy salad potatoes
4 scallions, finely chopped
$^1/_2$ cup mayonnaise or Piquant Mayonnaise (see page 101)
2 tablespoons scissored chives

Cook potatoes whole in their skins in boiling salted water until just tender. Drain and leave to cool a little. When still warm, thickly slice and put into a serving bowl with scallions. Season to taste and toss to combine. Spoon mayonnaise over salad and toss gently to mix. Scatter over chives. Serve immediately.

4 servings

CHEAT'S NIÇOISE

1 pound green beans, trimmed
2 x 6$^1/_2$ ounce cans tuna in oil, drained
6 hard-cooked eggs, halved
$^1/_3$ cup bottled French vinaigrette dressing (or see page 99), or Lemon and Oil Dressing (see page 99)

Cook green beans in boiling salted water until just tender. Drain and refresh under cold running water. Drain again. Put into a salad bowl. Break tuna into chunks and add to bowl with eggs. Pour over dressing and toss lightly to combine.

4 servings

SPICED COLE SLAW

5 tablespoons mayonnaise (store-bought or see page 101) or $^1/_2$ quantity Piquant Mayonnaise (see page 101)
1-2 teaspoons curry powder
$^1/_2$ head white cabbage, shredded
4 carrots, grated

Beat mayonnaise with curry powder to combine. Put cabbage and carrots into a serving bowl. Add dressing and toss to coat.

4 servings

VEGETABLE SALADS

MARINATED MUSHROOM AND POTATO SALAD

1 pound button mushrooms, very finely sliced
$^2/_3$ cup bottled French vinaigrette dressing or Walnut Dressing (see page 100)
$^1/_2$ pound new potatoes
$^1/_2$ head lettuce or other salad leaves

Put mushrooms onto a large plate. Pour half of dressing over mushrooms. Marinate for 1 hour, turning occasionally, until softened. Cook potatoes in their skins in boiling salted water until just tender. Drain and leave to cool a little. Place lettuce or salad leaves in a large bowl with warm potatoes. Add remaining dressing and toss to coat. Divide between 4 serving plates and arrange marinated mushrooms on top. Serve immediately.

4 servings

CHICORY SALAD

2 heads chicory
3-4 tablespoons bottled Italian vinaigrette dressing or Lemon and Oil Dressing (see page 99)
$^1/_4$ pound thickly sliced bacon, finely diced
1 cup shredded Parmesan or Pecorino cheese

Separate chicory leaves and put into a bowl. Add dressing and toss to coat. Arrange rounded-side down on a large serving platter. Heat a dry nonstick skillet over medium heat. Cook bacon, stirring, until fat runs and bacon is brown and crisp. Drain on paper towels. Sprinkle bacon inside chicory leaves. Sprinkle with cheese and pour over hot pan drippings. Serve immediately.

4 servings

CUCUMBER AND DILL

1 cucumber, peeled and very thinly sliced
$^1/_4$ cup thick plain yogurt
1 teaspoon white wine vinegar or Garlic Vinegar (see page 104)
2 tablespoons chopped dill, plus sprigs for garnish (optional)

Put cucumber slices into a colander set over a large plate. Sprinkle 2 teaspoons salt over cucumber and leave for 20-30 minutes, to allow excess moisture to drain away. Rinse cucumber under cold running water. Drain thoroughly and place in a shallow serving dish. Beat together yogurt, vinegar, and dill in a small bowl. Spoon over cucumber and toss gently to combine. Garnish with dill sprigs, if you like.
4 servings

CUCUMBER AND PINEAPPLE WITH GUACAMOLE

$^1/_2$ cucumber, peeled and very thinly sliced
$^1/_2$ ripe pineapple, peeled, cored, and cut into bite-size pieces
1 bunch cilantro
$^2/_3$ cup guacamole

Put cucumber slices into a colander set over a large plate. Sprinkle 1 teaspoon salt over cucumber and leave for 20-30 minutes, to allow excess moisture to drain away. Put pineapple into a bowl. Roughly tear about half the cilantro leaves into the bowl. Rinse cucumber under cold running water. Drain well, then tip onto paper towels to dry slightly. Add to pineapple mixture and season to taste. Toss gently to combine. Garnish guacamole with remaining cilantro and serve with salad.
4-6 servings

TOMATO AND CILANTRO SALAD

2 pounds mixed tomatoes (include yellow cherry tomatoes, if available), sliced or quartered

$^1/_2$ red onion, thinly sliced
1 tablespoon sesame seeds, toasted
Lime and Cilantro Dressing (see page 100)

Put tomatoes into a large serving bowl. Scatter over onion and sesame seeds. Pour dressing over salad and let stand for 30 minutes for the flavors to develop.

4 servings

CHEESE AND MEAT SALADS

MIXED LEAF SALAD WITH PECAN CHEESE BALLS

1 cup medium-soft chèvre (goat's cheese), derinded, or cream cheese
$^1/_2$ cup very finely chopped pecan nuts
$^1/_2$ pound mixed red and green salad leaves (radicchio, romaine lettuce, butterhead lettuce)
$^2/_3$ cup bottled ranch-style dressing or Yogurt Dressing (see page 101)

Blend together cheese and pecans in a small bowl. Shape into about 16 small balls. Transfer to a cookie sheet, cover, and chill for at least 20 minutes, or until required. Arrange salad leaves in a shallow serving bowl. Spoon over dressing. Add cheese balls and serve immediately.

4 servings

MOZZARELLA SALAD WITH PESTO DRESSING

2 heads romaine or other crisp green lettuce, separated into leaves
2 cups diced mozzarella
1 red onion, chopped
$^2/_3$ cup pesto sauce (or use Pistou, see page 85)

Tear lettuce into bite-size pieces and arrange in a shallow serving dish. Scatter over cheese, then onion. Season to taste. Spoon pesto (or pistou) over cheese.   4 servings

WARM CHORIZO SALAD

$^1/_2$ pound mixed salad leaves
$^1/_3$ cup bottled French vinaigrette dressing (or use recipe on page 99,
made with red wine vinegar)
10 ounces chorizo, skinned and thinly sliced
1 small red onion, thinly sliced

Tear leaves into bite-size pieces and put into a large salad bowl. Add
half the dressing and toss to coat. Heat a nonstick skillet over high heat.
Add chorizo and fry for 2 minutes, stirring. Add remaining dressing and
cook, stirring, for a minute or so. Spoon pan contents over salad, toss
gently to combine, and serve immediately.
4 servings

SMOKED CHICKEN AND ARUGULA

$^1/_2$ pound arugula
$^1/_3$ cup bottled Italian dressing or Tarragon and Lemon Dressing (see
page 99)
$^3/_4$ pound cold smoked chicken
$^1/_2$ cup roughly chopped walnuts

Put arugula into a salad bowl or onto a serving platter. Add half the
dressing and toss to coat. Cut chicken into thin strips. Arrange over leaves
and scatter with walnuts. Drizzle over remaining dressing.
4 servings

WARM DUCK AND ORANGE SALAD

4 boneless duck breasts
$^3/_4$ pound mixed salad leaves
2 small oranges, peeled and segmented (see page 35)
$^1/_3$ cup bottled French vinaigrette dressing or Orange Dressing (see
page 100)

Score skin of duck breasts. Heat a nonstick skillet over high heat. Cook, skin side down, for 4-5 minutes, until well browned. Turn over and cook for 3-4 minutes more, or to taste (duck can be pink inside). Keep warm. Arrange salad leaves and orange segments on individual plates. Slice duck breasts and arrange alongside salad. Spoon over dressing.

4 servings

COOK'S KNOW-HOW

Scoring the skin of duck breasts allows the fat to be released and the skin to crisp. Use a sharp knife to score the skin in a diamond pattern through to the flesh.

PASTA SALADS

SHRIMP AND CELERY

$^3/_4$ lb fusilli (twists) or other dried pasta shapes
1 pound peeled cooked shrimp
3 celery stalks, finely chopped
$^2/_3$ cup mayonnaise (or $^1/_2$ quantity Piquant Mayonnaise—see page 101)

Cook pasta in boiling salted water according to the package instructions, until just tender. Drain and refresh under cold running water. Drain again and set aside until completely cooled. Put into a large bowl with shrimp, celery, and mayonnaise, and mix well. Season to taste. Cover and chill for 20 minutes.

4-6 servings

TUNA AND OLIVE

$^1/_2$ pound conchiglie (shells) or other dried pasta shapes
$6^1/_2$ ounce can tuna in oil, drained and flaked or cut into chunks
3 tablespoons pimiento-stuffed olives, chopped
$^1/_3$ cup bottled Italian dressing or Horseradish Dressing (see page 100)

Cook pasta in boiling salted water according to the package instructions. Drain and refresh under cold running water. Drain again. Put into a large bowl with tuna, olives, and dressing. Season to taste and toss to combine. Serve at room temperature.

4 servings

CHICKEN AND CORN

$^3/_4$ pound penne or other dried pasta shapes

2 cups cold cooked chicken, diced or cut into strips

11 ounce can Mexican-style corn, drained

$^1/_4$–$^1/_3$ cup bottled French vinaigrette dressing or Tarragon and Lemon Dressing (page 99)

Cook pasta in boiling salted water according to the package instructions. Drain and refresh under cold running water. Drain again. Put into a large bowl with chicken, corn, and dressing. Season to taste and toss to combine. Serve at room temperature.

4-6 servings

SALAMI AND FAVA BEAN

1 pound shelled fava beans

1 pound conchiglie (shells) or fusilli (twists)

$^1/_2$ pound salami, diced

$^1/_3$ cup mayonnaise (store-bought or use recipe on page 101)

Cook fava beans in boiling salted water for 5 minutes, until tender. Drain and set aside. Cook pasta in boiling salted water according to the package instructions, until just tender. Drain and refresh under cold running water. Drain again. Put into a large bowl with beans and salami. Fold mayonnaise into pasta and bean mixture.

4-6 servings

ZUCCHINI AND CHERRY TOMATO

$^1/_2$ pound dried pasta shapes
$^1/_3$ cup bottled Italian vinaigrette dressing or Lime and Cilantro
Dressing (see page 100)
$^1/_2$ pound small zucchini, very finely sliced
$^1/_2$ pound cherry tomatoes, halved

Cook pasta in boiling salted water according to the package
instructions, until just tender. Drain pasta and immediately toss with
dressing in a bowl. Stir in zucchini and tomatoes, and leave to cool to
room temperature before serving.

4 servings

SWISS CHEESE AND BELL PEPPER

$^3/_4$ pound dried pasta shapes
$2^1/_2$ cups diced Swiss cheese
3 green bell peppers, cored, deseeded, and diced
$^1/_3$ cup bottled ranch-style dressing or French vinaigrette dressing
(store-bought or use recipe on page 99 made with white wine vinegar)

Cook pasta in boiling salted water according to the package
instructions, until just tender. Drain and refresh under cold running water.
Drain again. Put into a large bowl with cheese and bell peppers. Add
dressing and toss to combine. Season to taste.

4-6 servings

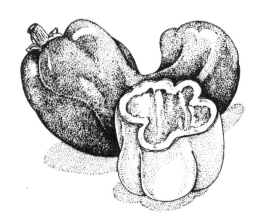

RICE AND GRAIN SALADS

CRAB RICE SALAD

1^1/$_2$ cups long-grain rice
5 tablespoons mayonnaise (or use ^{1}/$_2$ quantity Piquant Mayonnaise—
see page 101)
6^1/$_2$ ounce can crabmeat, drained and flaked
1 medium cucumber, diced

Cook rice in boiling salted water according to the package
instructions, until just tender. Rinse with boiling water and drain well.
Put into a large bowl while still warm, add mayonnaise, and toss to coat.
Leave until cool. Add crabmeat and cucumber, and toss to combine.
4 servings

SPICED FRUIT AND NUT RICE SALAD

1^1/$_2$ cups long-grain rice
3 slices Cumin Butter (see page 206)
1 cup golden raisins
1 cup mixed unsalted nuts or cashew or shelled pistachio nuts

Cook rice in boiling salted water according to the package
instructions, until just tender. Rinse with boiling water and drain well.
Put in a large bowl while still hot, add cumin butter, and toss to coat. Stir
in fruit and nuts. Serve at room temperature.
4 servings

HAM AND PINEAPPLE RICE SALAD

1^1/$_2$ cups long-grain rice
2^1/$_2$ cups diced cooked lean ham
^{1}/$_2$ x 14 ounce can pineapple chunks in natural juice, drained

$^1/_2$ quantity Yogurt Dressing (see page 101)

Cook rice in boiling salted water according to the package instructions, until just tender. Rinse with boiling water and drain well. Leave until cool. Add ham, pineapple, and dressing. Toss to combine. Season to taste.

4 servings

SHRIMP COUSCOUS SALAD

$1^1/_4$ cups pre-cooked couscous (see page 133)
about $^1/_3$ cup bottled French vinaigrette dressing or Lime and Cilantro Dressing (see page 100)
1 pound peeled cooked shrimp
6 scallions, thinly sliced

Put couscous in a large heatproof bowl. Pour over an equal volume of boiling water. Cover and let stand for about 15 minutes, until water is absorbed. Fluff up grains with a fork. Add dressing and toss to coat. Leave until completely cool. Add shrimp and scallions, and toss to combine.

4 servings

TABBOULEH

$1^1/_2$ cups bulghur wheat
4 tomatoes, skinned, deseeded, and chopped
6 tablespoons chopped mint
Lemon and Oil Dressing (see page 99)

Put bulghur in a large bowl. Add enough cold water to cover. Let stand for 30 minutes, until water is absorbed. Line a colander with a clean dish towel. Drain wheat into colander, then gather up sides and squeeze to extract as much moisture as possible. Tip bulghur into a salad bowl. Stir in tomatoes, mint, and dressing. Season to taste. Cover and let stand for 30 minutes before serving.

4 servings

SALAD DRESSINGS

FRENCH VINAIGRETTE

1 tablespoon white or red wine vinegar
1 teaspoon Dijon mustard
$^1/_3$ cup extra-virgin olive oil

Put ingredients into a screw-top jar and season to taste. Replace lid and shake well to combine.

LEMON AND OIL

1 tablespoon white wine vinegar
3 tablespoons olive oil
2 tablespoons lemon juice
1 teaspoon Dijon mustard

Put ingredients into a screw-top jar and season to taste. Replace lid and and shake well to combine.

TARRAGON AND LEMON

2 tablespoons Tarragon Vinegar (see page 104)
finely grated zest of 1 lemon
$^1/_4$ teaspoon Dijon mustard
5 tablespoons olive or grapeseed oil

Put ingredients into a screw-top jar and season to taste. Replace lid and shake well to combine.

MINTED YOGURT

$^2/_3$ cup plain yogurt
2 tablespoons mint jelly

Put ingredients into a small bowl. Beat together until well blended.

LIME AND CILANTRO

$^1/_3$ cup olive oil
1 tablespoon lime juice
2 tablespoons finely chopped cilantro
1 clove garlic, minced

Put ingredients into a screw-top jar and season to taste. Replace lid and shake well to combine.

ORANGE

3 tablespoons orange juice
$^1/_2$ teaspoon finely grated orange zest
$^1/_4$ cup grapeseed oil, or 2 tablespoons sunflower oil plus 2 tablespoons olive oil

Put ingredients into a screw-top jar and season to taste. Replace lid and shake well to combine.

WALNUT

5 tablespoons walnut oil
2 tablespoons red wine vinegar
$^1/_2$–1 teaspoon coarse-grain mustard
pinch of sugar

Put ingredients into a screw-top jar and season to taste. Replace lid and shake well to combine.

HORSERADISH

2 tablespoons finely grated horseradish or 1 tablespoon creamed horseradish
$^1/_4$ cup olive oil
2 teaspoons red wine vinegar
2 tablespoons chopped dill, flatleaf parsley, or oregano

Put ingredients into a small bowl and season to taste. Beat together until well blended.

YOGURT

²/₃ cup plain yogurt
1 tablespoon lemon juice
1 teaspoon clear honey
¹/₂ teaspoon Dijon mustard

Put ingredients into a small bowl and season to taste. Beat together until well blended.

BLENDER MAYONNAISE

1 egg
¹/₂ teaspoon powdered mustard
1 tablespoon wine vinegar
1¹/₄ cups olive or vegetable oil

Crack egg into a blender or food processor, add mustard, and season to taste with salt. Whizz for 30 seconds, then add vinegar and process again. With motor still running, pour in oil in a thin, steady stream through feed tube. The sauce will thicken after half the oil has been added. Continue to add oil until all is absorbed. Scrape mayonnaise into a bowl with a spatula. Cover and store in refrigerator.

Makes scant 2 cups

PIQUANT MAYONNAISE

¹/₂ cup mayonnaise (see above, or use store-bought mayonnaise)
3 tablespoons light cream
1 teaspoon Dijon mustard

Put ingredients into a small bowl. Beat together until well blended.

FLAVORED OILS

GARLIC

6 large, young cloves garlic, peeled and halved
2¹/₂ cups virgin olive oil

Add garlic to oil in a clean, sterilized bottle or jar. Screw lid down tightly. Store for three weeks before using.

CHILI

8 fresh hot chilies
1 fresh bayleaf
6 black peppercorns
2¹/₂ cups virgin olive oil

Add spices to oil in a clean, sterilized bottle or jar. Screw lid down tightly. Store for three weeks before using.

LEMON AND THYME

pared zest of 2 lemons
20 sprigs thyme
2 cloves garlic, peeled and halved
2¹/₂ cups virgin olive oil

Add zest, thyme, and garlic to oil in a clean, sterilized bottle or jar. Screw lid down tightly. Store for three weeks before using.

BASIL

8 tablespoons basil leaves
2¹/₂ cups virgin olive oil

Pound basil with a pestle and mortar. Gradually blend with ¹/₄ cup oil, adding a little at a time. Mix with remaining oil and pour into a clean, sterilized bottle or jar. Screw lid down tightly. Store for three weeks before using.

ROSEMARY

6 stems rosemary
$2^{1}/_{2}$ cups virgin olive oil

Add rosemary to oil in a clean, sterilized bottle or jar. Screw lid down tightly. Store for three weeks before using.

COOK'S KNOW-HOW
Sterilize bottles by washing them on the hottest cycle of the dishwasher. Alternatively, wash thoroughly by hand, then plunge into boiling water. Put them on a cookie sheet and dry in a warm oven.

Store flavored oils and vinegars up to six months in a cool, dry, dark place. Oils can be stored in the refrigerator to retain potency, although they will solidify at very low temperatures.

FLAVORED VINEGARS

TARRAGON

2¹/₂ cups white wine or cider vinegar
2 stems tarragon, plus extra for decoration (optional)
1 clove garlic, peeled and halved

Bring vinegar to boiling point in a pan. Put tarragon and garlic into a clean, sterilized bottle or jar. Pour over vinegar. Screw lid down tightly. Leave in a sunny place for 2-3 weeks. Strain, discarding herbs, into a clean, sterilized bottle or jar, adding extra tarragon stems for decoration if you like. Seal and store in a cool, dry, dark place.

BASIL

2¹/₂ cups white wine or cider vinegar
14 tablespoons basil leaves, plus extra for decoration (optional)

Bring vinegar to boiling point in a pan. Pound basil with a pestle and mortar. Put into a clean, sterilized bottle or jar. Pour over vinegar. Screw lid down tightly. Leave in a sunny place for 2-3 weeks. Strain, discarding herb, into a clean, sterilized bottle or jar, adding extra basil leaves for decoration if you like. Seal and store in a cool, dry, dark place.

GARLIC

5 large cloves garlic, minced
2¹/₂ cups white wine or cider vinegar

Add garlic to vinegar in a clean, sterilized bottle or jar. Screw lid down tightly. Leave in a sunny place for 2-3 weeks. Strain, discarding garlic, into a clean, sterilized bottle or jar. Seal and store in a cool, dry, dark place.

ORANGE AND BAY

2$\frac{1}{2}$ cups white wine or cider vinegar
pared zest of $\frac{1}{2}$ orange, plus extra for decoration (optional)
8 fresh bayleaves, plus extra for decoration (optional)

Bring vinegar to boiling point in a pan. Put zest and bayleaves into a clean, sterilized bottle or jar. Pour over vinegar. Screw lid down tightly. Leave in a sunny place for 2-3 weeks. Strain, discarding zest and herb, into a clean, sterilized bottle or jar. Add extra pared zest and bayleaves for decoration if you like. Seal and store in a cool, dry, dark place.

SPICY

2$\frac{1}{2}$ cups red wine vinegar
2 dried chilies
2 teaspoons black peppercorns
2 teaspoons lightly crushed coriander seeds

Put vinegar into a pan with spices. Bring to boiling point, then simmer for a few minutes. Pour into a clean, sterilized bottle or jar. Screw lid down tightly. Leave in a sunny place for 2-3 weeks. Strain, discarding spices, into a clean, sterilized bottle or jar. Seal and store in a cool, dry, dark place.

COOK'S KNOW-HOW
Fruit-flavored vinegars can be made by adding fresh raspberries, strawberries, or blueberries to vinegar. Strain after one week, discarding fruits, into clean, sterilized bottles or jars. Scented herb flowers can also be used, such as lavender, unsprayed rose petals, and elderflowers.

VEGETABLE DISHES

ZUCCHINI WITH OREGANO

$^1/_2$ cup olive oil
3 cloves garlic, roughly chopped
1$^1/_2$ lb small zucchini, thinly sliced diagonally
1 tablespoon chopped oregano or 2 teaspoons dried

Heat oil in a large skillet over low heat. Add garlic and cook for 1 minute, stirring, without browning. Add zucchini and stir well to coat in oil. Sauté for 2 minutes, stirring. Season to taste and stir in oregano. Cook for 5–6 minutes, stirring, until zucchini are just tender.
4 servings

HONEY-GLAZED TURNIPS

1$^1/_2$ pounds small turnips
4 tablespoons/$^1/_2$ stick/$^1/_4$ cup butter
2$^1/_2$ tablespoons clear honey
2 tablespoons slivered almonds

Cook turnips in boiling salted water for about 10 minutes, until tender but still firm to the bite. Drain. Melt butter with honey in a skillet over medium heat. Add turnips and cook for 35 minutes, stirring, until glossy. Toast almonds in a dry skillet over medium heat. Stir into turnips. Transfer to a warmed serving dish. Season to taste and pour over pan juices.
4–6 servings

GLAZED BABY CARROTS

2 tablespoons/$^1/_4$ stick butter
1 pound young carrots, quartered lengthwise
pinch of sugar
2 tablespoons orange juice

106

Melt butter in a pan over low heat. Add carrots and sugar, and season to taste. Pour in just enough water to cover and cook, uncovered, for 15-20 minutes, until carrots are tender and liquid has evaporated. Add orange juice toward end of cooking time.

4 servings

BUTTERNUT SQUASH WITH PARMESAN

2 pounds butternut squash, peeled, deseeded, and cut into small wedges or slices
6 tablespoons/$^3/_4$ stick butter
5 ounces Parmesan cheese

Heat griddle pan or nonstick skillet, add squash in batches, and cook for about 10 minutes on each side. As squash is cooked, place on a large plate and keep warm. Melt butter in a small pan until just beginning to brown. Pour over cooked squash and season to taste. Using a vegetable peeler, shave Parmesan directly onto squash. Serve immediately.

4 servings

FENNEL BAKED WITH CREAM AND PARMSAN

$1^1/_2$ pounds fennel bulbs
butter, for greasing
1 cup double cream
1 cup shredded Parmesan

Trim outside leaves from fennel, remove and discard hard central core, and slice fennel lengthwise. Cook in boiling water for 5 minutes. Drain well. Grease a shallow ovenproof dish, add fennel, and season to taste. Pour over cream and sprinkle with Parmesan. Bake on the top shelf of a preheated oven, 400°F, for 20 minutes, until top of fennel is well browned.

4 servings

PEPERONATA

$^1/_2$ cup Garlic Oil (see page 102)
2 onions, finely sliced
1 pound red and yellow bell peppers, cored, deseeded, and quartered
1 pound ripe tomatoes, skinned and chopped, or 14$^1/_2$ ounce can
chopped tomatoes

Heat oil in a heavy-bottomed pan, add onions, and sauté until lightly
colored. Add bell peppers, cover, and cook over low heat for 10-12
minutes. Add tomatoes and season to taste. Cook, uncovered, until bell
peppers are tender and liquid has reduced to a thick sauce. If using
canned tomatoes, raise heat toward end of cooking time to evaporate
extra liquid.

4 servings

POTATOES AND SPINACH WITH GINGER

$^1/_3$ cup Garlic Oil (see page 102)
1 inch piece of fresh gingerroot, chopped
1 pound potatoes, peeled and diced
1 pound frozen spinach, defrosted

Heat oil in a skillet, add ginger, and cook for 2 minutes, stirring. Add
potatoes and season with salt. Cover and cook for 10 minutes, stirring
occasionally. Drain spinach in a colander, pressing down firmly with a
wooden spoon to squeeze out excess moisture. Chop spinach, add to pan,
and cook for about 5 minutes, until both vegetables are tender.   4 servings

CURRIED CAULIFLOWER

$^1/_2$ cup vegetable oil
1$^1/_2$ pounds cauliflower, cut into flowerets
1$^1/_4$ cups plain yogurt
2 tablespoons curry powder

Heat half the oil in a large pan. Add cauliflower and cook over medium heat for 5 minutes. Using a slotted spoon, transfer cauliflower to a bowl and pour yogurt over the top. Heat remaining oil in pan. Add curry powder and fry for 2 minutes, stirring. Return cauliflower and yogurt to pan and stir gently to combine. Cook over low heat for 10 minutes. Pour in $1^1/_4$ cups hot water and simmer for 20 minutes, or until cauliflower is tender, stirring occasionally.

4 servings

STIR-FRIED CHINESE VEGETABLES

$2^1/_2$ tablespoons peanut oil
$1^1/_2$ pounds bok choy, sliced into 1 inch pieces
16 ounce can whole baby corn, drained
2 tablespoons oyster sauce

Heat wok or large skillet over high heat. Add oil and heat until just smoking. Add vegetables and stir-fry for 1 minute. Add sauce and $^1/_3$ cup water. Season with pepper to taste. Stir-fry for 2-3 minutes more.

4 servings

STIR-FRIED GINGER BROCCOLI WITH CASHEW NUTS

$1^1/_2$ pounds broccoli, divided into small flowerets
2–3 tablespoons peanut oil
$1^1/_2$ inch piece fresh gingerroot, finely shredded
$^1/_3$ cup cashew nuts

Peel and diagonally slice broccoli stems. Branch flowerets and stems in boiling salted water for 30 seconds. Drain well. Refresh under cold running water and drain again. Heat wok or large skillet over high heat. Add oil and heat until just smoking. Add ginger and stir-fry for 2-3 seconds. Add broccoli and nuts, and stir-fry for 2-3 minutes. Serve immediately.

4 servings

ARTICHOKE AND BELL PEPPER STIR-FRY

1 large red bell pepper
2–3 tablespoons Garlic Oil (see page 102) or olive oil
1 pound frozen artichoke hearts, thawed and sliced, or canned, drained and sliced
1 tablespoon balsamic vinegar

Broil bell pepper under medium heat, turning frequently, for 8–10 minutes, until blistered and charred all over. Wrap in aluminum foil or a clean damp dish towel. Leave for a few minutes. Peel away skin. Halve, core, and deseed bell pepper. Cut flesh into thin strips. Heat wok or large skillet over high heat. Add oil and heat until just smoking. Add artichokes and bell pepper strips and stir-fry for 2 minutes. Sprinkle over vinegar and season to taste. Serve immediately.

4 servings

JUST POTATOES

ROAST POTATOES WITH ROSEMARY AND GARLIC

$^1/_4$ cup olive oil
$1^1/_2$ pounds medium potatoes in their skins, quartered lengthwise
2 tablespoons chopped rosemary
4 cloves garlic, sliced

Put half the oil into a large roasting pan. Heat in a preheated oven, 450°F. Make sure potatoes are dry. Combine remaining oil and rosemary in a bowl. Add potatoes and toss to coat. Transfer potatoes to roasting pan. Shake to give an even layer. Roast on top shelf of oven for 20 minutes. Remove from oven. Rearrange potatoes so that they cook evenly. Scatter garlic amongst potatoes. Return to oven and cook for 5 minutes more. Season to taste and serve immediately.

4 servings

SCALLOPED POTATOES WITH ONIONS

2 pounds potatoes, thinly sliced
1 large onion, thinly sliced
$^2/_3$ cup beef broth
2 tablespoons/$^1/_4$ stick butter, melted

Make layers of potatoes and onion in a well-greased ovenproof dish. Season generously. Bring broth to a boil and pour over potatoes. Brush liberally with melted butter. Cover with aluminum foil and bake in a preheated oven, 350°F, for $1^1/_2$ hours. Remove foil and cook for 30 minutes more, until potatoes are cooked through and lightly browned. Broil under medium heat until potatoes are brown and crisp on top.

4-6 servings

NEW POTATOES WITH LEMON AND THYME

1$^1/_2$ pounds small new potatoes
$^1/_3$ cup Garlic Oil (see page 102) or olive oil
grated zest of 2 lemons
1 tablespoon chopped fresh thyme or 2 teaspoons dried

Cook potatoes in boiling salted water for about 10 minutes, until
partially cooked but still firm. Drain and leave to cool. Halve lengthwise.
Heat oil in a large skillet. Add potatoes, lemon zest, and thyme. Cook,
stirring frequently, for 10-15 minutes, until browned and cooked through.
4 servings

GRIDDLED WARM NEW POTATOES

1$^3/_4$ pounds small new potatoes, halved lengthwise
finely grated zest and juice of 2 limes
$^1/_2$ cup grapeseed oil
2 tablespoons chopped mint, plus a few leaves for garnish

Heat a griddle pan or nonstick skillet over high heat. Put a layer of
potato halves on pan and cook for 6 minutes each side, reducing heat as
required. Remove and keep warm while cooking remaining potatoes. Put
lime zest and juice, oil, and chopped mint into a screw-top jar. Replace
lid and shake well to combine. Toss potatoes in dressing. Transfer to
warmed serving dish and garnish with mint leaves.
4 servings

POTATO AND AVOCADO PURÉE

1 pound potatoes
sprig of mint
1 ripe avocado, halved, pitted, and peeled (see page 15)
finely grated zest of $^1/_2$ lemon

Put potatoes into a pan with mint. Add cold water to cover and bring to a boil. Reduce heat and simmer until potatoes are just tender. Drain well, discarding mint. Transfer potatoes to a food processor or blender. Add avocado and lemon zest, and season to taste. Whizz until smooth. Transfer purée to a heavy-bottomed pan and heat through over low heat, stirring.   4 servings

FLASH MASH
MASHED POTATOES WITH CILANTRO

2 pounds floury potatoes, peeled and cut into large chunks
$^1/_3$ cup olive oil
3 tablespoons chopped cilantro leaves and stems
milk

Cook potatoes in boiling salted water for 15–20 minutes, until tender. Drain well. Return to pan and mash until smooth. Meanwhile, heat oil in a small pan. Remove from heat and add cilantro. Transfer to a food processor or blender and process to form a smooth paste. Add cilantro paste to mashed potatoes and season to taste. Beat gently until combined. Add a little milk to soften mixture. Serve immediately.   4 servings

MASHED POTATOES WITH PESTO AND PARMESAN

2 pounds floury potatoes, peeled and cut into large chunks
2–3 tablespoons pesto sauce (or use Pistou, see page 85)
$^3/_4$ cup shredded Parmesan cheese
hot milk

Cook potatoes in boiling salted water for 15–20 minutes, until tender. Drain well. Return to pan and mash until smooth. Add pesto (or pistou) and Parmesan, and season to taste. Beat gently over low heat until combined. Add a little hot milk to soften mixture. Serve immediately.
4 servings

MASHED POTATOES WITH CHEDDAR AND SCALLIONS

2 pounds floury potatoes, peeled and cut into large chunks
6 scallions, finely chopped
4 tablespoons/$\frac{1}{2}$ stick/$\frac{1}{4}$ cup butter
1 cup shredded cheddar cheese

Cook potatoes in boiling salted water for 15–20 minutes, until tender. Drain well. Return to pan and mash until smooth. Beat in scallions, butter, and cheese over low heat, until combined and cheese has melted. Season to taste.

4 servings

PARSNIP AND POTATO MASH WITH ROASTED GARLIC

2 heads garlic
$\frac{2}{3}$ cup olive oil or Rosemary Oil (see page 103)
1 pound parsnips, peeled and thickly sliced
1 pound floury potatoes, peeled and cut into large chunks

Cut a small slice from top of each head of garlic. Put in a small baking pan. Pour over half the oil and season to taste. Cover with aluminum foil and bake in a preheated oven, 400°F, for 1 hour. Cook potatoes and parsnips in boiling salted water for 15–20 minutes, until tender. Drain well. Return to pan and mash until smooth. Remove baking pan from oven. When cool enough to handle, separate cloves and squeeze soft-roasted garlic from cloves into mash with any oil. Add remaining oil and beat over low heat until combined. Season to taste.

4 servings

PARSNIP AND CARROT SOUR CREAM MASH

$1^1/_4$ pounds parsnips, peeled and sliced
$^3/_4$ pound carrots, peeled and sliced
$^2/_3$ cup sour cream
1-2 teaspoons grated nutmeg

Cook parsnips and carrots in boiling salted water for 15-20 minutes, until tender. Drain well. Return to pan and mash until smooth. Beat in sour cream and nutmeg over low heat until combined. Season to taste.
4 servings

POTATO AND YELLOW TURNIP MASH

1 pound floury potatoes, peeled and cut into large chunks
1 pound yellow turnips, peeled and cut into chunks
$^1/_2$ cup bacon drippings, reserved from cooking bacon
3 tablespoons chopped chives

Cook potatoes and yellow turnips in boiling salted water for 15-20 minutes, until tender. Drain well. Return to pan and mash until smooth. Heat bacon drippings in a pan and add to mash with chives. Beat over low heat until combined. Season to taste.
4 servings

PASTA AND GRAINS

CHEESE AND HERB PASTA

FUSILLI WITH PARMESAN AND PINE NUTS

10 ounces fusilli (twists)
generous 1 cup pine nuts
$^1/_3$-$^1/_2$ cup Basil Oil (see page 102)
1 cup shredded Parmesan cheese

Cook pasta in boiling salted water according to the package instructions, until just tender. Toast pine nuts in a dry skillet over medium heat, stirring constantly, until golden. Heat oil over low heat. Drain pasta well, pour over hot oil, and toss to coat. Turn into a warmed serving dish and sprinkle with pine nuts and Parmesan.

4 servings

LEMON AND PARMESAN ORZO

10 ounces dried orzo
5 tablespoons Garlic Oil (see page 102)
zest and juice of 2 lemons
1$^1/_2$ cups shredded Parmesan cheese

Cook pasta in boiling salted water according to the package instructions, until just tender. Beat oil with lemon zest and juice. Add Parmesan and beat until combined. Season to taste. Drain pasta well. Turn into a warmed serving dish, pour over oil mixture, and toss to coat.

4 servings

PAPPARDELLE WITH PESTO AND POTATOES

$^3/_4$ pound new potatoes, or large red-skinned potatoes cut into chunks
2 tablespoons olive oil
10 ounces dried pappardelle
$^2/_3$ cup pesto sauce (or use Pistou, see page 85)

Cook potatoes in boiling lightly salted water for 15-20 minutes, until just tender. Drain and dry on paper towels. Put into a shallow dish with oil and 1 tablespoon coarse salt. Toss gently to combine. Cook pasta in boiling salted water according to the package instructions, until just tender. Drain well and return to pan. Add potatoes and pesto (or pistou) and toss well to combine.

4 servings

TWO CHEESE PASTA

$^3/_4$ pound penne
6 tablespoons/$^3/_4$ stick butter
1 cup shredded Gruyère or Swiss cheese
1 cup shredded Parmesan cheese

Cook pasta in boiling salted water according to the package instructions, until just tender. Drain, reserving a little cooking water. Melt butter in pasta pan over low heat. Add pasta and cheese, and toss to combine. Remove from heat as soon as cheese has melted. Add a little reserved cooking water if dry. Season to taste and serve immediately.

4 servings

TAGLIATELLE WITH LEMON AND TARRAGON BUTTER

8 tablespoons/1 stick/$^1/_2$ cup softened butter
grated zest and juice from $^1/_2$ small lemon
1 tablespoon chopped tarragon
$^3/_4$ pound dried tagliatelle verde

Put butter into a small bowl. Gradually beat in lemon juice, then zest and tarragon. Cook pasta in boiling salted water according to the package instructions, until just tender. Drain well. Turn into a warmed serving dish. Add butter and toss with pasta to coat.

4 servings

COOK'S KNOW-HOW

Add 1 tablespoon vegetable oil to pasta cooking water, to prevent pasta from sticking together and to keep water from boiling over.

FETTUCCINE WITH MASCARPONE AND WALNUTS

$^3/_4$ lb dried fettuccine
$^1/_4$ cup Garlic Oil (see page 102)
$1^3/_4$ cups chopped walnuts
1 cup mascarpone cheese

Cook pasta in boiling salted water according to the package instructions, until just tender. Meanwhile, heat oil in a pan over medium heat. Add nuts and sauté, stirring, for 2-3 minutes. Reduce heat to low and add mascarpone. Heat through, stirring. Drain pasta. Turn into a warmed serving dish and add sauce. Toss to combine.

4 servings

SPINACH TORTELLINI WITH BLUE CHEESE DRESSING

1 pound spinach-filled tortellini
$2^1/_2$ cups crumbled blue cheese
6 tablespoons/$^3/_4$ stick butter
$^2/_3$ cup heavy cream

Cook pasta in boiling salted water according to the package instructions, until just tender. Put cheese in a small pan over low heat. Add butter and cream. Stir until cheese is melted and mixture is warmed through. Season to taste with pepper. Drain pasta and return to pan. Add sauce and toss well to combine. Serve immediately.

4 servings

FETTUCCINE WITH CREAM, BUTTER, AND PARMESAN

$3/4$ pound dried fettuccine
1 cup heavy cream
2 tablespoons/$1/4$ stick butter
1 cup shredded Parmesan cheese

Cook pasta in boiling salted water according to the package instructions, until just tender. Put cream and butter in a pan over low heat. Drain pasta, reserving some of cooking water, and return to pan. Add cream and butter to pan with Parmesan. Briefly toss over low heat. Add a little reserved cooking water if dry. Season with pepper and serve.
4 servings

CREAM CHEESE AND HERB PASTA

1 pound dried spaghetti or linguine
1 cup cream cheese with garlic
1-2 tablespoons lemon juice
2 tablespoons chopped flatleaf parsley

Cook pasta in boiling salted water according to the package instructions, until just tender. Put cheese into a bowl. Beat in lemon juice and half the parsley. Drain pasta well. Return to pan. Add cheese mixture to pasta. Toss briefly over low heat until melted and combined. Serve immediately, scattered with remaining parsley.
4 servings

BROCCOLI AND STILTON TAGLIATELLE VERDE

$3/4$ pound dried tagliatelle verde
$1/2$ pound broccoli flowerets
$1 1/2$ cups crumbled Stilton or other blue cheese
$2/3$ cup heavy cream

Cook pasta in boiling salted water according to the package insructions, until just tender. Meanwhile, cook broccoli in boiling lightly salted water until tender. Put cheese and cream into a pan over low heat. Heat until cheese has melted and mixture is warmed through. Season to taste with pepper. Drain pasta well. Divide between individual plates and top with sauce and broccoli.

4 servings

PASTA WITH VEGETABLES

FUSILLI WITH ARTICHOKES AND TOMATOES

$14^{1}/_{2}$ ounce can seasoned tomatoes
2 tablespoons basil
$^{3}/_{4}$ pound fusilli (twists)
$^{3}/_{4}$ pound frozen artichoke hearts, thawed and halved, or canned, drained and halved

Put tomatoes in a pan with basil. Bring to a boil, cover, and simmer while pasta is cooking. Cook pasta in boiling salted water according to the package instructions, until just tender. Add artichokes to tomatoes and simmer for about 3 minutes. Drain pasta well. Divide pasta between serving plates. Top with sauce.

4 servings

SPAGHETTI WITH MUSHROOMS AND PARSLEY

$^{3}/_{4}$ lb dried spaghetti
$^{1}/_{4}$ cup Garlic Oil (see page 102)
$^{3}/_{4}$ pound mushrooms, finely silced
2 tablespoons chopped flatleaf parsley

Cook pasta in boiling salted water according to the package instructions, until just tender. Meanwhile, heat oil in a large skillet, add mushrooms, and sauté over a medium heat for about 5 minutes or so. Add half the parsley to the mushrooms and season to taste. Drain pasta well. Turn into a warmed serving dish. Add mushrooms and oil, and toss well to combine. Scatter with remaining parsley.

4 servings

PENNE WITH ROASTED RED BELL PEPPER AND OREGANO

$^3/_4$ pound penne
6 red bell peppers, quartered, cored, and deseeded
$^2/_3$ cup Garlic Oil (see page 102)
1 tablespoon dried oregano

Put the bell peppers, skin side up, in a roasting pan and drizzle with about half the oil. Scatter over oregano. Roast in a preheated oven, 400°F, for about 30 minutes, until softened and browned. Cook pasta in boiling salted water according to the package instructions, until just tender. Remove pan from oven. Slice bell peppers into strips. Drain pasta and return to pan. Add bell peppers and remaining oil. Briefly toss over low heat until combined.

4 servings

MOZZARELLA AND PLUM TOMATO LASAGNA

6 sheets dried lasagna verde
10 large plum tomatoes
$^1/_2$ pound mozzarella, sliced
2 tablespoons chopped oregano or 1 tablespoon dried

Cook lasagna in boiling salted water according to the package instructions, until just tender. Line a greased rectangular 5-cup ovenproof dish with 2 sheets lasgna, cutting to fit if necessary. Slice 6 tomatoes and arrange half the slices over pasta, packing them well. Season with salt and add a few slices of cheese and some oregano. Lay 2 lasagna sheets on top and cover with remaining tomato slices, half remaining cheese, and remaining oregano. Top with remaining lasagna sheets. Cut remaining tomatoes into wedges and scatter over pasta with rest of cheese. Cook in a preheated oven, 400°F, for 20-30 minutes. Remove lasagna from oven and leave to rest for 10 minutes before serving.

4 servings

COOK'S KNOW-HOW

To check the volume of an ovenproof dish or pan, pour in water up to just below rim. Pour into a measuring cup to measure.

SPAGHETTI WITH OLIVE SAUCE

$1^1/_2$ cups pitted black olives, chopped
3 cloves garlic, finely chopped
$^1/_2$ cup olive oil
1 pound dried spaghetti

Combine olives, garlic, and half the oil. Cover and let stand overnight. Cook pasta in boiling salted water according to the package instructions, until just tender. Meanwhile, heat remaining oil in a pan over low heat, add olive and garlic mixture, and continue cooking until pasta is done. Drain pasta well. Turn into a warmed serving dish. Add sauce, toss to combine, and season with pepper to taste.

4 servings

SEAFOOD PASTA

CREAMY SHRIMP AND CAPER CONCHIGLIE

$3/4$ pound conchiglie (shells)
$1^1/4$ cups heavy cream
1 pound peeled cooked shrimp
2-3 tablespoons chopped capers

Cook pasta in boiling salted water according to the package instructions, until just tender. Meanwhile, put cream into a pan over medium heat. Bring to a boil, stirring. Add shrimp and capers, and simmer for 5 minutes. Drain pasta well. Turn into a warmed serving dish. Add sauce and toss to combine. Season to taste.   4 servings

LINGUINE WITH FRESH SALMON

$3/4$ pound dried linguine verde
$1^1/4$ cups heavy cream
$3/4$ pound cooked salmon fillet, flaked
4 scallions, finely chopped

Cook pasta in boiling salted water according to the package instructions, until just tender. Meanwhile, put cream into a pan over medium heat. Bring to a boil, stirring. Add salmon and scallions, and simmer for 5 minutes, until heated through. Season to taste. Drain pasta. Turn into a warmed serving dish. Add sauce and toss to combine.
4 servings

PENNE WITH SMOKED SALMON

10 ounces penne
$1^1/4$ cups sour cream
1 tablespoon finely chopped dill, plus sprigs for garnish

$^1/_2$ pound smoked salmon, cut into strips

Cook pasta in boiling salted water according to the package instructions, until just tender. When pasta is almost ready, put sour cream into a pan and heat very gently, stirring, until hot but not boiling. Add dill and season to taste. Remove pan from heat and stir in smoked salmon. Drain pasta, reserving some of cooking water. Turn into a warmed serving dish. Add sauce and toss to combine. Add a little cooking water if dry. Garnish with dill sprigs.

4 servings

FETTUCCINE WITH TUNA AND FRESH TOMATO SAUCE

1 pound small plum tomatoes or cherry tomatoes, halved
1 fresh hot green chili, or to taste, deseeded and finely chopped
$^3/_4$ lb dried fettuccine
$6^1/_2$ ounce can tuna in olive oil

Put tomatoes and chili into a pan. Simmer over medium heat, stirring occasionally, while pasta is cooking. Cook pasta in boiling salted water according to the package instructions, until just tender. Drain tuna, reserving oil, and flake. When pasta is almost ready, add tuna to tomatoes with some of reserved oil and heat through. Season to taste. Drain pasta. Turn into a warmed serving dish. Add sauce and toss to combine.

4 servings

SPAGHETTI WITH CLAMS

2 pounds baby clams in their shells, cleaned
$^1/_4$ cup white wine
$14^1/_2$ ounce can seasoned tomatoes
$^3/_4$ pound dried spaghetti

Put clams into a pan with wine. Cover and cook over high heat, shaking pan vigorously at intervals, until clams open. Remove from pan with a slotted spoon, discard shells, and reserve clams. Strain cooking liquid into a pan with tomatoes. Cook, uncovered, over medium heat for 20 minutes, stirring occasionally. Cook pasta in boiling water according to the package instructions, until just tender. When pasta is almost ready, add clams to sauce and heat through. Season to taste. Drain pasta and turn into a warmed serving dish. Add sauce and toss to combine.

4 servings

PASTA WITH MEAT

PENNE WITH CHILI TOMATOES AND BACON

$^1/_2$ pound thinly sliced unsmoked bacon, cut into short strips
$14^1/_2$ ounce can seasoned tomatoes
1 teaspoon dried chili flakes or 1 fresh hot chili, deseeded and chopped, or to taste
$^3/_4$ pound penne

Heat a large nonstick skillet over medium heat. Add bacon and cook, stirring, until fat runs and bacon turns brown and crisp. Add tomatoes and chili to pan and simmer while pasta is cooking. Season to taste. Cook pasta in boiling salted water according to the package instructions, until tender. Drain pasta and turn into a warmed serving dish. Add sauce and toss to combine.

4 servings

PENNE WITH CHICKEN LIVERS

10 ounces penne
$^1/_3$ cup Garlic Oil (see page 102)
1 red onion, sliced
10 ounces chicken livers, trimmed

Cook pasta in boiling salted water according to the package instructions, until tender. Meanwhile, heat oil in a large skillet over high heat. Add onion and sauté for a few minutes, stirring frequently, until softened. Add chicken livers and sauté, stirring, until browned all over but still a little pink inside. Season to taste. Drain pasta and turn into a warmed serving dish. Add pan contents and toss to combine.

4 servings

LINGUINE WITH HAM AND CHEESE

1 cup light cream
$^1/_2$ pound cooked lean ham, diced
1 cup shredded Parmesan cheese
$^3/_4$ lb dried linguine

Put cream in a heavy-bottomed skillet over low heat. When hot, add ham and season to taste. Cook over low heat, stirring frequently, for 10 minutes. Do not allow to boil. Stir in Parmesan and remove from heat. Meanwhile, cook pasta in boiling salted water according to the package instructions, until tender. Drain and turn into a warmed serving dish. Add sauce and toss to combine.

4 servings

SPAGHETTI WITH PEPPERONI AND BACON

$^3/_4$ pound dried spaghetti
$^1/_4$ pound thickly sliced bacon, diced
$^1/_4$ pound pepperoni, sliced
1 cup frozen mixed peas and corn, or other frozen mixed vegetables

Heat a nonstick skillet over medium heat. Add bacon and cook, stirring, until fat runs. Add pepperoni and cook, stirring, until browned and bacon is crisp. Cook pasta in boiling salted water according to the package instructions, until tender. Meanwhile, cook vegetables in boiling salted water according to package instructions, until tender. Drain pasta and vegetables. Turn into a warmed serving dish. Add bacon and pepperoni with hot pan drippings. Toss to combine and serve immediately.

4 servings

PASTA WITH FAVA BEANS AND BACON

2 ounces thickly sliced smoked bacon, diced
1³/₄ pounds shelled fava beans
3 ounces Pecorino or Parmesan cheese
³/₄ pound dried tagliatelle or fettuccine

Heat a large nonstick skillet over medium heat. Add bacon and cook, stirring, until fat runs and bacon turns brown and crisp. Remove bacon from pan with a slotted spoon and drain on paper towels. Keep warm. Add beans to pan and cook over low heat, stirring, for 5 minutes. Add 1 cup warm water and simmer for 25 minutes, until tender. Season to taste. Cook pasta in boiling salted water according to the package instructions, until tender. Drain pasta and return to pan. Add cheese and toss briefly over low heat to combine. Divide between individual plates, spoon over beans, and scatter over bacon.

4 servings

NICE RICE

KEDGEREE

³/₄ cup long-grain rice
1 pound smoked haddock fillet
4 tablespoons/¹/₂ stick/¹/₄ cup butter
3 hard-cooked eggs, chopped

Cook rice in boiling salted water according to the package instructions, until just tender. Meanwhile, poach fish in a little water for 10 minutes. Drain and flake. Drain rice well. Melt butter in a large skillet over medium heat. Add fish, rice, and eggs, and heat through, stirring, until thoroughly hot. Season to taste.

4 servings

SEAFOOD PILAU

1 cup long-grain rice
$^1/_3$ cup olive oil or Garlic Oil (see page 102)
$1^1/_2$-2 tablespoons curry powder
1 pound peeled cooked shrimp or mixed cooked seafood, defrosted if frozen

Cook rice in boiling salted water according to the package instructions, until just tender. Drain, reserving a little cooking liquid. Heat oil in a large skillet over medium heat. Add curry powder and cook, stirring, for 2 minutes. Add rice and seafood, and heat through, stirring, until thoroughly hot, adding a little reserved liquid to moisten. Season to taste.
4 servings

RISOTTO MARINARA

4 tablespoons Garlic Oil (see page 102)
$1^1/_4$ cups long-grain rice
14 ounce can baby clams, drained
$2^1/_2$ cups fish or chicken broth

Heat oil in a large skillet over medium heat. Add rice and sauté, stirring constantly, for 2-3 minutes, until golden. Stir in clams and broth. Bring to a boil, stirring. Cover and simmer for 15 minutes, until rice is tender and liquid absorbed.
4 servings

GREEN RISOTTO

2 vegetable bouillon cubes
$1^2/_3$ cups long-grain rice
10 ounces frozen spinach, thawed and drained
$1^1/_4$ cups shredded Parmesan cheese.

Crumble bouillon cubes into a pan of boiling water. Stir to blend. Cook rice in broth according to package instructions, until just tender. Meanwhile, put spinach into a pan. Heat through over low heat, stirring frequently. Drain rice. Return to pan and add spinach and Parmesan. Stir briefly over low heat before serving.

4 servings

RICE WITH PEPPERONI AND PARMESAN

$1^2/_3$ cups long-grain rice
2 tablespoons/$^1/_4$ stick butter
5 ounces pepperoni, sliced
5 tablespoons shredded Parmesan cheese

Cook rice in boiling salted water according to the package instructions, until just tender. Meanwhile, melt butter in a large skillet. Add pepperoni and cook for a few minutes, until browned. Drain rice and return to pan. Add rice and cheese, and stir briefly over low heat before serving. Season to taste.

4 servings

COOK'S KNOW-HOW
It doesn't take any additional time to cook an extra batch of rice, to create another meal for the next day or so. Use for a salad (see pages 97-8) or as a filling for stuffed peppers (see page 254–5).

QUICK COUSCOUS

SHRIMP AND CILANTRO COUSCOUS

$1^1/_4$ cups pre-cooked couscous
$1^1/_4$ cups hot fish or chicken broth
$^3/_4$ pound peeled cooked shrimp
6 ounces cherry tomatoes, chopped

Put couscous into a large heatproof bowl. Pour over hot broth. Cover and let stand for 10 minutes. Stir in shrimp and tomatoes. Season to taste. Turn into a fine-mesh strainer over a pan of simmering water. Steam, covered, for about 10 minutes, stirring occasionally, until ingredients are thoroughly hot and couscous is tender.

4 servings

COUCOUS WITH CHICKEN AND MANGO

1¹/₄ cups pre-cooked couscous
1¹/₄ cups hot chicken broth or clear chicken soup
3 cups diced cooked chicken
1 ripe mango, pitted, peeled, and diced

Put couscous into a large heatproof bowl. Pour over hot broth or soup. Cover and let stand for 10 minutes. Stir in chicken and mango. Season to taste. Turn into a fine-mesh strainer over a pan of simmering water. Cover and steam for about 10 minutes, stirring occasionally, until ingredients are thoroughly hot and couscous is tender.

4 servings

APRICOT AND PISTACHIO COUSCOUS

1¹/₄ cups pre-cooked couscous
1¹/₄ cups hot vegetable broth
1¹/₄ cups dried ready-to-eat apricots, chopped
1 cup shelled pistachio nuts

Put couscous into a large heatproof bowl. Pour over hot broth. Cover and let stand for 10 minutes. Stir in fruits and nuts. Turn into a fine-mesh strainer over a pan of simmering water. Cover and steam for about 10 minutes, stirring occasionally, until ingredients are hot and couscous is tender.

4 servings

COUSCOUS WITH ROASTED BELL PEPPERS

6 mixed bell peppers (red, orange, and yellow), ccored, deseeded, and quartered
$^1/_4$ cup Garlic Oil (see page 102)
$1^1/_4$ cups pre-cooked couscous
$1^1/_4$ cups hot vegetable broth

Put bell peppers in a roasting pan. Pour over oil and toss to coat. Arrange bell peppers skin side up. Roast in a preheated oven, 400°F, for about 30 minutes, until tender and browned. Meanwhile, put couscous into a large heatproof bowl. Pour over hot broth. Cover and let stand for 10 minutes. Stir in roasted bell peppers and any pan juices or drippings. Season to taste. Turn into a fine-mesh strainer over a pan of simmering water. Cover and steam for about 10 minutes, stirring occasionally, until ingredients are thoroughly hot and grains are fluffed up.

4 servings

COOK'S KNOW-HOW
Most couscous now available has been pre-cooked, so it requires minimal preparation. However, always check the instructions on the package.

COUSCOUS WITH LAMB AND ROSEMARY

$^3/_4$ pound lean ground lamb
2 teaspoons very finely chopped rosemary, plus extra sprigs for garnish
$1^1/_4$ cups pre-cooked couscous
$1^1/_4$ cups hot lamb broth

Combine lamb with rosemary. Shape into small balls, pressing meat firmly to hold together. Heat a nonstick skillet over high heat. Add meatballs and brown on all sides. Lower heat to medium-low and cook, turning occasionally, for about 10 minutes, until cooked through. Meanwhile, put couscous into a large heatproof bowl. Pour over hot broth. Cover and let stand for 10 minutes. Stir in meatballs and any pan drippings. Season to taste. Turn into a fine-mesh strainer over a pan of simmering water. Cover and steam for about 10 minutes, stirring occaisonally, until ingredients are thoroughly hot and couscous is tender. Garnish with rosemary sprigs before serving.

4 servings

NOODLES AND RICE ON THE SIDE

STIR-FRIED VEGETABLE NOODLES

1 pound egg noodles
$^1/_4$ cup peanut or corn oil
14 ounce can bean sprouts, or mixed bean shoots and water chestnuts, drained
2 tablespoons teriyaki marinade

Cook noodles in boiling salted water according to the package instructions. Drain and refresh under cold running water until cool. Heat a wok or large skillet over high heat. Add oil and heat until just smoking. Add vegetables and stir-fry for 1 minute. Add noodles and teriyaki, and stir-fry for 2 minutes. Serve immediately.

4 servings

CELLOPHANE NOODLES WITH SHRIMP AND CILANTRO

2 fish or vegetable bouillion cubes
$^1/_2$ pound cellophane or bean thread noodles, soaked according to instructions on package
$^1/_2$ pound green shrimp, peeled and deveined (see page 173)
2 tablespoons chopped cilantro

Crumble bouillion cubes into a pan of boiling water. Stir well to dissolve. Add noodles to boiling broth and cook according to the package instructions. Add shrimp 5 minutes from end of cooking time. Drain, reserving about $^3/_4$ cup broth. Turn noodles into a warmed serving dish and pour over broth. Add cilantro and toss to combine.

4 servings

CRISPY NOODLES

1 pound egg noodles
vegetable oil, for deep-frying
1 tablespoon sesame oil or Chili Oil (see page 102)
1 tablespoon toasted sesame seeds

Cook noodles in boiling salted water according to the package instructions. Drain well. Dry on paper towels. Heat oil in a deep pan. Add noodles and fry for about 3 minutes, until crisp. Drain well. Turn into a warmed serving dish. Season with salt and sprinkle with sesame or chili oil and sesame seeds.

4 servings

EGG-FRIED RICE

3 tablespoons peanut oil
1 medium egg, beaten
$^3/_4$ pound cooked long-grain rice
1 tablespoon light soy sauce

Heat a wok or large skillet over high heat. Add oil and heat until just smoking. Pour in egg and cook until just beginning to set. Add rice and soy sauce, and stir-fry for 2-3 minutes.

4-6 servings

FRAGRANT RICE

1^1/$_4$ cups long-grain rice
1 cinnamon stick
seeds of 4-6 cardamom pods
3-4 cloves

Cook rice in boiling salted water according to the package insructions with spices. Drain and discard spices before serving.

4 servings

FINGER FOOD

PASTRY PLEASURES

SPICY SAUSAGE ROLLS

$1^1/_2$ pounds bulk sausage
2 tablespoons hot pepper sauce
1 pound puff pastry, defrosted if frozen
1 egg yolk, beaten

Combine bulk sausage and hot pepper sauce in a bowl. Divide pastry in half and roll out each piece to form a rectangle 20 x $4^1/_2$ inches. Divide sausage mixture in half and form a long sausage on each pastry strip, arranging it to one side. Dampen long edge of pastry with a little beaten egg yolk. Fold pastry over to enclose bulk sausage. Brush rolls with beaten egg yolk. Cut each roll into 25 equal pieces and arrange on cookie sheets. Bake in a preheated oven, 425°F, for 20 minutes. Serve warm or cold.
Makes 50

SAUSAGE TWISTS

1 pound chipolata sausages or thin link sausages
$^1/_2$ pound puff pastry, defrosted if frozen
1 egg yolk, beaten
caraway seeds, for sprinkling

Broil sausages for about 6 minutes, turning, until partially cooked. Leave to cool. Roll out pastry until wafer thin. Cut into strips and roll around sausages in a spiral. Arrange on a cookie sheet. Brush pastry with beaten egg yolk and sprinkle with caraway seeds. Bake in a preheated oven, 450–475°F, for 15 minutes. Reduce heat after 7–8 minutes if necessary. Serve warm or cold.

8 servings

SAUSAGE CHEESE SAVORIES

1 pound small link sausages
1 tablespoon Dijon mustard
6 ounces cheddar or Swiss cheese, cut into fingers the same length as sausages
4 ounces thin slices bacon, halved

Broil sausages until just brown all over. Spread one side with mustard. Press a finger of cheese against each. Wrap in bacon and secure with toothpicks. Broil under high heat, turning once or twice, until bacon is crisp and brown. Serve hot. They can be served on fingers of toast.

8 servings

SAUSAGE SLICE

1 pound bulk sausage (spicy or herb-flavored if available)
13 ounces puff pastry, defrosted if frozen
1 small cooking apple, peeled, cored, and sliced
1 egg, beaten

Combine bulk sausage with seasoning to taste. Roll out three-quarters of pastry to a 10 inch square. Put onto a greased cookie sheet. Spread bulk sausage over pastry to within $1/2$ inch of edge. Arrange apple slices on top. Dampen edges of pastry with water. Roll out remaining pastry. Cut into $1/2$ inch wide strips. Make a woven trellis with strips over top of apples. Brush with beaten egg. Cover loosely and chill for 30 minutes. Cook in a preheated oven, 425°F, for 15 minutes. Reduce temperature to 350°F and cook for a further 15-30 minutes. Slice and serve hot.

6 servings

HAM HORSESHOES

$^1/_2$ pound puff pastry dough, defrosted if frozen
$^1/_4$ pound sliced cooked lean ham
2-3 teaspoons Dijon mustard
1 egg, beaten

Roll out pastry thinly to a large square. Trim edges. Divide into 6 equal squares. Cut across each square to form triangles. Spread each slice of ham with mustard to taste. Put a slice onto each triangle. Starting from the longest edge working toward the point, roll up each pastry triangle, enclosing the ham. Damp corner with beaten egg and secure. Gently shape into curved horseshoes. Put onto a greased cookie sheet. Brush with beaten egg. Bake in a preheated oven, 425–450°F, for 15-20 minutes, until pastry is cooked and browned.   6 servings

PHYLLO PASTRY PARCELS

8 sheets phyllo pastry dough, defrosted if frozen
6 tablespoons/$^3/_4$ stick/3 ounces butter, melted

Cover pastry dough with a damp dish towel. Working with 1 sheet at a time, cut into 3 equal strips. Brush well with butter. Put a teaspoon of filling at one end of each strip. Fold one corner of pastry diagonally over to enclose filling. Continue folding to make a neat triangular parcel. Brush parcel with more butter and put on a cookie sheet. Repeat with remaining filling, dough, and butter to make 24 parcels. Bake in a preheated oven, 425°F, for 8-10 minutes, until golden brown. Serve hot.
Makes 24

RICOTTO AND SPINACH FILLING

$^1/_2$ pound frozen spinach, defrosted, chopped, and squeezed dry
1 cup ricotta cheese

Combine and season to taste.

140

FETA CHEESE AND MINT FILLING

$^3/_4$ pound feta cheese
4 tablespoons chopped mint

Mash cheese with mint. Season to taste with pepper.

SPICY POTATO FILLING

about $1^1/_4$ pounds small new potatoes
1 tablespoon curry powder

Cook potatoes in boiling salted water until just tender. Drain. Dice when cool enough to handle. Melt an extra 4 tablespoons/$^1/_2$ stick/$^1/_4$ cup butter in a pan. Add curry powder and cook, stirring, for 2 minutes. Add potatoes and cook, stirring frequently, for 5 minutes. Season to taste and leave to cool.

SMOKED MOZZARELLA AND TOMATO PUFF TARTLETS

$^1/_2$ pound puff pastry dough, defrosted if frozen and divided into 8
2 tablespoons pesto sauce (or use Pistou, see page 85)
2 large ripe tomatoes, each cut into 4 slices
$^1/_4$ pound smoked mozzarella, cut into 8 slices

Roll out each piece of pastry thinly. Using a 4 inch pastry cutter, stamp out 8 circles. Prick with a fork and transfer to cookie sheets. Spread each with sauce, leaving a thin border around edges. Top with a tomato, then a cheese slice. Season to taste. Bake tartlets at top of a preheated oven, 425°F, for 10-15 minutes, until puffed up and golden. Serve warm.

8 servings

MIXED PLATTER

POTATOES WRAPPED IN PARMA HAM

12 small new potatoes, boiled
12 very thin slices Parma ham
2 tablespoons olive oil
sea salt

Roll each potato in a slice of Parma ham, molding ham to shape of potato. Lightly oil a roasting pan. Add potatoes and cook in a preheated oven, 400°F, for 20 minutes. Turn or rearrange during cooking to cook evenly. Serve sprinkled with sea salt.

4 servings

FILLED CHERRY TOMATOES

24 cherry tomatoes
$^1/_3$ cup cream cheese with herbs
lemon juice
$^1/_3$ cup peeled cooked shrimp, finely chopped

Slice top off each tomato and reserve. Scoop out flesh and put a little into a bowl. Invert tomato shells on paper towels to drain. Add cheese, lemon juice to taste, and shrimp to tomato flesh. Beat to combine. Arrange tomato shells right way up on a serving platter. Spoon filling into each and replace tops.

6-8 servings

WALNUT AND GORGONZOLA CHICORY

2 heads chicory
1 cup diced Gorgonzola cheese
$^1/_2$ cup roughly chopped walnuts
$^1/_4$ cup sour cream

Remove leaves from chicory stalks. Discard any blemished leaves. Stir together cheese, walnuts, and sour cream. Arrange chicory leaves on a serving platter. Spoon cheese mixture onto leaves.

4 servings

MARINATED SHRIMP

24 large cooked shrimp, peeled but tails left on
3 cloves garlic, minced
grated zest and juice of 1 lime, plus lime wedges for garnish
2 tablespoons chopped cilantro, plus leaves for garnish

Put shrimp in a shallow nonmetallic dish with other ingredients. Toss well to combine. Cover and refrigerate for 2 hours. Turn into a serving dish. Garnish with lime wedges and cilantro leaves. Serve with toothpicks for spearing shrimp.

6-8 servings

SESAME CHICKEN WINGS

8 chicken wings
grated zest and juice of $1/2$ lemon
4 tablespoons clear honey
2 tablespoons sesame seeds

Put chicken wings in a single layer in an ovenproof dish. Combine lemon zest and juice with honey and sesame seeds. Season to taste. Pour over chicken. Cover and refrigerate for at least 30 minutes, turning wings once or twice. Cook in a preheated oven, 400°F, for 15 minutes. Pour off marinade and return wings to oven for 10 minutes more, until golden brown and cooked through.

8 servings

SKEWERS

SESAME CHICKEN SKEWERS

2 teaspoons sesame seeds
3 boneless, skinless chicken breasts
$^1/_4$ cup sesame oil

Toast sesame seeds in a dry skillet, stirring constantly, until golden. Cut chicken into thin strips. Thread onto 8 wooden skewers, previously soaked in water for 30 minutes. Drizzle with oil and sesame seeds. Broil under high heat for 15 minutes, turning frequently and brushing with oil.

8 servings

AROMATIC CHICKEN SKEWERS

1 pound boneless, skinless chicken breast, cut into thin strips
$^1/_4$ cup Garlic Oil (see page 102)
grated zest and juice of 1 lemon
2 tablespoons light soy sauce

Put chicken into a shallow nonmetallic dish. Beat together other ingredients. Season to taste. Pour over chicken and toss to coat. Cover and refrigerate for an hour or so. Thread onto 16 small wooden skewers, previously soaked in water for 30 minutes. Broil under high heat for 15 minutes, turning skewers frequently and brushing with marinade, until cooked through.

8 servings

LAMB SKEWERS

1 pound lean lamb, cut into small cubes or thin strips
juice of 1 lemon
$^1/_4$ cup olive oil
1 tablespoon dried oregano

Put lamb into a shallow nonmetallic dish. Beat together other ingredients. Season with black pepper. Pour over lamb and toss to coat. Cover and refrigerate for an hour or so. Thread onto 16 small wooden skewers, previously soaked in water for 30 minutes. Broil under high heat for about 6-8 minutes, turning frequently and brushing with marinade, until well browned.

8 servings

SHRIMP SATÉ

1 pound peeled and deveined green shrimp (see page 173)
$^1/_4$ cup coconut milk
grated zest and juice of 1 lime
2 cloves garlic, minced

Put shrimp into a shallow nonmetallic dish. Beat together other ingredients. Season to taste. Pour over shrimp and toss to coat. Cover and refrigerate for 1 hour. Thread onto 16 small wooden skewers, previously soaked in water for 30 minutes. Broil under high heat for about 4 minutes, turning and brushing with marinade, until cooked through.

8 servings

PORK SATÉ

1 pound pork tenderloin, cut into small cubes or thin strips
3 tablespoons peanut oil
2 tablespoons dark soy sauce
3 cloves garlic, minced

Put pork into a shallow dish. Beat together other ingredients. Season to taste. Pour over pork and toss to coat. Cover and refrigerate for an hour or so. Thread onto 16 small wooden skewers, previously soaked in water for 30 minutes. Broil under high heat for about 8 minutes, turning frequently and brushing with marinade, until cooked through.

8 servings

BEEF SATÉ

1 tablespoon cumin seeds
1 pound tenderloin steak, cut into small cubes or strips
3 tablespoons dark soy sauce
2 cloves garlic, minced

Toast the cumin seeds in a dry skillet over medium heat until the aroma rises. Cool, then grind with a pestle and mortar or in a coffee grinder. Put beef into a shallow dish. Combine soy sauce with cumin and garlic. Pour over beef and toss to coat. Cover and refrigerate for an hour or so. Thread onto 16 small wooden skewers, previously soaked in water for 30 minutes. Broil under high heat for 6-8 minutes, turning frequently and brushing with marinade, until tender.

8 servings

DIPPING SAUCES

GINGER AND CHILI

1 inch piece fresh gingerroot, finely chopped
2 cloves garlic, minced
1 small red chili, deseeded and finely chopped
$^1/_3$ cup teriyaki marinade

Stir together ingredients in a serving bowl with $^1/_4$ cup boiling water. Serve cooled with Sesame Chicken Skewers or Pork Saté, pages 144-5.

8 servings

SWEET AND SOUR

$^1/_4$ cup sugar
3 tablespoons rice or wine vinegar
$^1/_2$ teaspoon salt
1 teaspoon dried chili flakes

Put ingredients into a small pan with 2 tablespoons water. Heat gently, stirring, until sugar is dissolved. Bring to a boil. Remove from heat and leave until cold. Transfer to a serving bowl. Serve with Aromatic Chicken Skewers, page 144.

8 servings

PEANUT AND CHILI

3 tablespoons chunky peanut butter
$^1/_3$ cup canned coconut milk
2 cloves garlic, minced
1 teaspoon dried chili flakes

Beat together ingredients in a bowl until well combined. Serve with Shrimp, Pork, or Beef Saté, pages 145–6.

6-8 servings

CHEESE

$^2/_3$ cup mayonnaise
juice of $^1/_2$-1 lemon
1 cup finely shredded cheddar cheese
$^2/_3$ cup thick cream, lightly whipped

Beat together until well blended. Season to taste. Serve as a dipping sauce for store-bought seafood nuggets or fish goujons.

10 servings

WALNUT

1 cup chopped walnuts
1 tablespoon Garlic Oil (see page 102)
1 teaspoon lemon juice
1 cup plain yogurt

Put walnuts, oil, and lemon juice into a food processor or blender and blend until smooth. Add yogurt and blend quickly. Season to taste. Transfer to a serving bowl. Serve with Lamb Skewers, page 144.

8 servings

COOK'S KNOW-HOW

Bring lemons and limes up to room temperature before squeezing, to yield the maximum amount of juice with ease. Ideally, choose organic fruits or unwaxed fruits, particularly when using the zest.

TOOTHPICK TREATS

TRICOLORE

avocados, cubed
mozzarella, cubed
Lemon and Oil Dressing (see page 99), or lemon juice
cherry tomatoes

Toss avocado and mozzarella in dressing, or sprinkle avocado with lemon juice. Thread an avocado, then a mozzarella cube, then a tomato onto toothpicks or small wooden skewers.

SWISS CRUNCH

red-skinned apples, cored and cut into wedges
lemon juice
celery stalks, cut into chunks
Swiss or Gruyère cheese, cubed

Sprinkle apple wedges with lemon juice, to prevent discoloration. Thread a celery chunk, then a cheese cube, then an apple wedge onto toothpicks or small wooden skewers.

CHÈVRE AND BLACK OLIVE

  Italian-style bread, cubed
  pesto sauce (or use Pistou, see page 85)
  firm chèvre (goat's cheese), cubed
  pitted black olives

  Spread one side of bread cubes with pesto (or pistou). Thread a bread cube, then cheese cube, then an olive onto toothpicks or small wooden skewers.

FETA AND CUCUMBER

  cucumber, cut into chunks
  mint leaves
  feta cheese, cubed
  cherry tomatoes

  Thread a cucumber chunk, mint leaf, cheese cube, then a tomato onto toothpicks or small wooden skewers.

BLUE CHEESE AND GRAPE

  red bell pepper, cored, deseeded, and cut into chunks
  blue cheese, cubed
  green seedless grapes

  Thread a bell pepper chunk, cheese cube, then a grape onto toothpicks or small wooden skewers.

MELON AND PARMA HAM

  honeydew melon, scooped into balls
  very thin slices Parma ham, halved
  Cantaloupe melon, scooped into balls

Thread a honeydew melon ball, then a loosely rolled up piece of Parma ham, then a cantaloupe melon ball onto toothpicks or small wooden skewers. Alternatively, wrap ham loosely around melon balls.

CANAPÉS

DEVILLED SARDINE

$4^1/_2$ ounce can sardines in olive oil, drained and a little oil reserved
2 teaspoons tomato paste
$^1/_4$ teaspoon chili powder, or to taste
about 12 crackers or rounds whole-wheat bread, stamped out with a round pastry cutter

Mash sardines with a little reserved oil and remaining ingredients. Spread onto crackers or whole-wheat bread rounds.
enough for about 12 canapés

CAVIAR

12 crackers or slices melba toast (store-bought or see page 45) or whole-wheat bread rounds, stamped out with a round pastry cutter
$^1/_4$ cup mayonnaise
3 hard-cooked eggs, sliced
4 tablespoons lumpfish caviar

Spread the crackers, melba toast, or bread rounds with mayonnaise. Arrange egg slices on top. Spoon over caviar.
makes 12

SHRIMP AND EGG

3-4 scrambled eggs, cooled
2 tablespoons mayonnaise

$^2/_3$ cup peeled cooked shrimp, chopped, plus 12 whole peeled shrimp
12 crackers, melba toast (store-bought or see page 45), or whole-wheat
bread rounds, stamped out with a round pastry cutter

Blend scrambled eggs with mayonnaise and chopped shrimp. Spread on
crackers, melba toast, or bread rounds. Top each with a whole shrimp.
makes 12

ASPARAGUS ROLLS

12 small, thin slices brown bread
4–6 tablespoons cream cheese
lemon juice
12 cooked asparagus spears

Cut crusts from bread. Roll each slice with a rolling pin. Beat cream
cheese with lemon juice to taste. Spread onto bread. Lay one asparagus spear
diagonally on each bread slice. Roll up so that asparagus tips just show.
Makes 12

SMOKED SALMON PINWHEELS

thin slices very fresh brown bread, crusts removed
mayonnaise
thin slices smoked salmon
lemon juice

Spread one side of bread with mayonnaise. Top with smoked salmon.
Squeeze over lemon juice. Season with black pepper. Roll up each slice
to enclose filling. Wrap with plastic wrap and chill in the refrigerator for
an hour or so. Unwrap and slice crosswise.

NUTS AND NIBBLES

MARINATED OLIVES

$^3/_4$ cup pimiento-stuffed green olives
$^3/_4$ cup black olives
2 cloves garlic, minced
grated zest 1 lemon
about $1^1/_2$ cups extra-virgin olive oil

Put ingredients into a bowl and stir well. Spoon into a screw-top jar. Replace lid and store in a cool place for 3-4 days, turning frequently.
6-8 servings

SALTED ALMONDS

$^1/_3$ cup olive oil
$1^2/_3$ cups blanched almonds
sea salt

Heat oil in a small, heavy-bottomed skillet. Add nuts in several batches and stir-fry over medium heat, until evenly browned. Using a slotted spoon, transfer nuts to a bowl. Add plenty of sea salt and stir to coat nuts. They can be kept in an airtight container for up to 3 days.
8 servings

CURRIED NUTS

3 tablespoons/$1^1/_2$ ounces butter
1 tablespoon curry powder
1 pound mixed shelled, skinned nuts, such as almonds, brazils, walnuts, pecans, and hazelnuts
1 teaspoon salt

Melt butter over medium heat in a roasting pan. Blend in curry powder. Cook, stirring, for 30 seconds. Add nuts and stir until well coated. Roast in a preheated oven, 300°F, for 30 minutes, stirring at regular intervals. Remove nuts from oven and toss with salt. Allow to cool completely. Store in an airtight container for up to 2 weeks.

15 servings

SPICY-GLAZED CASHEWS

2 tablespoons/^{1}/$_4$ stick sweet butter
3 tablespoons clear honey
^{1}/$_4$ teaspoon cayenne pepper or chili powder
1^1/$_4$ cups unsalted cashew nuts

Melt butter in a small, heavy-bottomed pan over medium heat. Stir in honey and cayenne or chili powder with 1 tablespoon water and 1 teaspoon salt. Bring to a boil, stirring. Add nuts and stir over medium heat for 5 minutes, until nuts are toasted and well coated with glaze. Tip onto a greased cookie sheet. Leave to cool. These nuts are best eaten the same day.

8 servings

SPICED CHICKPEAS

14 ounce can chickpeas (garbanzo beans), drained
2 tablespoons olive oil
2 plump cloves garlic, minced
paprika and ground cumin, for sprinkling

Spread chickpeas on a cookie sheet. Combine oil and garlic. Pour over chickpeas and toss to coat. Cook in a preheated oven, 400°F, for about 15 minutes, stirring occasionally. Tip onto paper towels to dry. While still warm, toss with paprika, cumin, and seasoning to taste. Serve while warm or store in an airtight container in a cool place for up to 2 weeks.

4 servings

SPICY PALMIERS

$1/2$ pound puff pastry, defrosted if frozen
2 tablespoons olive oil
$1/2$ teaspoon paprika or chili powder to taste
3 tablespoons shredded Parmesan cheese

Roll out pastry thinly. Trim to make a rectangle about 8 x 10 inches.
Combine oil with paprika or chili powder. Brush three-quarters of paste
all over pastry to give an even coating. Fold over both long sides of pastry
to meet in middle. Spread over a layer of remaining paste and fold pastry
in half lengthwise. Press down firmly. Cut into 24 thin slices and transfer,
cut side down, to 2 greased cookie sheets. Bake in a preheated oven,
400°F, for 10 minutes. Turn over and bake for a further 4-5 minutes, until
crisp and golden. Cool on a wire rack.
Makes 24

CARAWAY CRACKERS

1 cup all-purpose flour
$1/2$ teaspoon ground cumin
4 tablespoons/$1/2$ stick/$1/4$ cup butter
1-2 teaspoons caraway seeds

Sift flour and cumin into a bowl with a little salt. Cut in butter until
mixture resembles fine bread crumbs. Stir in seeds to taste, then gradually
work in 2-3 tablespoons water to form a soft dough. Knead lightly until
smooth. Cover with plastic wrap and leave to rest for 30 minutes. Roll
out dough thinly. Using a 3 inch pastry cutter, stamp out rounds. Re-roll
trimmings and repeat to make 16-18 rounds. Transfer crackers to a large
cookie sheet. Prick with a fork. Bake in a preheated oven, 375°F, for 10
minutes. Turn over and bake for 5 minutes more, until crisp and lightly
golden. Cool on a wire rack. These crackers will keep in an airtight
container up to 2 days.
Makes 16-18

PARMESAN CURLS

1 pound puff pastry, defrosted if frozen
2 tablespoons coarse-grain mustard
$^1/_2$ cup shredded Parmesan cheese
2 tablespoons sesame seeds

Roll out pastry. Trim to make a rectangle 12 x 14 inches. Spread with mustard and sprinkle with Parmesan. Fold in half and roll lightly. Cut pastry into about 20 long, thin strips. Sprinkle with sesame seeds. Twist strips into loose spirals and arrange on cookie sheets. Bake in a preheated oven, 450°F, for 15 minutes, until puffy and golden.
Makes about 20

CHIVE BISCUITS

8 tablespoons/1 stick/$^1/_2$ cup butter
$^1/_2$ cup cream cheese
1 cup all-purpose flour, sifted
1 tablespoon chopped chives

Beat butter and cheese together until well blended. Stir in flour and chives. Mix with a fork until well combined. Roll dough into a ball and wrap in aluminum foil. Chill in the refrigerator for at least an hour. Roll out dough to $^1/_4$ inch thick. Cut into $1^1/_2$ inch rounds with a plain cutter. Arrange spaced out on greased cookie sheets. Bake in a preheated oven, 425°F, for 10 minutes. Cool on a wire rack.
Makes about 60

ROOT VEGETABLE CHIPS

2 large potatoes
2 small sweet potatoes
3 parsnips
vegetable oil, for deep-frying

Slice vegetables into fine wafers using a potato peeler. Slice parsnips lengthwise. Keep different vegetables separate. Heat 2 inches vegetable oil in a deep pan until it reaches 350-375°F, or until a cube of bread browns in 30 seconds. Pat vegetables dry with paper towels. Keeping vegetables separate, deep-fry in batches for 30 seconds-1$^{1}/_{2}$ minutes, until crisp and golden. Drain on paper towels and let cool on a wire rack. Transfer chips to a bowl and season to taste.

4-6 servings

SWEET SOMETHINGS

CREAM HORNS

$^{1}/_{2}$ pound puff pastry, defrosted if frozen

Roll out pastry into a rectangle about 10 x 13 inches. Trim edges. Cut into 10 strips 1 inch wide. Dampen one long edge of each strip with water and wind round a cornet mold, starting at the point and overlapping the dampened edge. Gently press edges together. Repeat with remaining strips and cornet molds. Place on a dampened cookie sheet, cover, and chill for 15 minutes. Bake in a preheated oven, 425°F, for 15-20 minutes, until lightly browned. Let stand for 5 minutes before carefully removing molds. Cool on a wire rack.

Makes 10

STRAWBERRY JAM AND CREAM FILLING

strawberry jam
$^{3}/_{4}$ cup heavy cream, whipped
confectioner's sugar, for dusting

Spoon a little jam into each horn. Pipe or spoon in cream. Dust with sugar.

CHOCOLATE CREAM FILLING

confectioner's sugar
2-3 ounces semisweet chocolate, grated, or $^1/_2$ cup chocolate chips
$^3/_4$ cup heavy cream, whipped

Blend a little sugar and chocolate with cream. Pipe or spoon into horns. Dust with sugar.

ALMOND SNAPS

whites of 2 large eggs
2-3 drops almond essence
$^1/_2$ cup superfine sugar
1 cup ground almonds

Beat egg whites in a large bowl until stiff peaks form. Add essence and fold in sugar and almonds. Divide mixture into about 18 balls. Arrange well spaced out, allowing them to spread to about 3 inches in diameter, on greased cookie sheets. Flatten with your fingers. Bake one batch at a time in a preheated oven, 350-375°F, just above the center, for about 12 minutes. Watch carefully as they cook. Remove from oven and let cool for about 1 minute, until set enough to handle. Lift first cookie and roll around greased handle of a wooden spoon. Remove and cool on a wire rack. Repeat with remaining cookies. Store in an airtight container when cold. Serve on their own or for dipping into whipped cream or other whipped desserts.
Makes about 18

COCONUT RUM ROCKIES

$^1/_2$ pound semisweet chocolate, broken into small pieces
2 teaspoons rum
$1^1/_4$ cups dry unsweetened shredded coconut

Melt chocolate in a heatproof bowl over a pan of hot water, stirring occasionally. Stir in rum and enough coconut to give a stiff, rocky consistency. Place in small rough heaps on greased aluminum foil. Leave to set in a cool place.

Makes about 10

CHOCOLATE TRUFFLES

11 ounces semisweet chocolate
3 tablespoons heavy cream
$^1/_2$-1 tablespoon whiskey or cognac
2 tablespoons cocoa powder

Heat cream in a pan until tepid. Break $^1/_4$ pound chocolate into small pieces. Melt in a small heatproof bowl over a pan of hot water, stirring occasionally. Remove bowl from heat and slowly pour in cream, stirring constantly. Let mixture cool. Add whiskey or cognac. Beat for 3-4 minutes, until mixture becomes lighter and forms peaks. Cool in the refrigerator for about 20 minutes. Dust work surface with cocoa powder. Form spoonfuls of chocolate paste into balls about 1 inch in diameter. Roll each in cocoa powder to cover. Leave to cool until firm. Melt remaining chocolate, broken into pieces, over hot water. Spear each truffle on a toothpick and dip one by one into melted chocolate. Place on a sheet of aluminum foil to set.

Makes about 10

COOK'S KNOW-HOW
Provide finger bowls when serving any foods to be eaten
with
the fingers. Use hand-hot water and add lemon slices, to cut
any grease. Supply paper napkins alongside.

FISH AND SHELLFISH

SEAFOOD BITES

CEVICHE SALMON

6 ounce piece salmon fillet
lemon juice, for sprinkling
olive oil, for sprinkling
chopped dill or fennel, to garnish

Using a sharp knife, cut down through salmon into very thin slices—
about the same as sliced smoked salmon. Arrange raw salmon on 2 plates
in a single layer. Sprinkle salmon with lemon juice and oil. Season to
taste. Garnish with dill or fennel. Serve with triangles of thin brown bread
and butter.

GRIDDLED LOBSTER TAILS WITH OREGANO BUTTER

8 tablespoons/1 stick/^{1}/$_2$ cup butter
1 large bunch oregano, chopped
4 raw lobster tails, halved lengthwise
2 lemons, cut into wedges

Beat butter and oregano together in a small bowl. Season to taste.
Spoon butter onto waxed paper. Wrap paper around and form into a roll.
Put in freezer to chill for 10 minutes. Heat a griddle pan or nonstick
skillet over high heat. Cook lobster tails for 5 minutes on each side. Put
lemons in pan for 3 minutes to color and warm juice. Remove butter
from freezer. Slice and arrange on top of cooked lobster. Serve with
lemon wedges.

4 servings

FISH WHIRLS

8 small flounder fillets or 4 plaice fillets, halved and skinned
triple quantity Anchovy Butter (see page 180), softened
3 tablespoons chopped parsley
3 large ripe tomatoes, sliced

Spread anchovy butter on skinned side of fillets, reserving a little. Sprinkle with parsley. Roll up firmly and secure with wooden toothpicks. Put tomato slices in a layer into an ovenproof dish. Season well. Arrange fish rolls on top. Melt remaining anchovy butter in a pan. Brush fish rolls with butter. Cover with aluminum foil. Bake in a preheated oven, 350°F, for about 20 minutes, until cooked through.

4 servings

TIMBALES OF SMOKED SALMON

6 ounces smoked salmon, thinly sliced
$^1/_4$ cup sour cream
1 tablespoon red lumpfish caviar, plus extra to garnish
2 ripe tomatoes, skinned, deseeded, and chopped

Rinse 2 small soufflé dishes and line with plastic wrap. Line with 5 ounces of the smoked salmon slices, allowing them to overlap sides. Chop remaining smoked salmon finely. Beat sour cream until soft peaks form. Fold in salmon and caviar. Fill molds with mixture, fold over sides of overlapping salmon, cover, and chill overnight. Rub tomatoes through a fine nylon strainer. Season to taste and chill. Unmold timbales onto individual serving plates. Spoon a circle of tomato purée around each. Garnish with extra lumpfish caviar.

2 servings

GRIDDLED SCALLOPS WITH SAGE

16 scallops, shelled and prepared
1 bunch sage leaves
3 tablespoons olive oil
1 tablespoon balsamic vinegar

Dry scallops thoroughly with paper towels. Heat a griddle pan or nonstick skillet over high heat. Cook scallops on each side for 2-3 minutes. Add sage leaves and cook until just wilting. Beat together oil and vinegar. Remove scallops and sage from heat. Toss well with dressing. Season to taste.

4 servings

COOK'S KNOW-HOW

To remove scallops from their shells, insert a strong, short knife between the two shells. Twist firmly to prise the shells apart. To clean, remove the flat grayish fringe around the scallop, reserving the nugget of white flesh and the orange coral. If it is visible, remove the black digestive cord from the side of the flesh.

FISH CLASSICS

FISH MEUNIÈRE

4 white fish fillets, about 6 ounces each
8 tablespoons/1 stick/$^1/_2$ cup butter
1-2 tablespoons lemon juice
1-2 tablespoons chopped parsley

Lightly season fish. Melt butter in a large heavy-bottomed skillet over medium heat. Cook fish until flesh flakes when tested with the tip of a knife. Lift fish onto a warmed dish. Heat butter over high heat until it turns golden brown. Add lemon juice and parsley, and stir to combine. Pour over fish.

4 servings

TROUT WITH ALMONDS

4 medium trout, cleaned
juice of 1 lemon
8 tablespoons/1 stick/$^1/_2$ cup butter
$^1/_2$ cup blanched slivered almonds

Season trout to taste. Sprinkle with lemon juice. Melt butter in broiler pan under medium heat. Broil trout for 5 minutes. Turn over and scatter with almonds. Broil for about 4 minutes more, until fish are tender and almonds well browned. Transfer fish, almonds, and pan drippings to a warmed serving dish. Serve immediately.

4 servings

SALMON FILLETS IN OATMEAL

4 salmon fillets, about 5 ounces each
$1^1/_3$ cups oatmeal
4 slices bacon, diced
lemon wedges

Season fish to taste. Spread out oatmeal on a board. Press fish onto oatmeal, to coat. Heat a large skillet over medium heat. Cook bacon until the fat runs and bacon becomes brown and crisp. Remove with a slotted spoon and keep warm. Cook fish in bacon drippings until light golden brown. Scatter over bacon and serve with lemon wedges.

4 servings

BROILED RED SNAPPER

3 tablespoons olive oil
2 red snapper, about 1 pound each, cleaned
4 cloves garlic, sliced
$^1/_4$ cup dry white bread crumbs

Put oil into a shallow dish. Season to taste. Add fish, turning to coat in oil. Leave to marinate for at least 1 hour, turning once. Drain fish, reserving marinade. Put a little garlic inside each fish. Broil under medium heat for 6-8 minutes each side, turning once. About 3 minutes before end of cooking, sprinkle fish with bread crumbs. Spoon over reserved marinade. Finish cooking and serve immediately.

4 servings

BAKED FISH WITH POTATO AND GARLIC

4 medium potatoes
12 young whole cloves garlic, peeled
$^3/_4$ cup olive oil or Lemon and Thyme Oil (see page 102)
1 or 2 red snapper or sea bream (porgy), weighing about 2 pounds, cleaned

Cook potatoes whole in boiling salted water for about 10 minutes, until softened. Leave to cool, then peel and slice. Arrange potato slices, slightly overlapping, in a roasting pan or ovenproof dish. Tuck garlic in between slices. Pour over about three-quarters of oil. Season to taste. Lay fish on top. Dizzle over remaining oil. Season well with sea salt. Cover tightly with aluminum foil and bake in a preheated oven, 325°F, for 50 minutes. Remove foil. Increase heat to 375°F. Bake for about 20 minutes more, until fish is cooked through, potatoes are browned at the edges, and garlic is soft-roasted.   4 servings

HERBED FISH

BROILED SALMON STEAKS WITH CUCUMBER AND CHIVE SAUCE

$1^1/_4$ cups sour cream
$^1/_2$ cucumber, finely chopped
2 tablespoons chopped chives
4 salmon steaks, about 6 ounces each

Combine first three ingredients. Season to taste. Cover and chill in the refrigerator for 1 hour. Season salmon to taste. Broil under a medium heat, turning twice, for 8-10 minutes, until flesh is cooked through and skin is brown and crisp. Serve immediately, with sauce spooned alongside.
4 servings

FISH STEAKS WITH ANCHOVY, LEMON, AND PARSLEY SALSA

5 anchovy fillets canned or bottled in oil, drained and
oil reserved ($^1/_2$ cup)
1 cup flatleaf parsley
juice and zest of 1 lemon
4 salmon or swordfish steaks, about 6 ounces each

Put anchovies and parsley into a food processor or blender. Process to form a paste. Add reserved oil, lemon zest and lemon juice, and seasoning to taste. Season fish steaks. Broil under medium heat for about 4-5 minutes on each side, until cooked through. Transfer to warmed serving plates and top with a spoonful of salsa.
4 servings

TROUT WITH PARMESAN AND BASIL DRESSING

$^1/_4$ cup Garlic Oil (see page 102), plus extra for brushing
4 trout fillets, about 7 ounces each
large handful basil leaves
$1^1/_4$ cups shredded Parmesan cheese

Lightly brush a cookie sheet with oil. Heat under a very hot broiler. Put trout onto hot sheet, season to taste, and broil for 5 minutes. Put basil into a bowl. Blend in oil using a hand-held blender. Alternatively, use a pestle and mortar. Sprinkle broiled fish with Parmesan. Broil for 3-5 minutes more, until Parmesan turns golden. Serve with basil sauce spooned over.   4 servings

BROILED MACKEREL WITH FENNEL AND GOOSEBERRY SAUCE

4 mackerel, about 10-12 ounces each, cleaned
fennel fronds and stalks, plus 1 tablespoon finely chopped
14 ounce can gooseberries, drained and juice reserved
$1/2$–1 tablespoon light brown sugar

Season mackerel inside and out. Stuff with fennel. Make 2-3 deep diagonal slashes in flesh on each side. Broil under medium heat for about 5-7 minutes each side depending on size, turning carefully, until cooked through. Meanwhile, put gooseberries into a food processor or blender with some of juice. Process until blended. Strain through a nylon strainer into a pan. Add sugar to taste. Bring to a boil, stirring. Lower heat and stir in fennel. Remove herb stuffing before serving mackerel, with the hot gooseberry sauce separately.

4 servings

RED SNAPPER WITH ALMOND DRESSING

large handful of cilantro
scant $1/2$ cup almonds
about $1/3$ cup olive oil or Garlic Oil (see page 102)
2 red snapper, about $1^1/2$ pounds each

Put cilantro and almonds into a food processor or blender. With the motor running, gradually add oil in a trickle to make a paste. Cut deep diagonal cuts in both sides of each fish. Spread paste over both sides of fish, working it well into slashes. Cover and refrigerate for 1 hour. Broil fish under medium heat for 6-8 minutes on each side, until flesh just flakes when tested with a fork.

4 servings

SEAFOOD SPECIALS

DEEP-FRIED SQUID

1 pound squid, cleaned
vegetable oil, for deep-frying
2-4 tablespoons all-purpose flour
2 eggs, lightly beaten

Cut squid into rings. Halve tentacles if large. Wash well and dry thoroughly on paper towels. Heat 2 inches oil in a deep pan to 350-375°F, until a cube of bread browns in 30 seconds. Meanwhile, liberally season flour. Dip squid into beaten egg, then coat with flour. Deep-fry in batches for 1-2 minutes, until crisp and golden. Drain each batch on paper towels. Keep cooked squid warm in a hot oven while cooking remainder. Serve immediately.

4 servings

BROILED SALMON WITH SPICED SOUR CREAM

3 tablespoons sour cream
1 tablespoon horseradish sauce
2 teaspoons sun-dried tomato paste, tomato paste, or tomato catsup
2 salmon steaks, about 6 ounces each

Blend together sour cream, horseradish, and tomato paste or catsup. Season to taste. Season salmon to taste. Broil under medium heat for 2-3 minutes on each side. Spread about half the sour cream mixture over each side of steaks. Broil for a further 2-3 minutes on each side. Serve with remaining sour cream mixture spooned alongside.

2 servings

GRIDDLED TUNA WITH SHALLOT JUS

4 tuna steaks, about $^1/_4$ pound each
4 shallots, finely chopped
$1^1/_4$ cups red wine
$^2/_3$ cup Marsala

Heat a griddle pan or nonstick skillet over high heat. Cook tuna steaks two at a time for 3 minutes on each side. Remove from pan and keep warm. Combine shallots, wine, and Marsala in a small pan. Season to taste. Bring to a boil and boil rapidly until reduced by half. Return tuna steaks to pan. Add shallot jus and simmer for 2 minutes.

4 servings

SOLE WITH PARMESAN

all-purpose flour, for coating
4 sole or flounder fillets, skinned
6 tablespoons/3 ounces/$^3/_4$ stick butter
$^1/_4$ cup shredded Parmesan cheese

Put flour into a shallow dish. Season well. Dip fillets into seasoned flour to coat lightly on both sides. Shake off excess flour. Melt butter in a large skillet over low heat. Add fillets and cook until golden brown on both sides, turning once. Sprinkle Parmesan over fillets. Cook very gently for 2-3 minutes more, until melted.

4 servings

ROAST ANGLER FISH WITH PARMA HAM

4 angler fish fillets, about 6 ounces each
4 rosemary sprigs
8 slices Parma ham
olive oil, for brushing

168

Season fillets to taste. Place a rosemary sprig on each. Wrap ham slices around fillets. Lightly brush an ovenproof dish with oil. Put fillets in dish. Cook in a preheated oven, 425°F, for 15 minutes.

4 servings

FISH TANDOORI

$^1/_3$ cup plain yogurt
$2^1/_2$ tablespoons ground cumin
1 teaspoon chili powder
4 halibut steaks, about 6 ounces each

Blend yogurt with spices in a bowl. Season well. Add halibut and turn to coat. Cover and refrigerate for 4-5 hours. Transfer fish to a shallow ovenproof dish. Bake, uncovered, in a preheated oven, 350°F, for 20-25 minutes, until cooked through. Serve with cooking juices spooned over.

4 servings

SALMON WRAPPED IN PARMA HAM WITH FONTINA AND BAY

4 salmon fillets, about 6 ounces each, skinned
4 thin slices fontina cheese
4-8 bayleaves, depending on size
8 thin slices Parma ham

Season fillets to taste. Trim any rind from cheese and cut slices to fit top of fillets. Arrange cheese slices on fillets, top with bayleaves, and wrap ham around salmon, securing cheese and bay. Heat a griddle pan or nonstick skillet over medium heat. Cook fillets for 4-5 minutes on each side, turning carefully.

4 servings

TARRAGON-INFUSED SEA BASS FILLETS

4 sea bass fillets, about 6 ounces each
large bunch tarragon
2 tablespoons olive oil
4 tablespoons lemon juice

Heat a griddle pan or nonstick skillet over medium heat. Cook fillets, skin side down, for 3 minutes. Put a quarter of the tarragon on each fillet, pressing it into fish. Turn fish so that it is resting on tarragon. Cook for 3 minutes more. To serve, drizzle fillets with oil and lemon juice. Season to taste. Serve with charred tarragon.

4 servings

SEARED SKATE WINGS WITH LEMON AND CAPERS

2 skate wings, about 10 ounces each
2 teaspoons olive oil
2 tablespoons capers
grated zest and juice of 1 lemon

Cut skate wings in half and pat dry with paper towels. Brush each side with oil. Heat a griddle pan or nonstick skillet over high heat. Sear skate for 3 minutes on each side. If wings are thick, cook for a little longer. Sprinkle capers on top with lemon zest and juice. Cook for a few seconds more. Season to taste and serve immediately.

4 servings

HADDOCK WITH SOUR CREAM AND MUSHROOMS

10 ounces haddock fillet
2 tablespoons/$^1/_4$ stick butter
generous $^1/_2$ cup button mushrooms, sliced
$^1/_2$ cup sour cream

Put haddock into a shallow $2^1/2$ cup ovenproof dish. Season to taste. Dot with half the butter and add $^1/4$ cup water. Cover tightly with aluminum foil. Cook in a preheated oven, 325°F, for 20 minutes. Meanwhile, melt remaining butter in a pan and fry mushrooms for 1 minute. Stir in sour cream and season to taste. Heat through over low heat, stirring. Drain fish. Pour over sauce.

2 servings

SPICED PRAWNS

2 tablespoons coriander seeds
$1^1/4$ cups plain yogurt
3 cloves garlic, minced
$1^1/2$ pounds green shrimp, in their shells

Toast coriander seeds in a dry skillet, stirring, until aroma rises. Leave to cool. Grind in a coffee grinder or with a pestle and mortar. Beat yogurt with ground coriander and garlic until well combined. Put shrimp in a shallow dish. Add yogurt mixture and turn to coat. Cover and refrigerate for about 2 hours, turning occasionally. Thread onto metal or wooden skewers, the latter previously soaked in water for 30 minutes. Broil under high heat for about 4-5 minutes, turning once, until flesh has turned pink.

4 servings

PAN-FRIED SQUID

2 pounds prepared small squid
$^1/4$ cup Chili Oil (see page 102)
3 cloves garlic, minced
$^1/4$ cup lemon juice

Slit squid down one side and lay flat. Score skin with a fine criss-cross pattern. Combine half the oil, garlic, and lemon juice in a bowl. Add squid and toss to coat. Cover and marinate for 15 minutes. Remove squid, reserving marinade. Heat remaining oil in a large skillet or wok over high heat until just smoking. Add squid and season to taste. Stir-fry for 2-3 minutes. The squid will curl up, but hold flat for a few seconds to brown outside. Strain marinade into pan. Stir-fry for a few seconds, then serve immediately.

4 servings

STIR-FRIED SQUID WITH GREEN BELL PEPPER AND GINGER

peanut oil, for deep-frying
$^1/_2$ pound prepared squid, cut into 2 x $1^1/_2$ inch pieces
2 inch piece fresh gingerroot, peeled and thinly sliced
2 green bell peppers, deseeded and sliced

Heat a wok or large skillet over high heat. Add oil and heat to 350-375°F, until a cube of bread browns in 30 seconds. Add squid and deep-fry for about 30 seconds, stirring with chopsticks to prevent pieces sticking together. Pour off all but 1 tablespoon oil. Add ginger and bell pepper. Stir-fry for 1 minute. Season to taste and stir-fry for 1 minute more. Serve immediately.

4 servings

SCALLOPS WITH MINTED PEA PURÉE

$^3/_4$ pound frozen peas
2 teaspoons mint jelly
3 tablespoons Garlic Oil (see page 102)
16 large scallops, shelled and cleaned

Cook peas in a pan of boiling salted water for about 10 minutes, until soft. Drain, reserving some of cooking liquid. Whizz in a food processor or blender, adding some of reserved cooking liquid to make a smooth purée. Add mint jelly and blend. Return to pan and keep warm over low heat, beating occasionally. Heat oil in a large heavy-bottomed skillet over high heat until just smoking. Add scallops and cook for 2-3 minutes on one side. Turn over and cook for about 2 minutes. Season to taste. Pile purée onto 4 dishes, top with scallops, and pour over pan drippings.

4 servings

JUMBO SHRIMP IN CREAM AND MUSTARD SAUCE

4 tablespoons/$^1/_2$ stick/$^1/_4$ cup butter
24 green jumbo shrimp, peeled and deveined
1 cup heavy cream
2-3 teaspoons Dijon mustard

Melt butter in a large skillet. Add shrimp and cook for a few minutes. Stir in cream. Season to taste with mustard and salt and pepper. Simmer very gently for 4-5 minutes, until shrimp are tender.

4 servings

COOK'S KNOW-HOW
To devein shrimp, make a fine cut down the back with a sharp knife. Lift out the black vein with the tip of the knife.

FISH BAKES AND PIES
MEDITTERANEAN TUNA

$^1/_3$ cup Garlic Oil (see page 102)
4 tuna steaks, about 5 ounces each
2 tablespoons chopped oregano or 1 tablespoon dried
14 ounce can seasoned tomatoes

Heat oil in a large skillet over medium heat. Add tuna and cook for 2 minutes on either side. Remove from pan and transfer to an ovenproof dish. Sprinkle with oregano. Add tomatoes to pan. Bring to a boil. Season to taste and simmer for 2-3 minutes. Spoon over tuna. Cover and bake in a preheated oven, 350°F, for about 25 minutes.   4 servings

CIDERED FISH BAKE

6 tablespoons/³/₄ stick butter
1¹/₂ cups sliced button mushrooms
4 halibut steaks, about 6 ounces each
1 cup hard cider

Melt butter in a skillet. Cook mushrooms for 3–4 minutes, stirring, until softened. Season fish to taste. Put in a shallow ovenproof dish. Top with mushrooms and pan drippings. Pour over cider. Cover and cook in a preheated oven, 350°F, for about 30 minutes, until fish is cooked and sauce well reduced.

4 servings

CREAMY FISH BAKE

6 cod or haddock fillets, defrosted if frozen, cut into chunks
³/₄ cup canned corn kernels, drained
10¹/₄ ounce can condensed cream of mushroom soup
2 teaspoons hot chili sauce

Put fish and corn into an ovenproof dish. Add soup and sauce, and toss well to combine. Bake, uncovered, in a preheated oven, 350°F, for 20–25 minutes, until fish flakes when tested with a fork.

4 servings

FISH PIE

1³/₄ pounds floury potatoes
1¹/₂ pounds smoked haddock fillet
1¹/₄ cups heavy cream
3 tablespoons pesto sauce (or use Pistou, see page 85)

Cook potatoes in boiling salted water until tender. Meanwhile, put haddock in a pan and cover with water. Season with freshly ground black pepper. Poach gently until flesh just flakes when tested with a fork. Drain, reserving cooking liquid. Drain potatoes. Mash with half the pesto (or pistou). Combine cream with remaining pesto. Thin with a little reserved cooking liquid. Flake fish and combine with cream and pesto mixture. Season to taste. Transfer to an ovenproof fish. Top with mashed potatoes. Bake in a preheated oven, 425°F, for about 20–25 minutes, until potato is browned and crisp.

4 servings

FISH IN PASTRY

$^1/_2$ pound puff pastry, defrosted if frozen
7 ounce can pink salmon, drained, bones removed, and flaked
$^1/_4$ cup mayonnaise
1 tablespoon capers, chopped

Roll pastry out thinly. Cut into 4 equal squares. Combine salmon with mayonnaise and capers. Lightly mark squares in half diagonally. Spoon filling onto one half, to the side. Moisten edges. Fold over to form a triangle and enclose filling. Press edges to seal. Moisten edges. Fold over again to form a smaller triangle. Press edges to seal. Transfer to a cookie sheet. Bake in a preheated oven, 425°F, for about 20-25 minutes, until crisp and brown.

2 servings

FISH PACKAGES

COD WITH VERMOUTH AND TARRAGON

4 cod steaks, about 7 ounces each
about 2 tablespoons/$^1/_4$ stick butter
2 tablespoons roughly chopped tarragon
$^2/_3$ cup dry vermouth

Cut 4 sheets of aluminum foil large enough to loosely enclose ingredients. Put a fish steak on each piece of foil. Season to taste. Dot each with butter. Scatter over tarragon. Sprinkle over vermouth. Fold over foil to seal in a loose package. Transfer packages to a cookie sheet. Cook in a preheated oven, 400°F, for 25 minutes. Open packages. Transfer fish and cooking juices to warmed individual plates to serve.

4 servings

TROUT WITH WINE AND THYME

4 medium trout, about 7 ounces each, cleaned
$^1/_4$ cup Garlic Oil (see page 102)
2 tablespoons chopped thyme
$^2/_3$ cup rosé wine

Cut 8 rectangles of waxed paper double the width of each trout and half as long again as fish. Brush one side of each with oil. Put 4 rectangles on a cooking sheet, oiled side up. Put a trout along the center of each. Pull up edges of paper and staple at each corner, to form a container. Put a fish in each. Season to taste. Drizzle with oil, scatter with thyme, and add 2 tablespoons wine to each. Cover with remaining rectangles of paper, oiled side down. Staple at corners to form a lid. Make sure packages loosely contain fish. Staple top and bottom layers of waxed paper together in two or three places. Bake in a preheated oven, 375°F, for 35-40 minutes, until fish is cooked and paper is turning brown. Serve in the packages.

4 servings

FISH STEAKS WITH GINGER

4 halibut or cod steaks, about 6 ounces each
$1^1/_2$ inch piece fresh gingerroot, finely chopped
$^1/_2$ cup dry sherry or rice wine
3–4 tablespoons teriyaki marinade

Cut 4 sheets of aluminum foil large enough to enclose ingredients loosely. Put a fish steak on each. Season to taste. Scatter over ginger. Sprinkle with sherry or wine and teriyaki. Fold over foil to seal. Transfer packages to a cookie sheet. Bake in a preheated oven, 400°F, for 25 minutes. Serve fish in packages.

4 servings

TUNA WITH TOMATES, CAPERS, AND OLIVES

4 tuna steaks, about 6 ounces each
$^1/_2$ pound canned plum tomatoes, drained
1 tablespoon capers, chopped
16 pitted black olives, chopped

Cut 4 sheets of aluminum foil large enough to enclose ingredients loosely. Divide half the tomatoes between each sheet. Scatter over half the capers and olives. Top with a tuna steak. Season to taste. Spoon over remaining tomatoes, capers, and olives. Fold over foil to seal. Transfer packages to a cookie sheet. Bake in a preheated oven, 400°F, for about 25 minutes. Serve fish in packages.

4 servings

HALIBUT WITH SHALLOTS AND OLIVES

4 halibut fillets, about 7 ounces each
2 shallots, finely chopped
8 pitted black olives, sliced
1 lemon

Cut 4 sheets of waxed paper large enough to enclose ingredients. Put a fillet on each piece of paper. Season to taste. Sprinkle with shallots and olives. Squeeze over lemon juice. Cut 4 lemon slices and put 1 on each fillet. Fold over paper to seal in a loose package. Staple to secure. Transfer to a cookie sheet. Cook in a preheated oven, 400°F, for 25 minutes.

4 servings

FISH PATTIES
SMOKED SALMON AND CHIVE

$1^1/_2$ cups mashed poatoes
6 ounces smoked salmon, finely chopped
2 tablespoons chopped chives
8 tablespoons/1 stick/$^1/_2$ cup butter

Combine mashed potatoes, smoked salmon, and chives. Season well.
Melt 2 tablespoons of the butter. Beat into mixture. With wet hands, form
into 8 patties about 1 inch thick. Cover and chill in the refrigerator for 30
minutes, until firm. Melt remaining butter in a skillet over medium heat.
Cook patties until well browned on both sides and heated through.
4 servings

COD AND CAPER

$^1/_2$ pound cooked cod or haddock fillets, flaked
$1^1/_2$ cups mashed potatoes
2-3 tablespoons tartare sauce
$^1/_3$ cup vegetable oil

Combine fish, mashed potatoes, and tartare sauce. Season well. With wet
hands, form into 8 patties about 1 inch thick. Cover and chill in the
refrigerator for 30 minutes, until firm. Heat oil in a skillet over medium
heat. Cook patties until well browned on both sides and heated through.
4 servings

SHRIMP AND PESTO

2 x $4^1/_2$ ounce cans shrimp, drained and chopped
$1^1/_2$ cups mashed potatoes
2-3 tablespoons pesto sauce (or use Pistou, see page 85)
$^1/_3$ cup vegetable oil

Combine shrimp, mashed potatoes, and pesto (or pistou). Season well. With wet hands, form into 8 patties about 1 inch thick. Cover and chill in the refrigerator for 30 minutes, until firm. Heat oil in a skillet over medium heat. Cook patties until well browned on both sides and heated through.

4 servings

TUNA

$3/4$ pound cooked potatoes, roughly chopped
handful of arugula or watercress
4 scallions, chopped
$6^1/_2$ ounce can tuna in olive oil, drained and flaked, oil reserved

Put potatoes into a food processor or blender with arugula or watercress, scallions, tuna, and a little reserved oil. Season to taste. Process to blend. With wet hands, form into 8 patties about 1 inch thick. Cover and chill in the refrigerator for 30 minutes, until firm. Heat remaining reserved oil in a skillet over medium heat. Cook patties until well browned on both sides and heated through.

4 servings

CRABMEAT AND CILANTRO

2 x $1^1/_2$ ounce cans dressed crabmeat
1 cup fresh white bread crumbs
1 tablespoon finely chopped cilantro
2 tablespoons Chili Oil (see page 102)

Combine crabmeat, bread crumbs, and cilantro. Season well. With wet hands, form into 2 patties. Cover and chill in the refrigerator for 30 minutes, until firm. Heat oil in a skillet. Cook patties until well browned on both sides and heated through.

1 serving

SALMON AND PARSLEY

1^1/$_2$ cups mashed potatoes
7 ounce can pink salmon, drained, bones removed, and flaked
2 tablespoons chopped parsley
8 tablespoons/1 stick/^{1}/$_2$ cup butter

Combine mashed potatoes, salmon, and parsley. Season well. Melt about 2 tablespoons of the butter. Beat into mixture. With wet hands, form into 8 patties about 1 inch thick. Cover and chill in the refrigerator for 30 minutes, until firm. Melt remaining butter in a skillet over medium heat. Cook patties until well browned on both sides and heated through.
4 servings

FLAVORED BUTTERS AND SAUCES

ANCHOVY BUTTER

2 tablespoons/^{1}/$_4$ stick butter, softened
1^1/$_2$ teaspoons mashed anchovy fillets
^{1}/$_2$ teaspoon lemon juice

Beat together ingredients. Season to taste. Spoon butter onto waxed paper. Wrap paper around and form into a roll. Refrigerate for 30 minutes. Cut butter into 8 equal slices. Serve on broiled salmon, tuna, or swordfish steaks.
4 servings

WASABI BUTTER

8 tablespoons/1 stick/^{1}/$_2$ cup butter, softened
grated zest and juice of 1 lime
2 teaspoons wasabi paste

Put butter, lime zest and juice, and wasabi paste into a food processor or blender. Process until well blended. Season to taste. Spoon butter onto waxed paper. Wrap paper around and form into a roll. Refrigerate for 30 minutes. Cut butter into 8 equal slices. Serve on broiled tuna and swordfish steaks.

4 servings

COOK'S KNOW-HOW

Wasabi is also called Japanese horseradish. Fresh wasabi can be grated in the same way as horseradish. Wasabi paste, available from specialty and Asian markets, has a hot, pungent flavor.

DILL CREAM

$^1/_4$ cup walnut oil
4 tablespoons chopped dill
1 tablespoon green peppercorns in brine, drained and crushed
$^1/_3$ cup sour cream

Heat oil in a small pan. Stir in dill and peppercorns. Remove from heat. Stir in sour cream. Serve with broiled salmon steaks or trout.

4-6 servings

HERB MAYONNAISE

2 anchovy fillets
2 tablespoons chopped parsley or chives
$^1/_2$ cup mayonnaise (store-bought or use recipe on page 101)
1 teaspoon tarragon vinegar (store-bought or use recipe on page 104)

Put anchovy fillets and herb into a food processor or blender and process until well blended. Add mayonnaise and process briefly to combine. Beat in vinegar and season to taste. Serve with shellfish.

2 servings

GARLIC SAUCE

6 cloves garlic, minced
2 egg yolks
$^1/_3$ cup olive oil
$^2/_3$ cup sour cream

Beat garlic with egg yolks in a bowl. Beat in oil in a fine trickle, until absorbed. Mix in sour cream. Serve with white fish and baked, broiled, or barbecued whole fish.

4 servings

POULTRY
AND GAME

POULTRY CLASSICS

TURKEY SCALLOPS WITH CRANBERRY SAUCE

4 tablespoons/$^1/_2$ stick/$^1/_4$ cup butter
4 turkey scallops or slices turkey breast, beaten to flatten if necessary
1$^1/_4$ cups button mushrooms, sliced
4 tablespoons cranberry sauce (store-bought or use Cranberry and
Orange Sauce, see page 204)

Melt butter in a large heavy-bottomed skillet over low heat. Cook
turkey for about 5 minutes on each side, until cooked through and tender.
Add mushrooms to pan and sauté for 1-2 minutes. Stir in sauce. Blend
with pan juices and a little water. Season to taste. Transfer to a warmed
serving dish.

4 servings

COOK'S KNOW-HOW
To test if poultry is cooked through, pierce the thickest part with a
skewer. If the juices run clear, it is properly cooked; if tinged pink, cook
for a few minutes more and test again.

CHICKEN AND RICE

1 cup long-grain rice
2$^1/_2$ cups cooked diced chicken
16 ounce can creamed corn
4 ounce jar pimientos, drained and chopped

Cook rice in boiling salted water according to the package instructions,
until just tender. Drain and return to pan. Stir in creamed corn and
pimientos. Season well. Cover and cook gently, stirring occasionally, for 8-
10 minutes, until thoroughly hot.

2 servings

CRISPY-BAKED CHICKEN

1 cup crushed potato chips
1¹/₄ cups shredded Parmesan cheese
4 chicken parts
¹/₂ quantity Garlic Butter (see page 205), melted

Mix crushed chips with cheese and freshly ground black pepper to taste. Spread onto a sheet of waxed paper or aluminum foil. Brush chicken with half the butter. Press chicken into crumb mixture. Transfer chicken to a cookie sheet or shallow ovenproof dish. Drizzle over remaining butter. Bake in a preheated oven, 350°F, for 45 minutes to 1 hour, until chicken is cooked through and tender.

4 servings

CHEAT'S CORONATION CHICKEN

1 tablespoon garam masala or curry powder
14 ounce can pineapple chunks in natural juice, drained and juice reserved
1¹/₄ cups mayonnaise
3 cups cold cooked chicken, cut into bite-size chunks

Heat a dry heavy-bottomed skillet over medium heat. Add spice mix and heat for 1-2 minutes, stirring. Blend in 1-2 tablespoons reserved pineapple juice and cook, stirring constantly, for 1 minute. Add another tablespoon or so of juice and cook again for 1 minute. Add one more tablespoon and cook again. Leave to cool. Stir cooled paste into mayonnaise. Toss with pineapple and chicken. Season to taste.

4 servings

COOK'S KNOW-HOW

As with all ground spices, buy curry powder or garam masala in small quantities because it loses its freshness if kept for longer than 6 months. Store in a cool, dry, dark place. Try making your own blend by combining and grinding whole spices.

CHICKEN IN THE OVEN

ROAST CHICKEN WITH LEMON AND ROSEMARY

3 pound oven-ready chicken
2 lemons
1 sprig rosemary
$^1/_2$ cup dry white wine

Season chicken generously. Halve 1 lemon and put inside body cavity, with half the rosemary sprig. Squeeze juice from remaining lemon and reserve. Put chicken into an ovenproof dish. Cook in a preheated oven, 400°F. After about 15 minutes, when skin begins to dry, prick all over with a fork to allow juices to escape. Sprinkle remaining rosemary, finely chopped, over chicken and in pan. Cook for 45 minutes, turning from time to time and basting halfway through with the reserved lemon juice and wine. Rest in a warm place for 10-15 minutes. To serve, slice meat and spoon over cooking juices.

4 servings

CHICKEN WITH MUSTARD AND LEMON

4 chicken parts with skin
2 tablespoons Dijon mustard
grated zest and juice of 2 lemons
vegetable oil, for brushing

Heat a nonstick skillet over medium heat. Cook chicken for about 6 minutes on each side, until skin is well-browned. Blend mustard with lemon zest and juice. Season to taste. Brush a roasting pan with a little oil. Transfer chicken to pan. Brush with mustard mixture. Roast in a preheated oven, 400°F, for about 35-40 minutes, until cooked through and tender.

4 servings

CHICKEN WITH ALMONDS

6 tablespoons/$^3/_4$ stick sweet butter
1 tablespoon olive oil
4 chicken breasts
1 cup slivered almonds

Melt butter with oil in a large heavy-bottomed skillet over medium heat. Fry chicken skin side down first and turning once, until well browned and skin is crisp. Transfer to a roasting pan. Brush liberally with pan drippings, reserving remainder in skillet. Roast near top of a preheated oven, 375°F, for about 45 minutes. Just before chicken is ready, heat reserved butter and oil in skillet over medium heat. Fry almonds, turning frequently, until golden brown. Remove from pan with a slotted spoon and drain on paper towels. Transfer chicken to a warmed dish. Top with almonds.

4 servings

HONEYED CHICKEN

8 tablespoons/1 stick/$^1/_2$ cup sweet butter
4 chicken parts with skin
$^1/_4$ cup clear honey
$^1/_4$ cup lemon juice

Melt half butter in a large heavy-bottomed skillet over medium heat. Arrange chicken in a shallow ovenproof dish or roasting pan. Season to taste. Pour over melted butter. Roast in a preheated oven, 375°F, for about 20 minutes. Melt remaining butter in a pan. Blend with honey and lemon juice. Remove chicken from oven. Turn over and brush with honey and lemon mixture. Return to oven and cook for about 30 minutes more, basting at intervals with honey and lemon, until well browned and crisp.

4 servings

CHICKEN AND CREAMED CORN PIE

$^1/_2$ pound shortcrust pastry dough (store-bought or use Short Crust recipe on page 294, made with 2 cups flour, $^1/_2$ cup fat)
2 cups cooked diced chicken
$^1/_2$ cup chopped cooked lean ham
16 ounce can creamed corn

Roll out pastry dough and use to line an 8 inch pie dish. Roll out a round for a lid. Combine remaining ingredients and put into pie shell. Season well. Damp dough edges and cover with dough lid. Crimp edges to seal. Make a vent in dough lid. Bake in a preheated oven, 425°F, for 15 minutes, then reduce to 375°F and cook for 25–30 minutes, until golden brown.

4 servings

CHICKEN AND MUSHROOM PIE

$^1/_2$ pound shortcrust pastry dough (store-bought or use Short Crust recipe on page 294, made with 2 cups flour, $^1/_2$ cup fat)
$2^1/_2$ cups cooked diced chicken
2 x 6 ounce cans button mushrooms, drained and liquid reserved
10 ounce can condensed cream of celery soup

Roll out pastry dough and use to line an 8 inch pie dish. Roll out a round for a lid. Combine remaining ingredients, adding a little reserved mushroom liquid if mixture is too dry. Put into pie shell. Season to taste. Damp dough edges and cover with dough lid. Crimp edges to seal. Make a vent in dough lid. Bake in a preheated oven, 425°F, for 15 minutes, then reduce to 375°F and cook for 25–30 minutes, until golden brown.

4 servings

MOM'S SCRATCH CHICKEN PIE

$^1/_2$ pound shortcrust pastry dough (store-bought or use Short Crust recipe on page 294, made with 2 cups flour, $^1/_2$ cup fat)
3 ounce package sage and onion stuffing mix
$2^1/_2$ cups cooked diced chicken
10 ounce can condensed cream of mushroom or chicken soup

Roll out pastry dough and use to line an 8 inch pie dish. Roll out a round for a lid. Make up stuffing according to the package instructions. Leave until cool. Combine chicken with soup, adding a little water if mixture is too dry. Put into bottom of pie shell. Top with a layer of stuffing. Damp dough edges and cover with dough lid. Crimp edges to seal. Make a vent in dough lid. Bake in a preheated oven, 425°F, for 15 minutes, then reduce to 375°F and cook for 25-30 minutes, until golden brown.

4 servings

CREAMED CHICKEN WITH ZUCCHINI

2 chicken breasts
$^1/_4$ cup vegetable oil
$^1/_2$ pound zucchini, sliced
7 ounce can creamed mushrooms

Season chicken to taste. Heat oil in a large heavy-bottomed skillet over medium heat. Add chicken and cook on both sides until browned. Lift out of pan with a slotted spoon and set aside. Sauté zucchini for about 5 minutes, until softened. Transfer to an ovenproof dish. Top with chicken, then spread over creamed mushrooms. Bake in a preheated oven, 375°F, for about 45 minutes, until chicken is cooked through and tender.

2 servings

CASSEROLES AND BRAISES
CHICKEN IN RED WINE

$^1/_4$ pound sliced smoked bacon, diced
4 chicken parts with skin
$1^1/_4$ cups button mushrooms
about $1^3/_4$ cups red wine

Heat a large heavy-bottomed sauté pan or deep skillet over medium heat. Add bacon and sauté, stirring frequently, until fat runs and bacon begins to brown and crisp. Remove from pan with a slotted spoon and set aside. Add chicken and cook, skin side down first, then turning occasionally, until browned all over. Remove from pan with a slotted spoon and keep warm. Add mushrooms and cook for about 5 minutes, stirring frequently, until softened. Return chicken and bacon to pan. Pour over red wine. Season well. Bring to a boil, stirring. Reduce heat, cover, and cook over low heat for about 40 minutes, until chicken is cooked through and tender. Remove chicken and mushrooms with a slotted spoon to a warmed serving dish. Reduce cooking liquid by boiling rapidly if necessary. Spoon over chicken to serve.   4 servings

CHICKEN WITH ORANGE AND HERBS

4 tablespoons/$^1/_2$ stick/$^1/_4$ cup butter
$3^1/_2$ pound oven-ready chicken
juice of 1 orange, plus orange slices for garnish
8 sprigs of mixed herbs (parsley, thyme, parsley, oregano)

Melt butter in a flameproof casserole dish over medium heat. Add chicken and brown all over. Pour over orange juice and scatter over herbs. Season well. Lay bird on its side and cover dish. Cook in a preheated oven, 300°F, for $1^1/_2$ hours, turning chicken over once or twice. Remove chicken from casserole. Carve and arrange meat on a warmed serving dish. Strain cooking juices, discarding herbs. Pour over chicken and garnish with orange slices.   4 servings

CHICKEN IN CIDER

$^1/_4$ pound sliced bacon, diced
4 chicken parts with skin
$1^1/_4$ cups cider
$^2/_3$ cup light cream

Heat a large heavy-bottomed sauté pan or deep skillet over medium heat. Add bacon and sauté, stirring frequently, until fat runs and bacon begins to brown and crisp. Remove from pan with a slotted spoon and set aside. Add chicken and cook skin side down first, then turning occasionally, until browned all over. Return bacon to pan. Add cider and season to taste. Bring to a boil. Reduce heat, cover, and cook over low heat for about 40 minutes, until chicken is cooked through and tender. Remove pan from heat. Stir in cream. Return to heat briefly to heat through for 1–2 minutes, stirring constantly.

4 servings

CHICKEN WITH CHICKPEAS AND CUMIN

4 boneless chicken breasts with skin
2 tablespoons ground cumin
$2^1/_2$ cups chicken broth
15 ounce can chickpeas (garbanzo beans), drained

Heat a nonstick skillet over moderate heat. Season chicken. Cook skin side down until fat runs and skin browns. Turn over and cook the other side until browned. Lift out of a pan with a slotted spoon. Allow to cool enough to handle. Remove skin and cut chicken into $1^1/_2$ inch cubes. Add cumin to pan and cook, stirring, for 1 minute. Return chicken to pan. Pour in broth. Bring to a boil, stirring. Reduce heat, cover, and simmer for 15 minutes. Add chickpeas and simmer for 10 minutes more, until chicken is tender.

3–4 servings

STUFFED CHICKEN

CHICKEN STUFFED WITH BLUE CHEESE

4 boneless, skinless chicken breasts
1³/₄ cups creamy blue cheese, e.g. Dolcelatte
8 thin slices bacon
1¹/₄ cups chicken broth

Lay chicken breasts flat between two sheets of waxed paper. Beat gently with a rolling pin or mallet to flatten. Mash cheese in a bowl. Season well with black pepper. Spread top of chicken pieces with cheese. Roll up. Wrap two slices bacon around each chicken roll to cover it completely. Secure with wooden toothpicks. Heat a nonstick skillet over medium heat. Add rolls and cook briefly on both sides, until fat begins to run. Cook for about 5 minutes in total on each side, until bacon browns. Add broth and bring to a boil. Reduce heat to low. Cover and simmer for about 30 minutes, turning occasionally, until chicken is tender. Serve rolls with pan juices spooned over. These can be reduced, if necessary, by boiling rapidly.

4 servings

CHICKEN STUFFED WITH PÂTÉ

4 chicken breasts with skin
¹/₄ pound pâté
2 teaspoons dried thyme or oregano
olive oil or vegetable oil, for brushing

Make a long horiziontal slit through thickness of each chicken breast without cutting right through. Divide paté between chicken breasts. Sprinkle in herb. Brush a shallow ovenproof dish with oil. Arrange chicken in dish. Brush all over with oil. Season well. Cook in a preheated oven, 350°F, for about 40 minutes, until tender.

4 servings

CHICKEN BREASTS WITH PESTO STUFFING

4 chicken breasts with skin, about 6 ounces each
4 tablespoons pesto sauce (store-bought or use Pistou, page 85)
Garlic Oil or Basil Oil (see page 102), or vegetable oil, for brushing
$^1/_2$ cup grated Parmesan cheese

Spread pesto (or pistou) under skin of each chicken breast. Brush
chicken all over with oil. Broil under medium heat for about 6-7 minutes
each side, or until cooked through. Sprinkle over Parmesan. Broil for 1-2
minutes more, until melted. Serve immediately.

4 servings

CHICKEN STUFFED WITH SPINACH AND RICOTTA

4 boneless, skinless chicken breasts
$^1/_2$ cup ricotta cheese
$^1/_2$ cup cooked spinach, squeezed dry
8 slices proscuitto or Parma ham

Make a long horiziontal slit through thickness of each chicken breast
without cutting right through. Combine ricotta and spinach in a bowl.
Season to taste. Divide stuffing between chicken breasts. Wrap each one
in 2 pieces ham, winding around chicken to completely cover meat. Heat
a large nonstick skillet with a heatproof handle over medium heat. Add
chicken breasts and cook briefly on both sides, until fat begins to run.
Cook for 4 minutes in total on each side, until ham starts to brown.
Transfer pan to a preheated oven, 400°F, for 15 minutes. The ham should
be browned and slightly crunchy on the outside and chicken moist and
tender.

4 servings

CHICKEN SPECIALS

CHICKEN BREASTS WITH HAM AND CHEESE

4 skinless, boneless chicken breasts
4 tablespoons/$^1/_2$ stick/$^1/_4$ cup sweet butter
4 thin slices proscuitto or lean cooked ham
4 tablespoons shredded Parmesan cheese

Lay chicken breasts flat between two pieces of damp waxed paper. Beat gently with a rolling pin or mallet to flatten. Season well. Melt butter in a large heavy-bottomed skillet over low heat. Cook chicken for about 10 minutes, turning once, until golden. Lay a ham slice on each piece of chicken. Top with Parmesan. Cover and cook for 5 minutes. Arrange chicken on a warmed serving dish. Pour over pan drippings.

4 servings

CHICKEN AND BACON ROLLS

4 skinless, boneless chicken breasts
juice of 1 lemon
3-4 tablespoons tahini
4 thin slices bacon

Put chicken into a nonmetallic dish. Sprinkle with lemon juice and season well. Cover and refrigerate for 2 hours, or overnight, turning occasionally. Lay chicken breasts flat between two pieces of waxed paper. Beat gently with a rolling pin or mallet to flatten. Spread top of chicken pieces with tahini. Roll up. Stretch bacon slices (see opposite). Wrap a slice around each roll. Secure with wooden toothpicks. Cut 4 sheets of aluminum foil large enough to enclose a chicken roll loosely. Put a roll onto each piece of foil. Sprinkle with lemon juice. Gather up foil loosely around roll and fold over to seal. Put packages onto a cookie sheet. Cook in a preheated oven, 375°F, for 30 minutes, until tender.

4 servings

194

COOK'S KNOW-HOW
To stretch bacon, hold a slice at one end. Pressing down with the blade of a dinner knife, draw along its length.

CHICKEN WITH OLIVES

1 cup black olives, bottled in olive oil, 2 tablespoons oil reserved, pitted and chopped
4 tablespoons chopped flatleaf parsley
$^2/_3$ cup butter, melted
4 chicken breasts with skin

Combine half the olives with parsley and butter. Season to taste. Put chicken breasts into an ovenproof dish. Rub butter mixture all over chicken. Transfer to a large ovenproof dish. Prick skin of chicken all over with a sharp knife. Sprinkle with reserved oil. Cook chicken in a preheated oven, 400°F, for about 40 minutes, until tender. Serve chicken garnished with remaining olives.

4 servings

CHICKEN WITH MUSTARD SAUCE IN FOIL

2 tablespoons Dijon mustard
2 tablespoons plain yogurt
4 chicken breasts
juice of 1 lemon

Combine mustard with yogurt. Coat chicken all over with mixture. Season well. Cut 4 sheets of aluminum foil large enough to enclose a chicken breast loosely. Put a chicken breast on each piece of foil. Sprinkle with lemon juice. Gather up foil loosely around chicken and fold over to seal. Put parcels onto a cookie sheet. Cook in a preheated oven, 375°F, for about 40 minutes, until tender.

4 servings

POULTRY PATTIES

CURRIED TURKEY PATTIES

1 pound ground turkey
1 cup fresh soft white bread crumbs
1 tablespoon garam masala or curry powder
$^1/_3$ cup Garlic Oil (see page 102)

Combine turkey, bread crumbs, garam masala, and seasoning with about
1-2 tablespoons oil. With wet hands, form into 12 small patties. Cover and
chill in the refrigerator for about 30 minutes, until firm. Heat remaining
oil in a large heavy-bottomed skillet over high heat. Cook patties briefly
on both sides. Reduce heat and cook for 12–15 minutes, turning
frequently, until cooked through.

4 servings

TURKEY AND STUFFING PATTIES

$^1/_2$ x 3 ounce package sage and onion or other poultry stuffing mix
1 pound ground turkey
1-2 tablespoons cranberry sauce (store-bought or use Cranberry and
Orange Sauce, see page 204)
$^1/_4$ cup vegetable oil

Make up stuffing according to instructions on the package. Leave to
cool. Combine with turkey and cranberry sauce. Season to taste. With wet
hands, form into 12 small patties. Cover and chill in the refrigerator for
about 30 minutes, until firm. Heat oil in a large heavy-bottomed skillet
over high heat. Cook patties briefly on both sides. Reduce heat and cook
for 12–15 minutes, turning frequently, until cooked through.

4 servings

MINTED TURKEY BURGERS

1 pound ground turkey
2 tablespoons chopped mint
2 tablespoons sour cream
$^1/_3$ cup Garlic Oil (see pages 102)

Combine turkey, mint, sour cream, 1 tablespoon oil, and seasoning, beating until well blended. With wet hands, form into 12 small burgers. Cover and chill in the refrigerator for about 30 minutes, until firm. Heat oil in a large heavy-bottomed skillet over high heat. Cook burgers briefly on both sides. Reduce heat and cook for 12–15 minutes, turning frequently, until cooked through.

4 servings

CHICKEN AND LEMON PATTIES

$^3/_4$ pound ground chicken
6 ounces herbed pork bulk sausage, or split skins and use meat from herbed pork link sausages
grated zest and juice of 1 small lemon
$^1/_3$ cup Lemon and Thyme Oil (see page 102)

Combine chicken, bulk sausage, lemon zest and juice, 1 tablespoon oil, and seasoning, mixing until well blended. With wet hands, form into 12 small patties. Cover and chill in the refrigerator for about 30 minutes, until firm. Heat oil in a heavy-bottomed skillet over high heat. Cook patties briefly on both sides. Reduce heat and cook for 12–15 minutes, turning frequently, until cooked through.

4 servings

THAI CHICKEN PATTIES

1 pound ground chicken
2 tablespoons thick plain yogurt

2 tablespoons finely chopped cilantro (stems and leaves)
$^1/_3$ cup Chili Oil (see page 102)

Combine chicken, yogurt, cilantro, 1 tablespoon oil, and seasoning, beating until well blended. With wet hands, form into 12 small patties. Cover and chill in the refrigerator for about 30 minutes, until firm. Heat oil in a large heavy-bottomed skillet over high heat. Cook patties briefly on both sides. Reduce heat and cook for 12–15 minutes, until cooked through.

4 servings

FAIR GAME

DUCK BREASTS WITH CRANBERRIES

4 boneless duck breasts
4 tablespoons balsamic vinegar
$^3/_4$ cup cranberries
$^1/_4$ cup packed brown sugar

Score skin of duck breasts (see page 94). Heat a nonstick skillet over medium heat. Cook duck breasts, skin side down, for 5 minutes. Reduce heat and cook for a further 10 minutes. Pour off excess fat. Turn duck over. Add vinegar, cranberries, and sugar. Cook for a further 10 minutes, until cranberries have broken down and duck is pink and juicy in the middle. Serve duck with sauce spooned.

4 servings

BUTTERFLY VENISON STEAKS

4 x $^1/_4$ pound venison fillet steaks
3 tablespoons butter
1 tablespoon olive oil
2 tablespoons brandy

Cut steaks almost in half horizontally. Open out flat to form a "butterfly" shape, pressing them with the hand to flatten. Season well. Heat butter and oil in a large heavy-bottomed skillet. Add steaks and cook for 15 seconds on each side, pressing down firmly. Transfer to a warmed serving dish and keep hot. Remove pan from heat. Pour in brandy, stirring to dissolve sediment. Pour over steaks. Serve with Horseradish and Chive Butter (see page 252), if you like.

4 servings

ROAST HONEY DUCK

5 pound oven-ready duckling
1 lemon
2 tablespoons clear honey
$1^1/_4$ cups chicken broth

Prick duck all over with a fine skewer. Squeeze 2 tablespoons juice from lemon. Cut lemon in half and put inside body cavity. Set duck on a wire rack in a roasting pan. Blend lemon juice and honey. Brush all over duck. Season well. Roast in a preheated oven, 425°F, for 10 minutes. Reduce to 375°F and cook for 25 minutes per pound, plus 10–15 minutes resting time at the end. Baste frequently during cooking time, brushing with lemon and honey mixture. Remove from oven. Keep duck warm while resting. Drain off almost all of fat. Add broth to pan over high heat. Bring to a boil, stirring to blend in any residue in bottom of pan. Serve gravy spooned over meat.

4 servings

CRISPY ROAST DUCK WITH ORANGE

4 pound oven-ready duckling
2 small oranges
3 tablespoons sherry
1 tablespoon clear honey

Dry duckling thoroughly inside and out with paper towels. Season cavity. Halve 1 orange. Squeeze 2 tablespoons juice. Put orange halves inside body cavity. Set duck on a wire rack in a roasting pan. Prick duck all over with a needle. Rub skin with salt. Roast in the center of a preheated oven, 375°F, for 1¹/₂ hours, until skin is crisp and golden. A few minutes before duckling is cooked, pare zest in fine strips from remaining orange. Put in a pan with orange juice, sherry, and honey. Bring to a boil. Reduce heat and simmer, stirring constantly, for 2 minutes. Carve duck into quarters. Transfer to a warmed serving dish. Spoon over sauce.

4 servings

PHEASANT FRENCH-STYLE

4 thick slices smoked bacon, diced
1 pheasant, cut into 4 pieces
4 tart apples, peeled, cored, and sliced
1 cup heavy cream

Heat a large heavy-bottomed skillet over medium heat. Cook bacon, stirring frequently, until fat runs and bacon begins to brown. Remove with a slotted spoon and set aside. Season pheasant. Add to pan and cook, turning frequently, until browned all over. Remove with a slotted spoon and put with bacon. Add apples to pan and cook until softened and browned. Return pheasant and bacon to pan. Stir in about ²/₃ cup water. Reduce heat to low. Cover and cook for about 30 minutes, until pheasant is tender. Stir in cream about 10 minutes from end of cooking time and season with freshly ground black pepper.

4 servings

STUFFINGS
SAGE AND ONION STUFFING

2 large onions, chopped
2 tablespoons/$^1/_4$ stick butter, softened
2 cups fresh soft bread crumbs
2 teaspoons dried sage

Put onions into a pan of water. Bring to a boil. Reduce heat and simmer for 5 minutes. Drain well. Melt butter in a skillet over medium heat. Sauté onions for about 2 minutes. Put bread crumbs into a bowl. Mix in sage and season well. Add onions and butter. Mix well to combine. Use to stuff the neck end of chicken, turkey, or goose. Carve with the meat.

4 servings

LEMON AND THYME STUFFING

2 cups fresh soft bread crumbs
1 tablespoon chopped fresh thyme or 1 teaspoon dried
grated zest and juice of 1 lemon
4 tablespoons/$^1/_2$ stick/$^1/_4$ cup butter, melted

Put bread crumbs, thyme, and lemon zest and juice into a bowl. Season well. Add melted butter and stir well to combine. Use to stuff the neck end of chicken, turkey, or guinea hen before roasting.

4-6 servings

APRICOT NUT STUFFING

14 ounce can apricot halves in natural juice
1 cup fresh soft bread crumbs
2-3 tablespoons chopped peanuts or walnuts
4 tablespoons/$^1/_2$ stick/$^1/_4$ cup butter, softened

Drain apricots, reserving juice. Dice fruit. Put into a bowl. Add remaining ingredients. Season to taste. Mix well together, adding a little reserved apricot juice to combine. Use to stuff chicken, turkey, goose, or duck. Can also be used to stuff lamb or pork.

4-6 servings

CHESTNUT STUFFING

1 pound chestnuts
1$^1/_4$ cups chicken, turkey, or ham broth, a little reserved
$^1/_4$ pound cooked lean ham, diced
$^1/_2$ pound pork bulk sausage

Slit chestnuts and put into a pan of water. Bring to a boil and boil for 5-10 minutes. Drain and allow to cool a little. Remove skins while still warm. Put broth into a pan. Add chestnuts and simmer until tender and nearly all broth is absorbed. Allow to cool, then finely chop. Put in a bowl with ham and bulk sausage. Add a little reserved broth and seasoning. Mix well together to combine. Use to stuff chicken, turkey, or goose.

4-6 servings

RICE STUFFING WITH PARSLEY AND CHIVES

1 cup long-grain rice
6 bacon slices, diced
1 medium onion
6 tablespoons chopped mixed parsley and chives

Cook rice in boiling salted water according to the package instructions, until almost tender. Drain. Heat a nonstick skillet over medium heat. Add bacon and cook, stirring frequently, until fat runs and bacon begins to color. Add onion and cook, stirring frequently, until softened and lightly colored. Remove pan from heat. Stir in rice. Season to taste. Stir in chopped herbs. Use to stuff chicken or guinea hen before roasting.

4 servings

SAUCES

GARLIC AND HERB SAUCE

$^2/_3$ cup plain yogurt
1 large clove garlic, minced
2 tablespoons chopped mixed parsley and tarragon, chives, or dill

Beat yogurt with garlic in a bowl. Beat in chopped herbs and seasoning to taste. Cover and chill until ready to serve. Serve with broiled, pan-fried, or barbecued chicken or turkey, or kabobs.
2-4 servings

LEMON HOLLANDAISE

12 tablespoons/$1^1/_2$ sticks/$^3/_4$ cup butter
2 large egg yolks
1 teaspoon Dijon mustard
$^1/_4$ cup lemon juice

Melt butter in a small pan over low heat. Put egg yolks, mustard, and lemon juice into a food processor or blender. Process until smooth. With motor running, slowly pour in melted butter. Season to taste. Pour sauce into a small heatproof bowl over a pan of warm water to keep warm until ready to serve. Serve with broiled, pan-fried, or roast chicken or turkey.
4 servings

MANGO SALSA

1 ripe mango, peeled, pitted, and finely chopped
1 red chili, deseeded and finely chopped
2 tablespoons finely chopped cilantro
2 tablespoons lime juice

Stir ingredients together in a serving dish. Cover and refrigerate for an hour or so, to allow flavors to develop. Serve with broiled, pan-fried, or barbecued chicken, turkey, or game.

4 servings

CRANBERRY AND ORANGE SAUCE

$^2/_3$ cup orange juice
$^3/_4$ cup sugar
$^1/_2$ pound cranberries, fresh or frozen
grated zest of $^1/_2$ orange

Put orange juice in a pan with sugar over low heat until sugar dissolves. Bring to a boil. Continue boiling for about 5 minutes, stirring occasionally. Add cranberries and orange zest. Reduce heat, cover, and simmer until berries have all popped. Remove lid and continue simmering for about 5 minutes, until fruit is tender. Leave to cool. Serve with roast turkey, game, or lamb.

6 servings

BREAD SAUCE

$2^1/_2$ cups milk
1 small onion, finely chopped
$1^1/_2$ cups fresh soft white bread crumbs
$^1/_2$ teaspoon freshly grated nutmeg

Put milk with onion in a pan over very low heat. Season with freshly ground pepper. Heat until milk has almost reached boiling point. Stir in bread crumbs and nutmeg. Season with salt to taste. Simmer over very low heat for about 15 minutes, stirring frequently. Add more milk if necessary–the sauce should be quite creamy. Serve with roast chicken, turkey, or game.

6 servings

FLAVORED BUTTERS
LIME AND CILANTRO BUTTER

8 tablespoons/1 stick/$^1/_2$ cup unchilled butter, diced
3 tablespoons finely chopped cilantro
grated zest and juice of 1 lime

Put ingredients into a food processor or blender. Process until well blended. Alternatively, blend together butter and cilantro with a fork, then beat in lime zest and lime juice. Season to taste. Form into a roll. Wrap in aluminum foil and chill in the refrigerator until firm. Slice into $^1/_2$ inch slices. Use to top hot broiled, pan-fried, or barbecued chicken or turkey, or kabobs.

4-6 servings

GARLIC BUTTER

8 tablespoons/1 stick/$^1/_2$ cup unchilled sweet butter, diced
3 young cloves garlic, minced
3 tablespoons finely chopped parsley
1 small shallot, finely chopped

Put ingredients into a food processor or blender. Process until well blended. Alternatively, blend ingredients together with a fork. Season to taste. Form into a roll. Wrap in aluminum foil and chill in the refrigerator until firm. Slice into $^1/_2$ inch slices. Use to top hot broiled, pan-fried, or barbecued chicken or turkey.

4-6 servings

BASIL BUTTER

8 tablespoons/1 stick/$^1/_2$ cup unchilled butter, diced
5 tablespoons finely chopped basil
1 clove garlic, minced

Put ingredients into a food processor or blender. Process until well blended. Alternatively, blend ingredients together with a fork. Season to taste. Form into a roll. Wrap in aluminum foil and chill in the refrigerator until firm. Slice into $^1/_2$ inch slices. Use to top hot broiled, pan-fried, or barbecued chicken or turkey.

4-6 servings

TARRAGON AND PARSLEY BUTTER

8 tablespoons/1 stick/$^1/_2$ cup unchilled butter, diced
2 tablespoons finely chopped tarragon
2 tablespoons finely chopped parsley
1 tablespoon lemon juice

Put ingredients into a food processor or blender. Process until well blended. Alternatively, blend together butter and herbs with a fork, then beat in lemon juice. Season to taste. Form into a roll. Wrap in aluminum foil and chill in the refrigerator until firm. Slice into $^1/_2$ inch slices. Use to top hot broiled, pan-fried, or barbecued chicken or turkey.

4-6 servings

CUMIN BUTTER

$1^1/_2$ tablespoons cumin seeds
8 tablespoons/1 stick/$^1/_2$ cup sweet butter, softened
1 shallot, finely chopped
$^1/_2$ teaspoon chili powder

Heat a dry heavy-bottomed skillet over low heat. Toast cumin seeds, stirring, until the aroma rises. Leave to cool. Grind with a pestle and mortar or in a coffee grinder. Blend together butter and shallot with a fork. Beat spices into butter. Wrap in aluminum foil and chill in the refrigerator until firm. Slice into $^1/_2$ inch slices. Use to top hot broiled, pan-fried, or barbecued chicken or turkey, or kabobs.

4–6 servings

DESIGNER
DRINKS

TEAS

RUSSIAN ICED TEA

$1^2/_3$ cups sugar
1 bunch mint leaves
1 cup lemon juice
$3^1/_2$ cups prepared Indian tea, cooled

Put sugar into a pan with 1 cup water over medium heat, until sugar dissolves. Bring to a boil and boil for 10 minutes to make a syrup. Add mint and let stand for about 2 hours. Strain into a pitcher. Stir in lemon juice and tea. To serve, divide tea among 10 glasses. Top with crushed ice. Decorate with lemon slices and mint sprigs, if you like.

10 servings

FRUITY ICED TEA

$2^1/_2$ cups strong prepared Indian tea
$^3/_4$ cup superfine sugar
$^1/_4$ cup freshly squeezed lemon juice
$1^1/_4$ cups freshly squeezed orange juice

Stir tea and sugar together in a pitcher, until sugar dissolves. Add fruit juices. Cover and chill for 1 hour. Serve with ice cubes and orange and lemon slices, if you like.

4 servings

MIDDLE EASTERN CINNAMON TEA

1 tablespoon aniseed
1 teaspoon ground cinnamon
sugar, to taste
chopped almonds and walnuts, to decorate

Put aniseed and cinnamon into a pan with $3^1/_2$ cups water over medium heat. Bring to a boil and boil for 3 minutes. Pour into cups. Add sugar to taste. Sprinkle over chopped nuts and serve immediately.

4 servings

AROMATIC TEA

2 tea bags, e.g. English breakfast
4 green cardamom pods, bruised
$^1/_2$ teaspoon ground ginger

Warm a teapot. Add tea bags and spices. Pour over $1^3/_4$ cups boiling water. Stir to mix. Let stand for 2 minutes. Pour through a strainer into glasses or cups. Add milk and sugar, if you like.

2 servings

MOROCCAN MINT TEA

2 teaspoons China tea
$^1/_4$ cup chopped mint, plus mint sprigs, to decorate
sugar, to taste
4 lemon slices

Warm a teapot. Add tea and mint. Pour over $3^1/_2$ cups boiling water. Let stand for 5 minutes. Pour through a strainer into glasses or cups. Add sugar to taste. Decorate with mint sprigs and lemon slices.

4 servings

CAMOMILE AND THYME TEA

1 lemon
honey, to taste
2 camomile tea bags

2 sprigs thyme

Cut lemon in half. Squeeze juice from 1 half into 2 glasses or cups. Add honey. Warm a teapot. Add tea bags and thyme. Pour over $1^3/_4$ cups boiling water. Leave to infuse for about 5 minutes. Pour through a strainer into glasses or cups. Stir well.

2 servings

COOLERS

MINTED LEMONADE

7 unsprayed lemons, 1 reserved for slicing
$^1/_2$ cup sugar
handful mint leaves, chopped, a few sprigs reserved to decorate
crushed ice

Grate zest of 6 lemons, being carefully to avoid white pith. Squeeze juice. Slice remaining lemon. Put zest, sugar, and mint in a pan over low heat. Add $2^1/_2$ cups water. Stir until sugar dissolves. Bring to a boil and boil for about 5 minutes. Leave to cool. Stir in lemon juice. Strain a little of mixture into glasses or into a pitcher. Add crushed ice and fill up with ice water. Decorate with mint sprigs and lemon slices.   8-10 servings

PINEAPPLEADE

4 unsprayed lemons
1 medium-sized pineapple, peeled, cored, and sliced, a few thin slices reserved to decorate
$^1/_2$ cup sugar
crushed ice

Grate zest from lemons, being careful to avoid white pith. Squeeze juice. Finely chop pineapple. Put zest, pineapple, and sugar into a pan over low heat. Add $2^1/_2$ cups water. Stir until sugar dissolves. Bring to a boil and boil for about 5 minutes. Leave to cool. Stir in lemon juice. Strain a little of mixture into glasses or into a pitcher. Add crushed ice and fill up with ice water. Decorate with pineapple slices.   8-10 servings

APPLEADE

2 large dessert apples
$^1/_2$ teaspoon sugar
ice cubes
apple slices, to decorate

Chop apples and put into a bowl. Pour over $2^1/_2$ cups boiling water.
Add sugar. Let stand for 10 minutes. Strain into a pitcher and leave to
cool. Pour over ice cubes in tall tumblers. Decorate with apple slices.
3 servings

TROPICAL COOLER

$^1/_2$ cup lime juice
2 tablespoons packed dark brown sugar
8 ounce can crushed pineapple
5 cups ginger ale

Put lime juice into a small pan with sugar over low heat, until sugar
dissolves. Leave to cool. Stir in pineapple. Transfer to a large pitcher. Chill
until required. Top up with ginger ale and serve immediately over ice.
6 servings

PINK GRAPEFRUIT FIZZ

4 tablespoons chopped mint, plus sprigs to decorate
2 teaspoons sugar
juice of 1 pink grapefruit
soda water or ginger ale

Put mint into a heatproof pitcher with sugar. Pour over $^2/_3$ cup boiling
water. Leave to cool. Stir in fruit juice. Chill for 2-3 hours in the
refrigerator. Strain into glasses with ice cubes. Top up with soda water or
ginger ale, decorate with mint sprigs, and serve immediately.   2-4 servings

FRUIT PUNCHES
CRANBERRY AND ORANGE PUNCH

2 cups cranberry juice
2¹/₂ cups orange juice
2¹/₂ cups sparkling apple juice
1 orange, sliced

Combine ingredients and chill well before serving.
6-8 servings

ORCHARD PUNCH

3 ripe peaches, peeled and pitted (see page 306)
3 ripe pears, peeled and cored
juice of 1 lemon
4 cups apple juice

Put fruit into a food processor or blender with lemon juice. Whizz until smooth. Combine with apple juice. Chill well before serving.
6 servings

CRANBERRY CRUSH

crushed ice
7¹/₄ cups sweetened cranberry juice
2¹/₂ cups fresh orange juice
2¹/₂ cups ginger ale

Half fill a punch bowl with crushed ice. Pour in fruit juices. Stir to mix. Top up with ginger ale. Decorate with orange and lemon wedges. Serve immediately.
15 servings

FRUIT PUNCH

2$^1/_2$ cups orange juice
2$^1/_2$ cups apple juice
$^1/_2$ teaspoon ground ginger
$^1/_2$ teaspoon allspice

Put fruit juices and spices into a pan with $^2/_3$ cup water over medium heat. Bring to a boil. Simmer for 5 minutes. Pour punch into a warmed bowl. Float apple slices on top to decorate, if you like.

6 servings

COOL PASSION

1$^1/_3$ cups orange juice
$^2/_3$ cup passionfruit juice
4 cups pineapple juice
6$^1/_4$ cups lemonade

Pour fruit juices into a large pitcher. Stir well to mix. Just before serving, stir in lemonade. Put crushed ice into bottom of glasses to serve.

20 servings

INDIAN TEA PUNCH

$^1/_4$ cup Indian leaf tea
2$^1/_2$ cups sparkling apple juice
2$^1/_2$ cups grape juice
2$^1/_2$ ginger ale

Put tea leaves into a pitcher. Pour over 2$^1/_2$ cups cold water. Cover and let stand overnight. Strain 1$^3/_4$ cups of tea liquor into a large bowl. Add remaining ingredients and stir well. To serve, pour punch into individual glasses. Add ice cubes and seedless grapes, if you like.

12 servings

PARTY PUNCHES

PEACH CUP

2 ripe peaches, skinned, halved, and pitted (see page 306)
2 bottles still Moselle, chilled
3 tablespoons superfine sugar
1 bottle sparkling Moselle, chilled

Chop peaches and put into a large bowl. Pour 1 bottle of still Moselle over fruit. Add sugar and stir gently. Cover and chill in the refrigerator for 30 minutes. Add second bottle of still Moselle. Just before serving, pour in sparkling Moselle.

8-10 servings

CHAMPAGNE STRAWBERRY CUP

1 cup strawberries, hulled
$^3/_4$ cup Fraises des Bois or other strawberry liqueur, chilled
1 bottle dry champagne or sparkling dry white wine, chilled

Slice strawberries and divide among individual glasses. Pour liqueur into a large pitcher. Gradually add champagne or sparkling wine, stirring gently to prevent losing bubbles. Pour over sliced strawberries and serve.

6 servings

SPARKLING SHERBET PUNCH

$2^1/_4$ cups lemon sherbet
$^1/_2$ bottle sweet or medium-sweet white wine, chilled
1 bottle sparkling white wine, chilled
lemon slices, to decorate

Scoop sherbet into a punch bowl. Add wine and garnish with lemon slices. Serve immediately.   8 servings

KIR PUNCH

1$\frac{1}{2}$ cups strawberries, hulled
1-2 measures Crème de Cassis
3 bottles dry white wine, chilled
chilled soda water, to taste

Put strawberries into a bowl. Add Crème de Cassis and stir. Chill in the refrigerator for 1-2 hours. Add wine and stir. Add soda water to taste.
18-20 servings

SUMMER FRUIT CUP

4 measures Grand Marnier
4 measures Kirsch or cherry brandy
$\frac{3}{4}$ pound mixed ripe summer fruits, e.g. peaches, apricots, nectarines, and strawberries, sliced
1 bottle medium-dry white wine, chilled

Combine Grand Marnier, Kirsch or cherry brandy, and fruits in a bowl. Stir well. Cover and chill in the refrigerator for about 1 hour. Add wine and stir.
8 servings

COOK'S KNOW-HOW
For a decorative effect, freeze herbs and herb flowers in ice cubes to add to fruit punches. Fill an ice-cube tray halfway up with water. Add herbs—mint sprigs, borage flowers, or unsprayed rose or nasturtium petals—and top up with water. Freeze until solid.

CLASSIC COCKTAILS

TEQUILA SUNRISE

2 measures tequila
4 measures orange juice
ice cubes
³/₄ measure grenadine

Combine tequila with orange juice in a glass. Stir to combine. Add several ice cubes. Slowly pour in grenadine, which will sink to the bottom, creating the "sunrise." Stir gently before drinking.
1 serving

PINA COLADA

2 measures light rum
2 measures creamed coconut
3-4 measures unsweetened pineapple juice
6-8 ice cubes, crushed

Put ingredients into a blender. Blend at high speed for about 10 seconds. Pour into a chilled glass. Serve with slices of fruit, if you like.
1 serving

GIN SLING

1 teaspoon sugar
2 measures gin
ice cubes
mineral water or soda water, to taste

Dissolve sugar in a little water in a tall tumbler. Add gin and several ice cubes. Top up with mineral water or soda water. Serve with straws.
1 serving

HIGHBALL

2 measures whiskey
ice
ginger ale or soda water, to taste
lemon and lime slices, to decorate

Pour whiskey over ice cubes in a glass. Fill with ginger ale or soda water. Stir gently. Deocrate with lemon and lime slices.
1 serving

HARVEY WALLBANGER

1-2 measures vodka
4 measures orange juice
ice cubes
$^1/_2$ measure Galliano

Pour vodka and orange juice into a glass. Add several ice cubes and stir. Float Galliano on top.
1 serving

CUBA LIBRE

1 lime
2 measures light rum
ice cubes
Coca-Cola, to taste

Cut lime in half. Squeeze juice from 1 half into a glass. Cut a wedge from remaining half and add to glass. Add rum and ice cubes. Top up with Coca-Cola. Stir gently to mix.
1 serving

JUST JUICE
WATERMELON, ORANGE, AND PINK GRAPEFRUIT

1 round watermelon, halved and deseeded
juice of 1 orange
juice of 1 pink grapefruit
crushed ice, to serve

Scoop out flesh of watermelon and put into a food processor or blender with fruit juices. Whizz until blended. To serve, pour over crushed ice in tall tumblers.

4 servings

MANGO AND PINEAPPLE

1 pineapple, about 2 pounds, peeled, sliced, and cored
1 ripe mango, pitted, peeled, and chopped
sparkling mineral water and ice cubes, to serve

Put pineapple flesh, in batches, into a food processor or blender. Whizz until fruit is well pulped, adding a little water if necessary. With a wooden spoon, press pulp through a nylon strainer to extract juice. Put mango into food processor or blender with pineapple juice. Whizz until smooth. Put ice into a pitcher. Add juice and top up with mineral water, to taste.

4 servings

MELON, RASPBERRY, AND ORANGE

1 Galia or Honeydew melon, about $1^1/_2$ pounds, halved and deseeded
$1^1/_2$ cups frozen raspberries, defrosted
about $2^1/_2$ cups orange juice
crushed ice

Scoop out melon flesh and put into a food processor or blender with with raspberries. Whizz until smooth. Add orange juice and whizz until well blended. Serve poured over crushed ice.   4 servings

CANTALOUPE AND GRAPE

1 Cantaloupe melon, about 1¹/₂ pounds, halved and deseeded
²/₃ cup grape juice
frozen grapes

Scoop out melon flesh and put into a food processor or blender with grape juice. Whizz until smooth. Pour into glasses. Add frozen grapes and stir to mix.
2 servings

MELON, MINT, AND GINGER

1 Cantaloupe melon, about 1³/₄ pounds, halved and deseeded
1 tablespoon chopped mint
1 inch piece fresh gingerroot, peeled and finely sliced
mineral water

Scoop out melon flesh and put into a food processor or blender with mint and ginger. Whizz until smooth. Add a little mineral water to make the desired consistency.   2 servings

CRANBERRY, BANANA, AND APPLE

1 large ripe banana, peeled and sliced
1 cup cranberry juice
²/₃ cup apple juice
light brown sugar, to taste

Put ingredients into a food processor or blender. Process until smooth.
2 servings

PAPAYA, KIWI, AND PINEAPPLE

1 ripe papaya, halved, deseeded, and diced
4 ripe kiwifruit, peeled and diced
1¹/₂ cups chilled pineapple juice

Put ingredients into a food processor or blender. Whizz until smooth.
2 servings

MANGO, PASSIONFRUIT, AND LIME

2 ripe mangos, pitted, peeled, and diced
3 passionfruit
juice of 2 limes
light brown sugar or honey, to taste

Put mango flesh into a food processor or blender. Scoop out seeds and flesh of passionfruit and add to mango with lime juice and sugar or honey to taste. Whizz until smooth.
2 servings

BLACKBERRY AND APPLE

1¹/₂ cups blackberries, defrosted if frozen
1¹/₄ cups chilled apple juice
¹/₄ teaspoon cinnamon
maple syrup, to taste

Put ingredients into a food processor or blender. Whizz until smooth.
2 servings

PEAR AND APPLE

16 ounce can pear halves in natural juice
$^2/_3$ cup apple juice
$^1/_4$ teaspoon ground ginger
honey, to taste

Put ingredients into a food processor or blender. Whizz until smooth.
2 servings

TOMATO JUICE WITH BASIL

2 pounds tomatoes, skinned
2 tablespoons torn basil leaves
2 tablespoons lemon juice
celery stalks with leaves, to serve

Put tomatoes and basil and into a food processor or blender. Blend
until puréed. With a wooden spoon, press through a fine nylon strainer.
Stir in lemon juice. Chill for 2 hours before serving. Serve in glasses with
a celery stalk standing in each.
2-4 servings

COOK'S KNOW-HOW
Always use a nylon rather than a metal strainer for acidic ingredients,
such as tomatoes and raspberries—the metal reacts with the acid and can
discolor the fruit.

SHAKES AND SMOOTHIES

RASPBERRY SHAKE

1$^1/_2$ cups frozen raspberries, defrosted
1 cup milk
1-2 scoops vanilla ice cream
1 level tablespoon clear honey

Put ingredients into a food processor or blender. Blend until smooth and frothy. Serve with crushed ice, if you like.

2 servings

STRAWBERRY, VANILLA, AND MINT SHAKE

1$^1/_2$ cups strawberries, hulled
1 cup milk
1-2 scoops vanilla ice cream
1 tablespoon chopped mint

Put ingredients into a food processor or blender. Blend until smooth and frothy. Serve with crushed ice, if you like.

2 servings

BANANA AND CHOCOLATE

2 ripe bananas, peeled and sliced
1 cup milk
2 scoops chocolate ice cream
$^1/_4$ teaspoon cinnamon

Put ingredients into a food processor or blender. Blend until smooth and frothy.

2 servings

SPICED PEACH AND ALMOND SMOOTHIE

16 ounce can sliced peaches in natural juice
²/₃ cup plain yogurt
¹/₂ teaspoon allspice
1 tablespoon toasted slivered almonds

Drain peaches, reserving juice. Put fruit in a food processor or blender with about half the juice. Whizz until blended. Add yogurt and cinnamon. Whizz again, adding more juice for the desired consistency, until well blended. Pour into glasses. Sprinkle almonds on top.
2 servings

CRANBERRY AND BLUEBERRY SMOOTHIE

1¹/₂ cups chilled blueberries
²/₃ cup chilled cranberry juice
²/₃ cup plain yogurt
clear honey, to taste (optional)

Put fruit and juice into a food processor or blender. Whizz until smooth. Add yogurt and honey, if using, and whizz again, until well blended.
2 servings

COOK'S KNOW-HOW
Use low-fat yogurt in smoothies for a lighter, slimmer alternative.

APRICOT AND VANILLA SMOOTHIE

5-6 ripe apricots, skinned, pitted, and diced (see page 306)
²/₃ cup vanilla yogurt
1 cup soy milk
¹/₃ cup amaretti crumbs

Put apricots, yogurt, and milk into a food processor or blender. Blend until smooth and frothy. Pour into glasses. Sprinkle over amaretti crumbs.
2 servings

BANANA AND MANDARIN SMOOTHIE

1 ripe banana, peeled and sliced
11 ounce can mandarin orange segments
$^2/_3$ cup sour cream
milk

Put banana, mandarins and juice, and cream into a food processor or blender. Blend until smooth, adding milk to make the desired consistency.
2 servings

SPICED MANGO COCONUT CREAM

2 ripe mangos, pitted, peeled, and diced
$1^1/_4$ cups canned coconut milk
$^1/_2$ teaspoon allspice
maple syrup, to taste

Put ingredients into a food processor or blender. Blend until smooth and frothy.
2 servings

PEACH, GINGER, AND PECAN SMOOTHIE

3-4 peaches, skinned, pitted, and diced (see page 306)
1¹/₄ cups evaporated milk
1 tablespoon chopped preserved ginger with a little syrup
2 tablespoons chopped pecan nuts

Put ingredients into a food processor or blender. Blend until smooth and frothy.

2 servings

PAPAYA AND PINK GRAPEFRUIT

2 ripe papayas, halved, deseeded, and diced
1 cup pink grapefruit juice
²/₃ cup plain yogurt
light brown sugar, to taste

Put ingredients into a food processor or blender. Blend until smooth and frothy.

2 servings

BANANA, CHOCOLATE, AND PEANUT BUTTER SMOOTHIE

2 ripe bananas, peeled and sliced
1¹/₄ cups milk
2 scoops chocolate ice cream
4 tablespoons smooth peanut butter

Put ingredients into a food processor or blender. Blend until smooth and frothy, adding a little more milk to make the desired consistency. Serve with crushed ice, if you like.

2 servings

MEAT

MEAT CLASSICS

PEPPERED STEAK

4 tenderloin steaks, about 1 inch thick
1 tablespoon cracked green peppercorns
vegetable oil, for brushing
$1/3$ cup heavy cream

Season steaks with salt. Press half peppercorns into one side, then turn and repeat on second side. Brush a large heavy-bottomed skillet with oil over high heat. When hot, add steaks and cook for $1^1/_2$-$2^1/_2$ minutes on each side, depending on thickness and to taste. Lower heat and cook 1 or 2 minutes longer on each side for medium to well-done steaks. Lift out steaks with a slotted spoon onto warmed plates. Add cream to pan and heat through gently, stirring for 1-2 minutes. Pour over steaks to serve.

4 servings

ROAST LAMB WITH GARLIC AND ROSEMARY

1 leg of lamb
1 rosemary sprig
2 cloves garlic, cut into slivers
$1^3/_4$ cups lamb broth

With a sharp knife, make deep, small cuts in the skin at intervals all over top of joint. Insert one or two rosemary leaves and a sliver of garlic into each. Season well all over lamb. Put into a roasting pan. Roast in a preheated oven, 350°F, for 20 minutes per pound, plus 20 minutes for pink, or 30 minutes per pound, plus 30 minutes for well done. Lift meat onto a warmed carving dish. Keep warm and leave to rest for 10 minutes. Meanwhile, pour off as much fat as possible from roasting pan. Add broth and bring to a boil over medium heat, stirring to incorporate any residue in bottom of pan. Continue to cook until gravy reduces and thickens. Carve lamb and serve gravy separately.

6 servings

COOK'S KNOW-HOW

Roasted meat and poultry must be allowed to rest in a warm place for 10-15 minutes once it is cooked. Resting settles the meat so that it is easier to carve and loses fewer juices.

LIVER AND ONIONS

$^1/_3$ cup olive oil
$2^1/_2$ cups very thinly sliced onions
1 pound liver
1 tablespoon chopped parsley

Heat oil in a large heavy-bottomed skillet over low heat. Sauté onions, covered but stirring frequently, for about 20 minutes, until soft and golden. Slice liver horizontally into wafer thin slices, then cut each slice into small pieces about 2 inches square. Season onions to taste. Increase heat. Add liver and cook, uncovered and stirring frequently, for about 2 minutes, until liver is just cooked but still pink inside. Serve immediately, sprinkled with parsley.

4 servings

BEEF-STUFFED PEPPERS

4 large red bell peppers
1 pound ground beef
$1^1/_4$ cups tomato and herb bottled spaghetti sauce
$^2/_3$ cup long-grain rice

Cut bell peppers in half lengthwise, leaving stalks in place. Core and deseed. Put bell peppers, cut side up and tightly packed, into an ovenproof dish. Bake in a preheated oven, 400°F, for about 25 minutes, until softened. Meanwhile, heat a large nonstick skillet over medium heat. Add beef and cook, stirring to break up, until browned. Stir in sauce and a little water. Cover and simmer over low heat for about 20 minutes, adding more water if needed. Cook rice in boiling salted water according to the package instructions, until just tender. Drain rice. Add to pan and stir to mix. Season to taste. Remove bell peppers from oven. Allow to cool a little. Add any liquid inside bell peppers to beef and rice mixture. Replace bell peppers in dish. Fill with beef and rice mixture. Return to the oven and cook for about 20 minutes.

4 servings

COOK'S KNOW-HOW

Red bell peppers have the fullest flavor for stuffing and baking, and certainly soften more easily in the oven than green bell peppers. However, mixing red with orange or yellow bell peppers gives added eye appeal.

WIENER SCHNITZEL

4 scallops of veal or pork
1 egg, beaten
about $1^1/_2$ cups fine fresh soft bread crumbs
4 tablespoons/$^1/_2$ stick/$^1/_4$ cup butter

Lay scallops flat between sheets of waxed paper. Beat with a rolling pin or mallet until thin but unbroken. Remove paper. Season meat to taste. Coat each slice in beaten egg, then bread crumbs. Melt butter in a large heavy-bottomed skillet over high heat. When foaming, add slices and cook quickly on either side, then lower heat and continue to cook, turning once again. Cook for about 10 minutes in all. Serve with lemon wedges.

4 servings

SPAGHETTI BOLOGNESE

3 tablespoons Garlic Oil (see page 102)
1 pound ground lean beef steak
3 tablespoons tomato paste, preferably sun-dried
$^3/_4$ pound dried spaghetti

Heat 2 tablespoons of the oil in a large heavy-bottomed skillet over high heat. Add beef and cook, stirring, until browned and broken up. Lower heat and stir in tomato paste. Season well. Cover and cook over very low heat while pasta is cooking, stirring frequently and adding a little of pasta cooking liquid to moisten. Cook pasta in boiling salted water according to the package instructions, until just tender. Drain. Return pasta to pan, add remaining oil, and toss to coat. Transfer to a warmed plates and toss with meat sauce.

4 servings

SPICED COTTAGE PIE

1 pound potatoes, peeled and cut into chunks
2 tablespoons/^{1}/$_4$ stick butter
15 ounce can chili
^{1}/$_2$ cup shredded cheddar cheese

Cook potatoes in boiling salted water for 15-20 minutes until tender. Drain well. Return to pan and mash with butter. Season to taste. Put chili into an ovenproof dish. Top with mashed potato. Sprinkle with cheese. Bake in a preheated oven, 400°F, for about 40 minutes, until top is well browned and meat sauce is piping hot.

2-3 servings

SHEPHERD'S PIE ITALIAN STYLE

1^3/$_4$ pounds potatoes, peeled and cut into chunks
1^1/$_2$ pounds ground lamb
about 2 cups lamb or vegetable broth
5 tablespoons red pesto sauce

Cook potatoes in boiling salted water for 15-20 minutes, until tender. Meanwhile, heat a large nonstick skillet over medium heat. Add lamb and cook, stirring to break up, until browned. Stir in broth. Season to taste. Cover and cook for about 15 minutes, stirring occasionally. Drain potatoes. Return to pan and mash with 1 tablespoon pesto. Add remaining pesto to lamb mixture with a little more broth if needed. Transfer sauce to an ovenproof dish. Top with mashed potatoes. Bake in a preheated oven, 400°F, for about 45 minutes, until top is well browned.

4–6 servings

VEAL WITH CREAM SAUCE

4 scallops of veal, about $1/4$ lb each
$2/3$ cup dry white vermouth
$1^1/4$ cups heavy cream
2-3 tablespoons butter

Put veal in a single layer into a shallow dish. Season to taste. Pour over vermouth. Cover and refrigerate for 2 hours. Put cream in a heavy-bottomed pan with pinch of salt over low heat. Bring to a boil. As soon as it reaches boiling point, lower heat and simmer gently, stirring frequently, for 10-15 minutes, until thick and golden. Drain veal. Gradually beat marinade into cream over a very low heat, until sauce thickens slightly. Meanwhile, melt butter in a skillet over high heat. Fry veal for 3 minutes each side, until browned. Transfer to warmed serving plates. Pour sauce over veal.

4 servings

CLASSIC HAMBURGER

$1^1/2$ pounds ground lean beef steak
1 small onion, grated
2 tablespoons Worcestershire sauce
4 burger buns, split in half

Put beef, onion, and Worcestershire sauce in a bowl. Season well. Combine with a fork. With wet hands, shape into 4 patties. Broil under medium heat for 3-5 minutes each side, according to taste. Serve in buns.

4 servings

SPICY HAMBURGER

1¹/₂ pounds ground lean beef steak
1-2 tablespoons cracked green peppercorns
1 tablespoon chopped thyme
Mustard Mayonnaise (see page 250), to serve

Put beef, peppercorns, and thyme in a bowl. Season well with salt.
Combine with a fork. With wet hands, shape into 4 patties. Broil under
medium heat for 3-5 minutes each side, according to taste. Serve with
Mustard Mayonnaise.

4 servings

CHEAT'S CHILI

1 pound ground lean beef
2 tablespoons ground cumin
about 1 cup chunky salsa, or to taste
15 ounce can red kidney beans, drained

Heat a large nonstick skillet over medium heat. Add beef and cook,
stirring to break up, until browned. Add cumin and cook for about 1
minute, stirring. Stir in salsa and thin with a little water. Bring to a boil,
then reduce heat to low. Season to taste. Cover and cook for 20 minutes,
stirring occasionally. Add beans and stir to mix. Cover and cook for 10
minutes more, stirring occasionally.

4 servings

BEEF IN RED WINE

¹/₄ pound sliced bacon, diced
1 pound stewing beef steak, cut into 1¹/₂ inch cubes
²/₃ cup herb broth
²/₃ cup red wine

Heat a large nonstick skillet over medium heat. Add bacon and cook, stirring, until fat runs and bacon begins to brown. Transfer with a slotted spoon to an ovenproof casserole dish. Increase heat to high. Cook meat in bacon drippings, in batches, until browned, transferring with a slotted spoon to casserole dish. Pour a little of the broth into pan and scrape up any residue. Pour into casserole dish with remaining broth and wine. Season to taste. Cover and cook in a preheated oven, 400°F, for about 20 minutes. Reduce heat to 300°F and continue cooking for 2 hours, until meat is very tender.

4 servings

BEEF OLIVES

2 pound tip roast
$^1/_2$ cup cream cheese with garlic and herbs
2 slices proscuitto or cooked lean ham, chopped
$1^3/_4$ cups beef broth

Cut beef into thin slices. Put between 2 sheets waxed paper. Flatten with a rolling pin or mallet. Season well. Blend cheese with ham in a bowl. Spread mixture onto top of beef slices. Roll up, folding in sides, and secure with cotton or fine string. Heat a nonstick skillet over high heat. Brown beef rolls on all sides. Transfer to a shallow casserole dish or ovenproof dish. Add broth. Cover and cook in a preheated oven, 300°F, for $1^1/_2$–2 hours, until tender. To thicken sauce, pour into a pan over high heat and cook until reduced. Cut and remove cotton or string around rolls to serve.

4 servings

STEAKS
BEEF STEAKS WITH FRESH TOMATO SAUCE

4 top round steaks, about $^3/_4$ inch thick
2 tablespoons Garlic Oil (see page 102), plus extra for sprinkling and brushing
$2^1/_2$ cups skinned, deseeded, and chopped tomatoes
a few basil leaves or 1 teaspoon dried oregano

Beat steaks with a rolling pin or mallet to tenderize. Season to taste and sprinkle with oil. Set aside. Heat 2 tablespoons oil in a small pan over low heat for 1-2 minutes. Add tomatoes and season to taste. Bring to a boil and cook for 5-6 minutes, until tomatoes are just softened. Roughly tear basil leaves and add to pan or add oregano. Brush a large skillet with oil over high heat. Cook steaks for 2 minutes on each side, until lightly browned. Top each steak with a layer of tomato sauce. Cover pan tightly and cook over low heat for 6-10 minutes, according to taste.

4 servings

BEEF STEAKS WITH BLUE CHEESE

2 beef tenderloin steaks, $1^1/_2$ inches thick
4 tablespoons/$^1/_2$ stick/$^1/_4$ cup butter
$^1/_4$ pound blue cheese, preferably Cashel Blue, rinded and sliced
croutons (store-bought or see pages 58–9)

Season steaks all over. Melt about two-thirds butter in a heavy-bottomed skillet over high heat. When foaming, add steaks and cook briefly on both sides to seal. Use remaining butter to grease a baking sheet. Arrange steak on sheet. Top with cheese slices. Cook in a preheated oven, 425°F, for 5 minutes for rare, 8 minutes for medium rare, and 15 minutes for well done, allowing cheese to melt and lightly color. Transfer steak to a warmed serving plate. Scatter croutons around steak and pour over cooking juices. Serve immediately.

2 servings

BEEF STEAKS WITH PESTO SAUCE

8 top round beef steaks, about 3 ounces each
2 tablespoons/^{1}/$_4$ stick butter
^{1}/$_3$ cup pesto sauce (or use Pistou, see page 85)

Flatten steaks with a dampened meat mallet. Melt butter in a large
heavy-bottomed skillet over high heat. Add steaks and cook for 1 minute
on each side. Reduce heat to low and season to taste. Spread pesto (or
pistou) over steaks and add some to cooking juices. Cover and cook over
low heat for about 10 mnutes, until steaks are tender.
4 servings

BEEF STEAKS WITH SMOKED OYSTERS

2 tenderloin steaks, about 5 ounces each
vegetable oil, for brushing
^{1}/$_4$ cup beef broth
3^3/$_4$ ounce can smoked oysters, drained

Carefully cut three-quarters of the way through each steak. Open out
butterfly fashion. Lay between 2 sheets of waxed paper. Beat gently with a
rolling pin or mallet to an even thickness. Season and brush both sides
lightly with oil. Broil under high heat for about 6 minutes, turning once.
Put broth into a small pan. Bring to a boil. Simmer for 3-4 minutes, until
liquid is slightly reduced. Stir in oysters. Transfer cooked steaks to serving
plates. Spoon over sauce.
2 servings

BEEF STEAKS WITH ORANGE

4 thin top round steaks
^{1}/$_4$ cup white wine
2 tablespoons Garlic Oil (see page 102)
juice of 1 orange, plus orange slices to garnish

Beat steaks with a rolling pin or mallet to tenderize. Put in a large shallow dish. Blend together remaining ingredients and pour over meat. Season to taste. Toss meat to coat in marinade. Cover and refrigerate for at least 2 hours, preferably overnight. Lift out steaks with a slotted spoon. Broil under high heat for about 10 minutes. Transfer to warmed serving plates. Garnish with orange slices.

4 servings

BANGERS AND BACON

PORK, HERB, AND CARROT MEATLOAF

$1^1/_2$ pounds pork and herb bulk sausage
$^1/_2$ pound carrots, grated
$^1/_4$ pound onion, grated
2 teaspoons Worcestershire sauce

Mix all ingredients together. Press mixture into an ovenproof dish to a depth of $1^1/_2$ inches. Cover and refrigerate for at least 2 hours, or overnight. Bake in a preheated oven, 400°F, for about an hour, until well browned.

4-6 servings

SAUSAGE HOTPOT

1 pound fat pork link sausages
10 ounce package frozen mixed vegetables, defrosted
$14^1/_2$ ounce can seasoned tomatoes
1 pound potatoes

Heat a nonstick skillet over high heat. Cook sausages briefly until browned all over. Transfer to a casserole or ovenproof dish. Reserve drippings. Add mixed vegetables and tomatoes with 3 cups water. Season to taste. Parboil potatoes in boiling salted water. Drain and leave to cool a little. Cut into $^1/_4$ inch slices. Overlap potatoes on top of casserole. Brush or dot with sausage drippings. Bake in a preheated oven, 350°F, for about 1 hour, until sausages are cooked and potatoes browned.

4 servings

SAUSAGE PIE

$^1/_2$ pound shortcrust pastry dough (store-bought or use Short Crust recipe on page 294, made with 2 cups flour, $^1/_2$ cup fat)
$^1/_2$ pound pork and herb bulk sausage
$^3/_4$ cup shredded cheddar cheese
$^2/_3$ cup heavy cream

Roll out pastry dough and use to line an 8 inch pie dish. Roll out a round for a lid. Heat a nonstick skillet over medium heat. Add bulk sausage and fry, stirring constantly, until browned. Season to taste. Spread half the cheese in pie shell. Cover with bulk sausage. Top with remaining cheese. Pour over cream. Damp dough edges and cover with dough lid. Crimp edges to seal. Make a vent in dough lid. Bake in a preheated oven, 400°F, for 30 minutes, until golden brown and cooked.

6 servings

TOAD IN THE HOLE

1 cup all-purpose flour, sifted
2 eggs
$1^1/_4$ cups milk
8 pork link sausages

Put flour, eggs, and half the milk with a little salt into a food processor or blender. Process until mixed. With motor running, gradually add remaining milk, to form a smooth, thin batter. Add a little water if mixture is too thick. Heat a nonstick skillet over medium heat. Cook sausages, turning frequently, until browned all over. Arrange sausages in an ovenproof dish or rectangular roasting pan, about 11 x 7 inches, with pan drippings. Heat in a preheated oven, 425°F, for about 5 minutes, until hot.

Remove and pour over batter. Return to oven and cook for about 35-40 minutes, until batter is well risen and browned. Serve immediately.

4 servings

BACON-STUFFED TOMATOES

8 slices smoked bacon, diced
1 large onion, finely chopped
6 beefsteak tomatoes
1 cup fresh soft white bread crumbs

Heat a nonstick skillet over medium heat. Cook bacon, stirring frequently, until fat runs and bacon begins to brown. Add onion and cook, stirring frequently, for about 5 minutes, until softened and golden. Meanwhile, cut tops off tomatoes. Scoop out flesh and seeds from bases and tops, discarding hard cores. Add flesh and seeds to pan and simmer for a few minutes to evaporate liquid. Stir in bread crumbs and season well. Spoon mixture into tomatoes. Replace tops. Cook in a preheated oven, 325°F, for about 30 minutes, until tender.

2-3 servings

BRAISES

VEAL ROLLS

8 scallops of veal, about 2 ounces each
8 thin slices cooked bacon or ham
1 tablespoon Basil Oil (see page 102)
$^2/_3$ cup white wine

Lay scallops flat between sheets of waxed paper. Beat with a rolling pin or mallet until thin but unbroken. Remove paper. Lay a slice of bacon or ham on each piece of veal. Season to taste. Roll up and secure with wooden toothpicks. Heat oil in a skillet over medium heat. Cook rolls, turning gently, until browned all over. Pour wine over rolls. Cover tightly and simmer over very low heat for 20-25 minutes, until tender, turning once. Alternatively, cook in an ovenproof dish in a preheated oven, 350°F. Lift rolls onto a warmed serving dish. Boil pan juices until reduced and thickened. Remove cocktail sticks. Serve with cooking juices poured over.

4 servings

PORK AND APPLE PACKAGES

4 tablespoons/^{1}/$_2$ stick/^{1}/$_4$ cup butter
4 pork loin steaks
2 tart apples, peeled and sliced
^{1}/$_2$ cup cider

Cut 4 sheets of aluminum foil large enough to enclose ingredients loosely. Spread butter onto each. Top with pork and season to taste. Top with apple slices. Sprinkle about 1 tablespoon cider over each steak. Gather up foil loosely around ingredients and fold over to seal. Arrange packages on a baking sheet. Bake in a preheated oven, 350°F, for 20-25 minutes, until meat is tender. Serve in packages.

4 servings

PORK WITH SPICED APRICOTS

1 pound boneless pork loin, cubed
1-2 tablespoons Jamaican jerk seasoning
^{1}/$_4$ cup Chili Oil (see page 102)
14 ounce can apricot halves in natural juice

Coat pork in jerk seasoning. Heat oil in a large heavy-bottomed skillet over medium heat. Add pork and cook, stirring, until browned all over. Drain apricots, reserving juice. Cut into quarters and add to pan with a little of juice. Bring to a boil, stirring. Reduce heat, cover, and simmer, stirring occasionally and adding more juice if necessary, for about 25 minutes, until pork is tender.

4 servings

BRAISED LAMB WITH ORANGE SAUCE

2 large oranges
4 lamb leg steaks
$^2/_3$ cup lamb or chicken broth
2 tablespoons light brown sugar

Thinly pare zest from oranges. Shred zest finely. Cook in a pan of boiling water for 5 minutes. Drain. Squeeze juice from oranges. Season lamb liberally. Heat a large nonstick skillet over high heat. Add lamb and cook until browned on both sides. Add orange juice, broth, sugar, and zest. Cover and braise over low heat for 40 minutes, or until lamb is tender.

4 servings

LAMB AND BEAN HOTPOT

$14^1/_2$ ounce seasoned tomatoes
15 ounce can cannellini beans
4 lamb leg steaks
3 tablespoons Garlic Oil (see page 102)

Put tomatoes and beans into a pan over medium heat. Season to taste. Bring to a boil. Reduce heat, cover, and simmer for 5 minutes. Transfer to an ovenproof dish. Top with lamb in a single layer. Drizzle over oil. Cook in a preheated oven, 400°F, for 30–40 minutes, until lamb is tender and well browned.

4 servings

MEAT SPECIALS

PORK ON A SKEWER

1 pound pork tenderloin
2-3 slices firm bread, $^1/_2$ inch thick
$^1/_4$ pound thinly sliced proscuitto
olive oil

Cut pork into 12 cubes. Remove crusts from bread. Cut bread into 12 cubes about the same size as meat. Cut proscuitto into 12 pieces. Divide pork, proscuitto, and bread equally between 4 greased long metal skewers. Thread onto skewers alternately. Lay skewers flat, slightly apart, in a well-oiled baking pan. Season lightly with salt and generously with pepper. Sprinkle liberally with oil. Bake in the center of a preheated oven, 375°F, for 30-40 minutes, until meat is cooked and bread is crisp and crunchy. Turn skewers once halfway through cooking.

4 servings

MUSTARD BEEF

$^2/_3$ cup Garlic Oil (see page 102)
$1^1/_4$ pounds tip roast
2 teaspoons Dijon mustard
1 pound young carrots, partly cooked

Heat 2-3 tablespoons oil in a large skillet over a high heat. Add meat and cook for 2 minutes on each side. Remove to a cutting board. Discard any fat. Cut meat into medium-thick slices. Arrange slices in an oiled ovenproof dish. Season with salt and plenty of coarsely ground black pepper. Blend 4-6 tablespoons of remaining oil with mustard. Pour over meat. Cover and refrigerate for 1-2 hours. Heat remaining oil in a skillet. Add carrots and sauté for 2 minutes. Add to dish with with meat. Cover and cook in a preheated oven, 350°F, for 25 minutes.

4 servings

HONEYED PORK CHOPS

4 pork loin chops
4 tablespoons set honey
4 teaspoons Dijon mustard
2 cups small button mushrooms

Heat a large nonstick skillet over medium heat. Add chops and cook for 2 minutes each side, until browned. Stir in honey, mustard, and mushrooms. Cover and cook for 8-10 minutes, turning frequently.
4 servings

LAMB WITH MINT CRUST

1 shoulder of lamb
3 tablespoons fresh soft white bread crumbs
3 tablespoons mint sauce (store-bought or use recipe on page 250)
2 cloves garlic, finely chopped

Put lamb on a rack in a roasting pan. Season well. Roast in a preheated oven, 350°F, for 25 minutes per pound. Mix bread crumbs with mint sauce and garlic to form a paste. Season to taste. 30 minutes before end of cooking time, remove lamb from oven. Spread bread crumb mixture over fat surface, pressing down well with a spatula. Baste with pan drippings and return to oven to finish cooking. The crust should be golden brown at the end of the cooking time.
4-6 servings

LAMB CHOPS WITH ROSEMARY AND LEMON

1 rosemary sprig, finely chopped
1 tablespoon olive oil
finely grated zest and juice of 1 lemon
8 lamb loin chops

Combine rosemary, oil, and lemon zest and juice in a shallow nonmetallic dish. Season to taste. Add lamb and turn to coat with marinade. Leave to marinate for 15 minutes. Broil, spooning over marinade, under very high heat for about 5 minutes on each side.

4 servings

MEATBALLS AND PATTIES

LAMB PATTIES WITH MINT

$1^1/_4$ pounds ground lean lamb
2 tablespoon vegetable oil or Garlic Oil (see page 102)
$^1/_2$ cup finely chopped onion
2 tablespoons mint jelly

Put lamb in a bowl. Season well. Heat half the oil in a large skillet over medium heat. Sauté onion, stirring constantly, until lightly colored. Blend onion into lamb with mint jelly. With wet hands, form into small patties. Heat remaining oil in a nonstick skillet over high heat. Add patties and cook for 2 minutes on each side. Lower heat and cook, turning frequently, for about 20 minutes, until cooked through. Serve with Yogurt and Mint Sauce (see page 248).

4 servings

SAUSAGE PATTIES WITH MOZZARELLA

$1^1/_4$ pounds bulk sausage
2 cloves garlic, minced
2 teaspoons dried oregano
3 ounces mozzarella, cut into 8 cubes

Put bulk sausage, garlic, and oregano into a bowl. Season to taste. Mix together well to combine. With wet hands, shape into 8 even-sized patties. Press a cheese cube into center of each. Reform mixture around cheese to enclose. Cover and chill in the refrigerator for 30 minutes, until firm. Heat a griddle pan or nonstick skillet over medium heat. Cook patties for about 20 minutes, turning frequently, until well browned and cooked through.

4 servings

LAMB AND OLIVE PATTIES

1¹/₄ pounds ground lean lamb
2 cloves garlic, minced
1 tablespoon chopped pitted olives
2 tablespoons freshly grated Parmesan cheese, plus extra for sprinkling

Put all ingredients into a bowl and season well. Mix together well to combine. With wet hands, shape into 8 even-sized patties. Heat a griddle pan or nonstick skillet over medium heat. Cook patties for about 8 minutes on each side, until well browned and cooked through. Sprinkle patties with Parmesan. Broil under high heat until just melted. Serve immediately.

4 servings

LAMB AND CUMIN PATTIES

1¹/₄ pounds ground lean lamb
2 tablespoons ground cumin
grated zest and juice of 1 lemon
2-3 tablespoons thick plain yogurt

Put all ingredients into a bowl. Season well. Mix together well to combine. With wet hands, shape into 8 even-sized patties. Chill in the refrigerator for 30 minutes, until firm. Heat a griddle pan or nonstick skillet over medium heat. Cook patties for about 8 minutes on each side, until well browned and cooked through.

4 servings

PORK AND MANGO PATTIES

1$^1/_4$ pounds ground pork
2 tablespoons curry powder or garam masala
1-2 teaspoons chili powder, to taste
2-3 tablespoons mango preserves

Put all ingredients into a bowl. Season well. Mix together well to combine. With wet hands, shape into 8 even-sized patties. Chill in the refrigerator for 30 minutes, until firm. Heat a griddle pan or nonstick skillet over medium heat. Cook patties for about 20 minutes, turning frequently, until well browned and cooked through.

4 servings

SAUCES

PORT SAUCE

1 teaspoon French mustard
few drops Worcestershire sauce
$^1/_4$ cup port
$^2/_3$ cup heavy cream

Put all the ingredients into a small pan over low heat. Bring to a boil, stirring constantly. Simmer gently for 1-2 minutes. Serve with broiled or sautéed meat.

4 servings

SESAME AND PARSLEY SAUCE

$^2/_3$ cup tahini
3 cloves garlic, minced
$^2/_3$ cup lemon juice
1 cup finely chopped parsley

Beat tahini with garlic. Beat in lemon juice, about 4 tablespoons cold water, and seasoning to taste to form a fairly thick creamy consistency. Stir in parsley. Serve with broiled or roast lamb, or lamb kabobs.

4 servings

TOMATO AND BASIL SAUCE

3 tablespoons olive oil
3 cloves garlic, chopped
2 x 14^1/$_2$ ounce cans plum tomatoes
2 tablespoons chopped basil

Heat oil in a pan over low heat. Add garlic and cook, stirring, for 2 minutes. Do not brown. Add tomatoes and break up with a wooden spoon. Season well. Increase heat to medium and cook, stirring frequently, for about 15 minutes, until reduced and thickened. Add basil and cook for only 2-3 minutes more. Serve hot with grilled or sautéed meat.

6 servings

ASPARAGUS SAUCE

10^1/$_2$ ounce can asparagus spears
^{2}/$_3$ cup vegetable or chicken broth
1 tablespoon sour cream
1 egg yolk

Drain asparagus. Put into a food processor or blender and purée. Transfer to a heatproof bowl over a pan of gently simmering water. Add remaining ingredients and season to taste. Cook, stirring frequently, until hot and slightly thickened. Serve with broiled or sautéed meat.

4 servings

MUSTARD AND DILL SAUCE

$1/2$ tablespoon Dijon mustard
$1/2$ tablespoon olive oil
$1/4$ cup sour cream
2 tablespoons chopped dill

Put mustard into a bowl and blend in oil drop by drop. When all oil is incorporated and smoothly blended, stir in cream and dill. Serve with broiled or pan-fried pork chops or steaks.

2-4 servings

YOGURT AND MINT SAUCE

1 cucumber
$1^1/4$ cups plain yogurt
1-2 cloves garlic, minced
24 mint leaves, roughly chopped

Peel cucumber and grate it coarsely. Squeeze out excess liquid. Add to a food processor or blender with yogurt, garlic, mint, and seasoning to taste. Whizz until blended. Cover and chill in the refrigerator. Serve with hot or cold roast lamb or lamb kabobs.

4 servings

SWEET PEPPER CATSUP

3 large red bell peppers
3 tablespoons Garlic Oil (see page 102)
1 large onion, chopped
1-2 teaspoons Tabasco sauce, to taste

Broil bell peppers under medium heat, turning frequently, for about 10 minutes, until blistered and charred all over. Wrap in aluminum foil or a clean damp dish towel. Leave for a few minutes. Meanwhile, heat 2 tablespoons of the oil in a skillet over medium heat. Cook onion, stirring, for about 5 minutes, until softened. Leave to cool a little. Peel away skin from bell peppers. Halve, core, and deseed. Roughly chop flesh and put into a food processor or blender with onion, Tabasco, and remaining oil. Whizz until blended. Serve with broiled or pan-fried beef steaks, pork chops or steaks, or kabobs.

4 servings

SALSA CRUDA

1 pound ripe cherry tomatoes
$^1/_2$ red onion, finely chopped
1-2 cloves garlic, minced
3 tablespoons finely chopped cilantro

Dice tomatoes. Put into a bowl with any juice. Add onion, garlic, and cilantro. Mix well. Season with salt. Cover and chill in the refrigerator for 30 minutes, to allow flavors to develop. Serve with broiled or pan-fried beef steaks, pork chops or steaks, lamb steaks, kebabs, or cold roast meats.

6 servings

APPLE AND SAGE SAUCE

2 tart apples, peeled, cored, and sliced
$^1/_2$ teaspoon sugar
2 teaspoons finely chopped sage
1 tablespoon/$^1/_8$ stick butter

Put apple slices in a small pan with just enough water to cover bottom of pan over very low heat. Cook until soft. Add sugar and freshly ground black pepper to taste. Remove from heat. Stir in sage and beat in butter. Leave for 5 minutes before serving. It can also be served cold. Serve with roast pork or broiled pork chops, or duck.

4 servings

HORSERADISH SAUCE

1^1/$_4$ cups sour cream
1^1/$_2$-2 tablespoons grated horseradish, to taste
2 teaspoons lemon juice

Beat cream with horseradish, adding a little at a time, to taste. Beat in lemon juice and season well. Serve with hot or cold roast beef.

4 servings

MINT SAUCE

^{1}/$_4$ cup finely chopped mint
1 teaspoon sugar
2 tablespoons lemon juice
1 tablespoon white wine vinegar

Pound chopped mint with sugar using a pestle and mortar until well blended. Transfer to a heatproof bowl. Beat in lemon juice, vinegar, and ^{1}/$_4$ cup boiling water. Leave to cool. Serve with roast lamb or broiled lamb chops or steaks.

4-6 servings

MUSTARD MAYONNAISE

2 egg yolks
1 tablespooon white wine vinegar
2 tablespoons coarse-grain or Dijon mustard
1^1/$_4$ cups grapeseed oil

Put egg yolks, vinegar, and mustard into a food processor or blender. Process briefly to blend. With motor running, add oil in a thin trickle, until mixture is smooth and creamy. Season to taste. Serve with hamburgers and beef steaks.

4 servings

FLAVORED BUTTERS

MINT BUTTER

8 tablespoons/1 stick/$^1/_2$ cup unchilled butter, diced
4 tablespoons finely chopped mint
1 tablespoon lemon juice

Put ingredients into a food processor or blender. Process until well blended. Alternatively, blend together butter and mint with a fork, then beat in lemon juice. Season to taste. Form into a roll. Wrap in aluminum foil and chill in the refrigerator until firm. Slice into $^1/_2$ inch slices. Use to top hot broiled or pan-fried lamb chops or steaks.

4-6 servings

SAGE BUTTER

8 tablespoons/1 stick/$^1/_4$ cup unchilled butter, diced
2 tablespoons finely chopped sage
1 tablespoon lemon juice
2 teaspoons onion juice

Put ingredients into a food processor or blender. Process until well blended. Alternatively, blend together butter and sage with a fork, then beat in lemon and onion juice. Season to taste. Form into a roll. Wrap in aluminum foil and chill in the refrigerator until firm. Slice into $^1/_2$ inch slices. Use to top hot broiled or pan-fried lamb or veal chops or steaks.

4-6 servings

PARSLEY BUTTER

8 tablespoons/1 stick/$^1/_2$ cup unchilled butter, diced
5 tablespoons finely chopped parsley
1 clove garlic, minced

juice of 1 lemon

Put ingredients into a food processor or blender. Process until well blended. Alternatively, blend together butter, parsley, and garlic with a fork, then beat in lemon juice. Season to taste. Form into a roll. Wrap in aluminum foil and chill in the refrigerator until firm. Slice into $^1/_2$ inch slices. Use to top hot broiled or pan-fried beef steaks.

4-6 servings

CHIVE AND LEMON BUTTER

8 tablespoons/1 stick/$^1/_2$ cup unchilled butter, diced
5 tablespoons chopped chives
grated zest and juice of $^1/_2$ lemon

Put ingredients into a food processor or blender. Process until well blended. Alternatively, blend together butter and chives with a fork, then beat in lemon zest and juice. Season to taste. Form into a roll. Wrap in aluminum foil and chill in the refrigerator until firm. Slice into $^1/_2$ inch slices. Use to top hot broiled or pan-fried lamb chops or steaks.

4-6 servings

HORSERADISH AND CHIVE BUTTER

8 tablespoons/1 stick/$^1/_2$ cup unchilled butter, diced
4 tablespoons chopped chives
1–2 tablespoons grated horseradish, to taste

Put ingredients into a food processor or blender. Process until well blended. Alternatively, blend together by hand with a fork. Season to taste. Form into a roll. Wrap in aluminum foil and chill in the refrigerator until firm. Slice into $^1/_2$ inch slices. Use to top hot broiled or pan-fried beef or venison steaks.

4-6 servings

VEGETARIAN

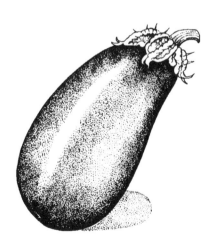

STUFFED VEGETABLES

STUFFED ZUCCHINI

4 large zucchini, trimmed and halved lengthwise
1 cup ricotta cheese
2 tablespoons finely chopped mint
milk, for blending

Cook zucchini in salted boiling water for 5 minutes. Drain well. Halve lengthwise. Carefully scoop out centers with a teaspoon to create "boats" to hold filling. Finely chop scooped-out flesh and mix with ricotta, mint, seasoning, and a little milk to make a soft consistency. Arrange courgette cases close together in a single layer in a well-oiled shallow ovenproof dish. Fill cases with cheese mixture. Bake in a preheated oven, 375°F, for 35-40 minutes, until zucchini are tender and filling is golden brown.

4 servings

AVOCADO-STUFFED TOMATOES

8 beefsteak tomatoes
1 ripe avocado, halved, pitted, and peeled (see page 15)
4 hard-cooked eggs, finely chopped
$^1/_4$ cup mayonnaise

Cut off tops of tomatoes. Scoop out flesh and seeds from tops and bottoms, discarding hard cores. Mash avocado in a bowl. Add tomato pulp, eggs, and mayonnaise. Mix together well. Pile into tomato shells and replace tops. Serve immediately.

4 servings

STUFFED BELL PEPPERS WITH BEANS AND CORN

4 large red bell peppers

15 ounce can chili beans or beans in a spicy sauce
11 ounce can Mexican-style corn, drained
$^3/_4$ cup shredded cheddar cheese

Cut bell peppers in half lenghwise, leaving stalks in place. Core and deseed. Put bell peppers, cut side up and tightly packed, into an ovenproof dish. Bake in a preheated oven, 400°F, for about 25 minutes, until softened. Allow to cool a little, then invert onto paper towels to drain. Put beans and corn into a pan over low heat, stirring frequently, until heated through. Return bell peppers to dish. Fill with hot bean mixture. Sprinkle with cheese. Return to oven and cook for about 20 minutes, until cheese is melted and lightly browned.

4 servings

STUFFED BELL PEPPERS WITH RICE AND SALSA

4 large red bell peppers
$1^1/_4$ cups long-grain rice
$1^1/_2$ cups chunky salsa
4 tablespoons sour cream

Cut bell peppers in half lenghwise, leaving stalks in place. Core and deseed. Put bell peppers, cut side up and tightly packed, into an ovenproof dish. Bake in a preheated oven, 400°F, for about 25 minutes, until softened. Cook rice in boiling salted water according to the package instructions, until just tender. Return to pan and add salsa. Heat through over low heat, stirring. Remove bell peppers from oven. Allow to cool a little. Pour any liquid inside bell peppers into rice mixture and season to taste. Fill bell peppers with rice mixture. Return to oven and cook for about 15 minutes. Remove from oven. Top each bell pepper half with a spoonful of cream. Return to oven for about 5 minutes, to warm cream.

4 servings

STUFFED BELL PEPPERS WITH COUSCOUS, OLIVES, AND FETA

4 large red bell peppers
1 cup pre-cooked couscous (see page 133)
$^3/_4$ cup pitted olives in oil, chopped, 1-2 tablespoons oil reserved
$1^1/_2$ cups crumbled feta cheese

Cut bell peppers in half lenghwise, leaving stalks in place. Core and deseed. Put bell peppers, cut side up and tightly packed, into an ovenproof dish. Bake in a preheated oven, 400°F, for about 25 minutes, until softened. Meanwhile, put couscous in a heatproof bowl. Pour over an equal quantity of hot water. Cover and let stand for 10 minutes. Remove bell peppers from oven. Allow to cool a little. Pour any liquid inside bell peppers into couscous. Add olives to couscous with oil. Turn into a fine-mesh strainer over a pan of simmering water. Cover and steam for about 10 minutes, stirring occasionally, until couscous is tender. Remove from heat and stir in cheese. Season with black pepper. Fill bell peppers with couscous mixture. Return to oven and cook for about 20 minutes.
4 servings

BAKES

POTATO AND LEEK BAKE

$1^1/_2$ pounds potatoes
1 pound leeks, trimmed and sliced
$^2/_3$ cup heavy cream
$^3/_4$ cup shredded cheddar cheese

Cook potatoes in boiling salted water for 3 minutes. Drain and slice. Put leeks into a greased ovenproof dish. Season with pepper. Arrange potatoes on top. Pour over cream. Cover with aluminum foil. Bake in a preheated oven, 375°F, for 45 minutes, until potatoes are tender. Sprinkle with cheese. Broil under moderate heat until top is browned.
4-6 servings

ROOT VEGETABLE AND CREAMED MUSHROOM BAKE

$^3/_4$ pound potatoes, peeled and sliced
$^1/_2$ pound parsnips, peeled and sliced
2 x 7$^1/_2$ ounce cans creamed mushrooms
$^3/_4$ cup shredded Monterey Jack or cheddar cheese

Cook potatoes and parsnips in boiling salted water for 4 minutes.
Drain. Put into an ovenproof dish. Top with creamed mushrooms. Season
liberally with freshly ground black pepper. Sprinkle over cheese. Bake in
a preheated oven, 400°F, for about 40 minutes, until top is well browned
and vegetables are tender.

3-4 servings

CREAMED CORN AND POTATO BAKE

4 large potatoes
16 ounce can creamed corn
1$^1/_2$ cups shredded cheddar cheese
2 medium onions, thinly sliced

Cook potatoes in boiling salted water for 3 minutes. Drain and slice.
Layer corn, cheese, potatoes, and onions in an ovenproof dish, finishing
with a layer of cheese. Bake in a preheated oven, 400°F, for about 45
minutes, until potatoes are tender.

2-3 servings

MACARONI AND CHEESE WITH BROCCOLI

1 pound broccoli, broken into flowerets
14 ounce can macaroni and cheese
2 teaspoons Dijon mustard
1 cup shredded cheddar cheese

Cook broccoli in boiling salted water until just tender. Meanwhile, put macaroni and cheese in a pan over low heat. Stir in mustard. Heat through, stirring. Drain broccoli and gently combine with macaroni and cheese. Transfer to an ovenproof dish. Sprinkle with cheese. Bake in a preheated oven, 400°F, for about 20 minutes, until well browned.
2-3 servings

BEETS WITH PARMESAN

$^1/_4$ cup olive oil
2 tablespoons butter
1 pound beets, sliced into rings
1 cup shredded Parmesan cheese

Heat oil and butter in a small pan until foaming. Put about one-third of beets into an ovenproof dish. Drizzle with some of oil and butter. Cover with about one-third of cheese. Season to taste. Repeat these layers until all ingredients are used. Bake in a preheated oven, 400°F, for 15 minutes. Serve hot straight from the dish.   4 servings

EASY EGGPLANT

BAKED EGGPLANT AND CHEDDAR

2 x 14$^1/_2$ ounce cans seasoned tomatoes
6 eggplants, thickly sliced lengthwise
2 tablespoons olive oil
2$^1/_2$ cups shredded cheddar cheese

Put tomatoes into a pan over medium heat. Bring to a boil. Reduce heat and simmer for about 10 minutes, until reduced. Season well. Meanwhile, brush eggplant slices with oil. Arrange on 2 large cookie sheets. Roast at the top of a preheated oven, 400°F, for 10 minutes on each side, until golden and tender. Spoon a little of tomatoes into an ovenproof dish. Top with a layer of eggplant slices and cheese. Continue with layers, finishing with cheese. Bake in the oven for 30 minutes, until cheese is bubbling and golden.

6 servings

BAKED EGGPLANT AND GORGONZOLA

14$^{1}/_{2}$ ounce can seasoned tomatoes
3 tablespoons Garlic Oil (see page 102)
2 eggplants, thickly sliced
1 cup crumbled Gorgonzola cheese or other blue cheese

Put tomatoes into a pan over medium heat. Bring to a boil. Reduce heat and simmer for about 10 minutes, until reduced. Season well. Heat oil in a large skillet over medium heat. Cook eggplant slices until golden on each side. Put a layer of eggplant into a shallow ovenproof dish. Spoon over half the tomatoes. Make another layer of eggplant, then add remaining tomatoes. Top with cheese. Bake in a preheated oven, 375°F, for 15 minutes.

4 servings

EGGPLANT, TOMATO, AND MOZZARELLA MOUNTAINS

1 eggplant, cut into 8 slices
2 beefsteak tomatoes, skinned and cut into 8 slices
$^{1}/_{2}$ pound mozzarella (preferably buffalo), cut into 8 slices
$^{1}/_{3}$ cup pesto sauce (or use Pistou, see page 85)

Broil eggplant slices under high heat until browned on both sides. Put 4 slices onto a lightly oiled baking sheet. Put a tomato slice and cheese slice on each one. Make a second layer of eggplant, tomato, and cheese, adding seasoning to each layer as you go. Skewer with a wooden toothpick through the center to hold stacks together. Bake in a preheated oven, 375°F, for 10 minutes. Transfer stacks to individual serving plates. Carefully remove toothpicks. Top with a generous spoonful of pesto (or pistou). Serve warm or at room temperature.   4 servings

POTATO, ZUCCHINI, AND EGGPLANT BAKE

3 medium potatoes, peeled and thinly sliced
3 medium zucchini, thinly sliced
1 eggplant, thinly sliced
$^1/_2$ cup Garlic Oil (see page 102)

Arrange vegetables in layers in an ovenproof, flameproof dish, brushing each liberally with oil and seasoning to taste, finishing with a layer of potato. Drizzle any remaining oil over top. Cover with aluminum foil. Bake in a preheated oven, 350°F, for about 1$^1/_2$ hours, stirring occasionally, until vegetables are tender. Remove foil. Broil under high heat to brown top.

3-4 servings

COUSCOUS WITH EGGPLANT AND FETA

3 tablespoons olive oil or Garlic Oil (see page 102)
1 eggplant, cut into 1 inch cubes
1$^1/_4$ cups pre-cooked couscous (see page 133)
1 cup crumbled feta cheese

Heat oil in a large skillet over medium heat. Add eggplant and cook, stirring occasionally, for about 10 minutes, until tender. Put couscous into a heatproof bowl. Pour over an equal volume of boiling water. Cover and let stand for 5 minutes. Add cooked eggplant and oil from pan. Season to taste. Turn into a fine-mesh strainer over a pan of simmering water. Cover and steam for about 10 minutes, stirring occasionally, until ingredients are thoroughly hot and couscous is tender. Scatter over cheese, cover, and steam for about 3 minutes more, until cheese warms and begins to melt.

4 servings

BEAN FEAST

CURRIED KIDNEY BEANS

$^1/_2$ cup vegetable oil
2 tablespoons garam masala or curry powder
14$^1/_2$ ounce can seasoned tomatoes
2 x 15 ounce cans red kidney beans, drained

Heat oil in a large skillet over medium heat. Add spice mix and cook, stirring, for about 2 minutes. Stir in tomatoes. Season to taste. Reduce heat and cook for about 5 minutes. Add beans and stir to mix. Cook for 10-15 minutes, stirring occasionally.

4 servings

BAKED BEANS

2 x 15 ounce cans red kidney beans
2 tablespoons tomato paste
1 tablespoon molasses or black treacle
1 tablespoon Worcestershire sauce or dark soy sauce

Drain liquid from beans and pour half into a bowl, reserving remainder. Beat tomato paste, molasses or black treacle, and Worcestershire or soy sauce into liquid until well combined. Season to taste. Put beans and bean liquid mixture into a casserole dish. Cover with a tight-fitting lid. Bake in a preheated oven, 350°F, for 2 hours. Check beans during cooking time and add a little more reserved bean liquid if too dry.

4-6 servings

POTATO AND CHICKPEA PATTIES

2 x 15 ounce cans chickpeas (garbanzo beans), drained

2 medium potatoes, cooked and mashed
2-3 tablespoons tahini
$^1/_3$ cup Garlic Oil (see page 102)

Put chickpeas into a bowl. Mash well. Combine with mashed potatoes, tahini, about 1 tablespoon of the oil, and seasoning. With wet hands, form into 12 patties. Cover and chill in the refrigerator for 30 minutes, until firm. Heat oil in a large heavy-bottomed skillet. Cook patties for 4-5 minutes on each side, until well-browned and thoroughly hot.

4-6 servings

SPICY BEAN BURGERS

2 x 15 ounce cans red kidney beans, drained and liquid reserved
2 red chilies, deseeded and finely chopped
Garlic Oil (see page 102)
2–3 ounces Monterey Jack or sharp cheddar cheese, sliced

Put beans into a food processor or blender with chilies and about 1 tablespooon of the oil. Season to taste. Process, adding a little of bean liquid to work mixture if needed, until blended but still chunky. With wet hands, form mixture into 8 small burgers. Cover and chill in the refrigerator for about 30 minutes, until firm. Heat oil to a depth of $^1/_2$ inch in a skillet over high heat. Fry burgers in batches for 2-3 minutes on each side, turning carefully, until browned. Transfer to a flameproof dish. Keep warm while cooking remainder. Top burgers with cheese. Broil briefly under high heat to melt and brown. Serve immediately.

4 servings

FALAFEL

2 x 15 ounce cans chickpeas (garbanzo beans), drained and liquid reserved
grated zest and juice of $^1/_2$ lemon
1 tablespoon ground cumin

Garlic Oil (see page 102)

Put chickpeas into a food processor or blender with lemon zest and juice, cumin, and about 1 tablespoon of the oil. Season to taste. Process, adding a little of bean liquid to work mixture if needed, until blended but still chunky. With wet hands, form mixture into 8 small burgers. Cover and chill in the refrigerator for about 30 minutes, until firm. Heat oil to a depth of $^1/_2$ inch in a skillet over high heat. Fry falafel in batches for about 3 minutes on each side, turning carefully, until browned and crisp. Serve immediately.

4 servings

PASTA

PENNE WITH HERBED RICOTTA

$^3/_4$ pound penne
1 cup ricotta cheese
2 tablespoons Garlic Oil (see page 102)
3 tablespoons chopped basil or flatleaf parsley

Cook pasta in boiling salted water according to the package instructions, until just tender. Put cheese into a bowl. Beat in oil and herb. Season well. Drain pasta, reserving a little of cooking liquid. Turn pasta into a warmed serving dish. Top with sauce and toss to coat, adding a little reserved cooking liquid if dry.

4 servings

TAGLIATELLE VERDE WITH SNOWPEAS AND LEMON

$^3/_4$ pound dried tagliatelle verde
$^1/_4$ cup olive oil
1 pound snowpeas
grated zest of 1 lemon and 1 tablespoon juice

Cook pasta in boiling salted water according to the package

instructions, until just tender. Drain pasta and keep warm. Heat a wok over high heat. Add oil and heat until just smoking. Add snowpeas and stir-fry for 2 minutes. Add lemon zest and juice. Season to taste. Stir-fry for a few seconds more. Turn pan contents onto pasta and toss to mix.

4 servings

LINGUINE WITH FAVA BEANS AND PESTO

$^3/_4$ pound dried linguine
1 pound frozen fava beans
$^2/_3$ cup pesto sauce (or use Pistou, see page 85)
$^3/_4$ cup freshly grated Parmesan cheese

Cook pasta in boiling salted water according to the package instructions, until just tender. Cook beans in a separate pan of boiling water according to the package instructions, until tender. Drain pasta, reserving some of cooking liquid. Return to pan over low heat. Drain beans and add to pan with pesto (or pistou) and cheese. Season well with black pepper. Toss to coat, adding a little reserved cooking liquid.

4 servings

SPAGHETTI WITH CHERRY TOMATOES AND CILANTRO

$^3/_4$ pound dried spaghetti
$^1/_4$ cup olive oil or Garlic Oil (see page 102)
$1^1/_2$ pounds cherry tomatoes, halved
4 tablespoons chopped cilantro, plus a few leaves to garnish

Cook pasta in boiling salted water according to the package instructions, until just tender. Meanwhile, heat oil in a large heavy-bottomed skillet over medium heat. Cook tomatoes, stirring frequently, for 5 minutes. Season well. Stir cilantro into tomatoes. Drain pasta and turn into a warmed serving dish. Add sauce and toss to combine. Serve immediately, garnished with cilantro leaves.

4 servings

TAGLIATELLE VERDE WITH CREAMED OLIVES AND PARSLEY

$^3/_4$ pound dried tagliatelle verde
$1^1/_4$ cups light cream
$^2/_3$ cup pitted olives, halved or sliced
4 tablespoons chopped flatleaf parsley

Cook pasta in boiling salted water according to the package instructions, until just tender. Drain pasta, reserving a little of cooking liquid. Return pasta to pan over low heat. Add cream and olives. Season liberally with freshly ground black pepper. Toss for a few minutes, until warmed through, adding a little reserved cooking water if too dry. Add half the parsley. Toss again. Serve immediately, sprinkled with remaining parsley.

4 servings

PASTA SALAD WITH ASPARAGUS AND PINE NUTS

$^3/_4$ lb fusilli (twists) or other dried pasta shapes
1 pound fresh asparagus spears, trimmed and cut into 1 inch lengths
$^1/_2$ cup pine nuts
Lemon and Oil Dressing (see page 99) or bottled Italian vinaigrette dressing

Cook pasta in boiling salted water according to the package instructions, until just tender. Drain pasta and leave to cool. Cook asparagus in a pan of simmering salted water for 3-4 minutes, until just tender. Drain. Turn pasta into a serving dish. Add asparagus and pine nuts. Season to taste. Add dressing and toss to coat. Serve at room temperature.

4 servings

VEGETARIAN SPECIALS

PANIR MATTAR

2-3 tablespoons Chili Oil (see page 102)
$^1/_4$ pound panir (curd cheese), cut into $^1/_2$ inch cubes
10 ounce package frozen peas
2 tablespoons finely chopped cilantro

Heat oil in a heavy-bottomed pan. Add panir and fry until golden, turning gently and taking care not to burn it. Remove from pan and set aside. Add $^1/_3$ cup water and salt to taste to pan. Bring to a boil. Add peas. Reduce heat, cover, and cook until almost tender. If necessary, uncover and cook for 1 minute to evaporate any liquid. Very gently stir in panir Heat through for 2 minutes, then stir in cilantro. Serve immediately.
2-4 servings

ALOO SAG

$^1/_3$ cup Garlic Oil (see page 102)
1 inch piece fresh gingerroot, chopped
1 pound potatoes, cut into small pieces
2 x 10 ounce packages frozen chopped spinach, defrosted

Heat oil in a large skillet over low heat. Add ginger and cook for 5 minutes, stirring frequently. Add potatoes and salt to taste. Stir well, cover, and cook for 10 minutes. Drain spinach in a colander, pressing down firmly with a wooden spoon to squeeze out moisture. Add to potatoes and cook for 5 minutes, until vegetables are tender and hot.
4 servings

SMOKED TOFU SIR-FRY

$^1/_4$ cup sesame oil

266

$^1/_2$ pound firm smoked tofu (soybean curd), cubed
$1^1/_2$ pounds frozen mixed Chinese stir-fry vegetables, defrosted
3 tablespoons Hoisin sauce

Heat a wok over high heat. Add 3 tablespoons of the oil and heat until just smoking. Add tofu and stir-fry for about 3 minutes, until browned. Add vegetables and stir-fry for about 3 minutes, until slightly softened. Add sauce and stir-fry for another minute or so. Drizzle over remaining oil and serve immediately.

4 servings

ASPARAGUS WITH EGGS AND PARMESAN

1 pound fresh asparagus spears
4 tablespoons/$^1/_2$ stick/$^1/_4$ cup butter
4 eggs
$^1/_2$ cup shredded Parmesan cheese

Trim tough part of asparagus. Peel skin from about 2 inches of base of each stalk. Simmer in a pan of simmering salted water until just tender. Meanwhile, melt half the butter in a large skillet and cook until it turns golden brown (about 1 minute). Break eggs into pan and season well. Cook until egg whites have set. Drain asparagus and divide between 2 warmed serving dishes. Top each dish with 2 eggs. Melt remaining butter in pan and pour over asparagus. Sprinkle with Parmesan and serve.

2 servings

OEUFS FLORENTINE

$1^1/_2$ pounds fresh leaf spinach
2 tablespoons/$^1/_4$ stick butter
4 eggs
$^1/_2$ cup shredded cheddar cheese

Rinse spinach under cold water but do not dry. Put in a large pan over low heat. Season with salt. Cover and cook for about 5 minutes, until wilted. Drain well and chop. Return to rinsed-out pan with butter and freshly ground black pepper to taste. Toss to coat. Cover and leave over very low heat. Meanwhile, lightly poach eggs. Transfer spinach to a large flameproof serving dish. Drain eggs and put on top. Sprinkle with cheese. Broil under high heat for 2-3 minutes. Serve immediately.

4 servings

COOK'S KNOW-HOW

To poach eggs, pour water into a skillet to a depth of $1^1/_2$ inches. Bring to simmering point. Break each egg onto a saucer. Gently lower egg into water. Cook for about 3 minutes for a lightly cooked egg. Lift out with a slotted spoon and drain well.

SPINACH TART

1 quantity Short Crust pastry dough (see page 294) or use store-bought
10 ounce package frozen chopped spinach, defrosted
$1^1/_4$ cups mascarpone cheese
3 eggs

Use pastry dough to line a 9 inch fluted tart or quiche pan with a removable base. Chill in the refrigerator for 30 minutes. Bake pie shell blind (see page 294), until just set. Reduce oven to 325°F. Drain spinach in a colander, pressing down firmly with a wooden spoon to squeeze out moisture. Put mascarpone into a large bowl. Beat in 1 whole egg, plus 2 egg yolks. Add spinach and season well. Mix until well blended. Spoon into pie shell. Bake in the oven for 30 minutes, covering edge of dough with foil if overbrowning. Leave to stand for 10-15 minutes before serving. It can also be served cold.

4-6 servings

FETA AND ROASTED BELL PEPPER PIE

1 quantity Short Crust pastry dough (see page 294) or use store-bought
5 mixed red, orange, and yellow bell peppers, cored, deseeded, and cut
into thick strips
3 tablespoons Garlic Oil or Rosemary Oil (see pages 102-3)
1¹/₄ cups crumbled feta cheese

Use pastry dough to line a 9 inch tart or quiche pan. Chill in the
refrigerator for 30 minutes. Bake pie shell blind (see page 294). Remove
foil and bake for 5 minutes more, until light golden brown. Meanwhile,
arrange bell pepper strips in a roasting pan. Drizzle over oil and season
well. Toss bell pepper strips with oil to coat. Roast skin side up in top of
oven (same as for pie shell) for about 30 minutes, or until tender, turning
occasionally. Remove with a slotted spoon and arrange in pie shell.
Scatter over cheese. Return to oven for 10 minutes, until top is crisp and
golden. Serve warm or cold.

6 servings

MIXED VEGETABLE TART

1 quantity Short Crust pastry dough (see page 294) or use store-bought
10 ounce package mixed frozen vegetables (carrots, cauliflower,
broccoli, etc.)
²/₃ cup heavy cream
³/₄ cup shredded cheddar cheese

Use pie dough to line a 9 inch tart or quiche pan. Chill in the
refrigerator for 30 minutes. Bake pie shell blind (see page 294), until just
set. Remove foil and bake for 5 minutes more, until light golden brown.
Meanwhile, cook vegetables in boiling salted water according to the
package instructions, until just tender. Leave to cool. Mix cooled
vegetables with cream. Season well. Allow pie shell to cool. Fill with
vegetable mixture, smoothing top. Sprinkle with cheese. Return to oven
for about 15 minutes, until cheese is melted and beginning to brown.

4-6 servings

VEGETARIAN CHILI

$^1/_2$ cup green lentils
14$^1/_2$ ounce can seasoned tomatoes
2 teaspoons chili powder, or to taste
15 ounce can red kidney beans, drained

Put lentils, tomatoes, and chili powder into a heavy-bottomed pan with about 1$^1/_2$ cups water over medium heat. Season with pepper to taste and and stir well. Bring to a boil. Reduce heat, cover, and simmer for about 50 minutes, stirring occasionally, until lentils are tender. Add more water if necessary. Stir beans into pan. Season with salt to taste. Cover and simmer for about 10 minutes more. Serve with boiled rice or baked potatoes.
4 servings

PIZZA TOPPINGS

ARTICHOKE AND CHÈVRE

$^3/_4$ pound bottled artichokes in oil, drained and oil reserved
1 red onion, finely sliced
1 tablespoon pitted black olives
6 ounces chèvre (goat's cheese), thinly sliced or crumbled

Slice artichokes in half. Combine with onion. Season well. Brush dough with reserved oil. Spread onion and artichokes over dough. Sprinkle with olives and top with cheese. Season to taste. Bake in a preheated oven, 450°F, for 15-20 minutes, or according to the pizza base package instructions. Serve immediately.
Enough to cover one 9-10 inch pizza base—2 servings

BLUE CHEESE AND WALNUT

$^1/_4$ cup olive oil
1 pound sweet onions, thinly sliced

$^1/_2$ cup crumbled blue cheese
$^1/_2$ cup chopped walnuts

Heat oil in a large heavy-bottomed skillet over low heat. Cook onions, stirring, for about 20 minutes, until soft and golden. Leave to cool. Spread over dough. Top with cheese. Scatter over walnuts. Season with black pepper. Bake as before or according to the pizza base package instructions.
Enough to cover one 9-10 inch pizza base—2 servings

PESTO, TOMATO, AND SPINACH

3 tablespoons pesto sauce (or use Pistou, see page 85)
6 ounces young leaf spinach
about 6 ounces ripe tomatoes, thinly sliced
2 tablespoons olive oil

Spread dough with pesto (or pistou). Pile spinach on top. Cover with tomato slices. Drizzle with oil. Season to taste. Bake as before or according to the pizza base package instructions. Serve immediately.
Enough to cover one 9-10 inch pizza base—2 servings

ROASTED RED BELL PEPPER AND MOZZARELLA

3 red bell peppers
2 tablespoons Garlic Oil (see page 102)
$1^1/_2$ cups coarsely shredded mozzarella cheese
1 red onion, chopped

Broil bell peppers under high heat, turning frequently, for 8-10 minutes, until charred and blistered on all sides. Cover with aluminum foil or a damp dish towel until cool. Peel away skins. Slice flesh. Brush dough with oil. Spread bell peppers evenly over dough. Top with cheese and sprinkle over onion. Season well. Drizzle with any remaining oil. Bake as before or according to pizza base package instructions. Serve immediately.
Enough to cover one 9-10 inch pizza base—2 servings

TOMATO, BASIL, AND LEMON

3 sun-dried tomatoes in oil, drained and oil reserved, roughly chopped
$^1/_2$ pound cherry tomatoes, halved
small handful of basil leaves, torn
1 teaspoon grated lemon zest

Brush dough with a little of the reserved oil. Spread over tomatoes. Scatter over basil and lemon zest. Season well. Drizzle over a little more of reserved oil. Bake as before or according to pizza base package instructions. Serve immediately.

Enough to cover one 9-10 inch pizza base—2 servings

ARTICHOKE AND MUSHROOM

$^3/_4$ pound bottled artichokes in oil, drained and oil reserved
$1^1/_4$ cups button mushrooms
$^1/_2$ lemon
2 teaspoons dried oregano

Heat 2 tablespoons of reserved oil in a skillet over medium heat. Sauté mushrooms for about 5 minutes, until softened. Halve artichokes and add to mushrooms. Stir to mix. Brush dough with more of reserved oil. Spread artichoke and mushroom mixture evenly over dough. Squeeze over lemon juice. Sprinkle with oregano. Season to taste. Bake as above or according to pizza base package instructions. Serve immediately.

Enough to cover one 9-10 inch pizza base—2 servings

HEALTHY
EATS

LITE BITES
TUNA TERRINE

10 ounce can water-packed tuna, drained and flaked
$^1/_2$ cup light garlic and herbs spreadable cheese
1 teaspoon horseradish sauce
1 tablespoon lemon juice

Blend ingredients together. Season to taste. Put into a serving dish and smooth top. Cover and chill in the refrigerator for at least 30 minutes before serving. Serve with Crudités or Pita Chips or Fingers (see pages 44-5), or toasted whole-wheat bread.

4 servings

PEA AND MINT SOUP

10 ounce package frozen tiny peas, defrosted
2 tablespoons chopped mint, plus sprigs to garnish
$1^1/_2$ cups fat-free chicken or garlic and herb broth
1 cup reduced-fat sour cream

Put peas, mint, and broth into a food processor or blender. Season to taste. Process until smooth. Strain into a pan over medium heat. Heat through, stirring frequently, until hot but not boiling. Remove from heat. Stir in sour cream. Return to heat briefly, stirring, until warmed through. Serve garnished with mint sprigs.

4 servings

SARDINE-STUFFED TOMATOES

6 large tomatoes
$4^1/_2$ ounce can sardines, drained
1 teaspoon Dijon mustard
2 rounded tablespoons fresh soft whole-wheat bread crumbs

Cut off tops of tomatoes. Scoop out flesh and seeds, discarding hard cores. Mash sardines in a bowl. Add tomato pulp, mustard, and bread crumbs. Season to taste. Blend together well. Spoon into tomato shells and replace tops. Cover and chill for a few minutes before serving.

2-3 servings

CHILLED FRESH TOMATO AND RED BELL PEPPER SOUP

2 red bell peppers
$1^1/_2$ pounds tomatoes, skinned and roughly chopped
2 cups fat-free chicken or garlic and herb broth
$^1/_4$ pint orange juice

Broil bell peppers under medium heat, turning frequently, for 8-10 minutes, until blistered and charred all over. Wrap in aluminum foil or cover with a damp dish towel. When cool enough to handle, halve, core, and deseed. Roughly chop flesh. Put into a food processor or blender with tomatoes. Process until blended but still slightly chunky. Pour into a bowl. Stir in broth and orange juice. Season to taste. Cover and chill in the refrigerator for 2 hours before serving. Serve with a swirl of low-fat or nonfat plain yogurt, if you like.

4-6 servings

BEAN PÂTÉ

15 ounce can cannellini beans, drained
2-3 tablespoons lemon juice
2 tablespoons chopped flatleaf parsley
2 teaspoons ground cumin

Put all ingredients into a food processor or blender. Season well. Process until blended and fairly smooth. Serve with Crudités or Pita Chips or Fingers (see pages 44–5).

4 servings

SEAFOOD SENSE
SHRIMP WITH LIME AND GINGER

1 pound fresh or frozen peeled cooked shrimp, defrosted if frozen
juice of 2 limes
1 1/2 inch piece of fresh gingerroot
3 tablespoons chopped cilantro

Combine ingredients in a nonmetallic dish. Season with freshly ground black pepper. Cover and refrigerate for 2 hours, stirring occasionally.
4 servings

MACKEREL AND APPLE PACKAGES

4 medium mackerel, cleaned and boned
juice of 1 lemon
2 dessert apples, peeled, cored, and chopped
1/2 cup sunflower seeds

Cut 4 sheets of aluminum foil large enough to enclose each fish loosely. Put a fish on each. Lay open fish. Sprinkle with lemon juice. Combine apples with seeds. Divide between each fish. Season well. Gather up foil loosely around fish. Fold over to seal. Transfer to a cookie sheet. Bake in a preheated oven, 350°F, for about 30 minutes. Serve in packages.
4 servings

TROUT WITH LIME AND CILANTRO

2 medium rainbow trout, cleaned
2 tablespoons chopped cilantro, plus sprigs to garnish
juice of 1 lime, plus lime wedges to garnish

Make 3 deep diagonal slashes in both sides of each fish. Push cilantro into cuts in fish. Squeeze over lime juice. Season to taste. Broil under medium heat, turning twice and squeezing over more lime juice, for about 6-8 minutes on each side, until flesh flakes when tested with a knife. Serve garnished with cilantro sprigs and lime wedges.

2 servings

SALMON AND SWEET POTATO PATTIES

7 ounce can pink salmon, drained, bones removed, and flaked
1 cup mashed sweet potatoes
2 teaspoons Cajun seasoning
Garlic Oil (see page 102) or olive oil, for brushing

Mix together salmon, mashed potatoes, spice mix, and seasoning to taste, until well blended. With wet hands, form into 4 patties. Cover and chill in the refrigerator for about 30 minutes, until firm. Brush a nonstick cookie sheet with oil. Put patties onto sheet. Cook in a preheated oven, 400°F, for about 20-25 minutes, carefully turning once, until piping hot. Broil under medium heat for about 5 minutes, until well browned.

2 servings

SARDINE AND SCALLION PATTIES

4¹/₂ ounce can sardines in tomato sauce
1 cup mashed potatoes
4 scallions, finely chopped
Lemon and Thyme Oil (see page 102) or olive oil, for brushing

Mash sardines with sauce, mashed potatoes, and scallions in a bowl. Season well with freshly ground black pepper. With wet hands, form into 4 patties. Cover and chill in the refrigerator for about 30 minutes, until firm. Brush a nonstick cookie sheet with oil. Put patties onto sheet. Cook in a preheated oven, 400°F, for about 20-25 minutes, carefully turning once, until piping hot. Broil under medium heat for about 5 minutes, until well browned.

2 servings

HONEY-BROILED TROUT

4 medium rainbow trout, cleaned
4 tablespoons/$^1/_2$ stick/$^1/_4$ cup butter
1$^1/_2$ tablespoons clear honey
2 tablespoons lemon juice

Make 3 deep diagonal slashes in both sides of each fish. Season to taste. Put into a broiler pan. Put remaining ingredients into a small pan over low heat, stirring, until melted. Pour over trout. Broil under medium heat for 6-8 minutes each side, until cooked through, basting from time to time with cooking juices. Transfer trout to a warmed serving platter with any pan juices.

4 servings

TUNA AND PINEAPPLE STUFFED BELL PEPPERS

4 large red bell peppers
$^2/_3$ cup long-grain rice
10 ounce can water-packed tuna, drained and flaked
1 cup drained canned pineapple chunks in natural juice, juice reserved

Cut bell peppers in half lenghwise, leaving stalks in place. Core and deseed. Put bell peppers, cut side up and tightly packed, into an ovenproof dish. Bake in a preheated oven, 400°F, for about 25 minutes, until softened. Meanwhile, cook rice in boiling salted water according to the package instructions, until just tender. Drain and return to pan over low heat. Add tuna and pineapple with some of juice. Season to taste. Heat through, stirring frequently, adding more juice if necessary to moisten. Remove bell peppers from oven. Add any liquid inside bell peppers to rice mixture. Replace bell peppers in dish. Fill with rice mixture. Reture to oven and cook for about 15 minutes.

4 servings

SHRIMP AND VEGETABLE STIR-FRY

2 tablespoons peanut oil
1 pound package fresh or frozen stir-fry vegetables, defrosted if frozen
$1/2$ pound peeled cooked shrimp
2 tablespoons Hoisin sauce or teriyaki marinade

Heat a wok or large skillet over high heat. Add oil and heat until just smoking. Add vegetables and stir-fry for about 2 minutes. Add shrimp and stir-fry for 1 minute. Add sauce or marinade and stir-fry for 1 minute more. Season to taste and serve immediately.

2-3 servings

BAKED COD WITH LEMON AND CHIVE CRUST

finely grated zest of 1 lemon and juice of 2 lemons
4 cod fillets with skin, about 5 ounces each
$1^1/2$ cups fresh soft white bread crumbs
5 tablespoons finely chopped chives

Sprinkle juice of 1 lemon over fish. Season to taste. Arrange skin side down in a shallow ovenproof dish. Combine bread crumbs, chives, and zest and remaining juice. Season well. Pile crumb mixture onto fish and press down. Bake in a preheated oven, 425°F, for about 20 minutes, until fish flakes when tested with the tip of a knife.

4 servings

BROILED SALMON STEAKS WITH CUCUMBER AND HORSERADISH SAUCE

$1^1/4$ cups low-fat or nonfat plain yogurt
$1/2$ cucumber, finely chopped
1 tablespoon horseradish sauce
4 salmon steaks, about 4 ounces each

Combine first three ingredients. Cover and chill in the refrigerator for 1 hour. Season salmon to taste. Broil under a medium heat, turning twice, for 6-8 minutes, until flesh is cooked through and skin is brown and crisp. Serve immediately, with sauce spooned alongside.

4 servings

LIGHT AND LEAN MEAT AND POULTRY

LAMB WITH ZUCCHINI

8 lamb loin chops
$14^1/_2$ ounce can seasoned tomatoes
2 cups sliced zucchini
3 tablespoons chopped basil

Heat a large heavy-bottomed pan over high heat. Add chops and brown on both sides. Add tomatoes and zucchini. Season to taste. Cover pan, reduce heat, and simmer for about 30-40 minutes, until meat is tender. Stir in basil and cook for 3-4 minutes more.

4 servings

CHICKEN WITH APRICOTS

4 boneless, skinless chicken breasts, about 5 ounces each
8 ready-to-eat apricots
Lemon and Thyme Oil or Garlic Oil (see pages 102), or olive oil, for brushing
2 tablespoons honey

Make a horizontal slit in each chicken breast. Tuck 2 apricots into each breast. Brush lightly with oil, then brush with honey. Season with freshly ground black pepper. Brush a shallow ovenproof dish lightly with oil. Arrange chicken in dish. Cook in a preheated oven, 350°F, for about 40 minutes, until cooked through and tender.

4 servings

TURKEY AND LEEK STIR-FRY

1 tablespoon Garlic Oil (see page 102)
3 leeks, thinly sliced diagonally
³/₄ pound turkey breast meat, cut into 1 inch cubes
1 tablespoon chili sauce

Heat a wok or large heavy-bottomed skillet over high heat. Add oil
and heat until just smoking. Add leeks and stir-fry for 30 seconds. Add
turkey and stir-fry until browned for 2 minutes. Add sauce and stir-fry
for 1 minute more.

2 servings

STEAMED CHICKEN WITH BOK CHOY

oven-ready chicken, about 3 pounds
1¹/₂ pounds bok choy (Chinese cabbage)
5 slices fresh gingerroot
2 chicken bouillon cubes

Bring a large pan of water to a boil. Add about 2 teaspoons salt.
Immerse chicken in water. Boil for 5-6 minutes, skimming off scum from
surface. Meanwhile, cut bok choy into 2 inch slices. Put gingerroot into a
large, deep heatproof bowl. Put chicken on top. Pour in just enough
water to cover. Cover top of bowl tightly with aluminum foil. Put bowl
in a large pan of water to come no more than halfway up sides of bowl.
Bring water to a boil. Simmer for 1 hour, topping up with boiling water
if necessary. Lift out chicken. Put sliced bok choy in bottom of bowl.
Crumble over bouillon cubes. Replace chicken. Tightly cover bowl again
with foil. Simmer gently for 1 hour more. Arrange bok choy and chicken
on a warmed platter.

4-6 servings

PORK CHOPS WITH TOMATOES AND OREGANO

2 pork loin chops, fat trimmed
1 onion, chopped
$^1/_2$ x 14$^1/_2$ ounce can seasoned tomatoes
1 teaspoon dried oregano

Season chops to taste. Put into a casserole dish. Cover with onion and tomatoes. Sprinkle over oregano. Cover and cook in a preheated oven, 275°F, for 3 hours. It will not spoil if left for a few minutes longer.
2 servings

NUTRITIONAL KNOW-HOW
Lycopene, a carotenoid pigment that gives tomatoes and red bell peppers their red color, is a powerful antioxidant. There is evidence to suggest that lycopene may significantly reduce the risk of heart disease.

PASTA LIGHT

FUSILLI WITH CREAMED CORN AND BEANS

$^1/_2$ pound fusilli (twists)
16 ounce can creamed corn
15 ounce can red kidney beans, drained
4 tablespoons chopped flatleaf parsley

Cook pasta in boiling salted water according to the package instructions, until just tender. Meanwhile, put corn and beans into a pan over low heat, stirring frequently, until heated through. Season to taste. Add parsley just before pasta is ready. Drain pasta, reserving some of cooking liquid. Turn into a warmed serving dish. Add sauce and toss to combine, adding a little reserved cooking liquid if necessary.
4 servings

TAGLIATELLE VERDE WITH CREAMY MUSHROOM AND SMOKED SALMON SAUCE

10 ounces dried tagliatelle verde
7^1/$_2$ ounce can creamed mushrooms
^{1}/$_4$ pound smoked salmon, chopped
juice of ^{1}/$_2$ lemon

Cook pasta in boiling salted water according to the package instructions, until just tender. Meanwhile, put creamed mushrooms into a small pan over low heat, stirring frequently, until heated through. Stir in smoked salmon and lemon juice. Season well with freshly ground black pepper. Drain pasta, reserving some of cooking liquid. Turn into a warmed serving dish. Add sauce and toss to combine, adding a little reserved cooking liquid if necessary.

4 servings

PASTA WITH TUNA, TOMATO, AND OLIVE SAUCE

14^1/$_2$ ounce can seasoned tomatoes
10 ounces dried linguine or spaghetti
10 ounce can water-packed tuna, drained and flaked
^{1}/$_2$ cup pimiento-stuffed olives, sliced

Put tomatoes into a pan over medium heat. Bring to a boil. Reduce heat and simmer while pasta is cooking. Stir in tuna and olives just before pasta is ready. Season to taste. Cook pasta in boiling salted water according to the package instructions, until just tender. Drain. Turn into a warmed serving dish. Top with sauce and toss to combine.

4 servings

CHILI SEAFOOD PASTA

14^1/$_2$ ounce can tomatoes with chilies
^{3}/$_4$ pound frozen mixed seafood, defrosted

$^{1}/_{4}$ cup ricotta cheese
10 ounces dried linguine or spaghetti

Put tomatoes into a pan over medium heat. Bring to a boil. Reduce heat and simmer while pasta is cooking. Stir in seafood and cheese just before pasta is ready. Season to taste. Cook pasta in boiling salted water according to the package instructions, until just tender. Drain. Turn into a warmed serving dish. Top with sauce and toss to combine.

4 servings

FETTUCCINE WITH BELL PEPPERS AND BASIL

4-5 red bell peppers
10 ounces dried fettuccine
2 tablespoons sun-dried tomato paste
4 tablespoons torn basil leaves

Broil bell peppers under medium heat, turning frequently, for 8-10 minutes, until blistered and charred all over. Wrap in aluminum foil or cover with a damp dish towel. Cook pasta in boiling salted water according to the package instructions, until just tender. When bell peppers are cool enough to handle, peel away skins. Halve, core, and deseed. Chop or slice flesh. Drain pasta, reserving some of cooking liquid, and return to pan over low heat. Add bell peppers, tomato paste, and a little of cooking liquid. Season well. Toss to combine. Remove from heat. Add basil and toss to combine. Serve immediately.

4 servings

NUTRITIONAL KNOW-HOW

Bell peppers are not only a great source of vitamin C, which helps guard against invading bacteria and viruses, they also contain beta carotene, an antioxidant which is converted into vitamin A as and when the body requires, and bioflavonoids. Both beta carotene and bioflavonoids help to boost the body's immunity against infection and disease, and neutralize an excess of harmful free radicals in the body.

SUPERSALADS
TURKEY AND APPLE COLE SLAW

2 cups reduced-calorie cole slaw
1 teaspoon curry powder
2 cups cold diced cooked turkey
2 crisp apples

Put cole slaw into a bowl. Blend in curry powder. Stir in turkey.
Season to taste. Slice apple and add to bowl. Toss to mix.
2 servings

MARINATED MUSHROOM AND ARTICHOKE SALAD

$^1/_2$ pound bottled artichoke hearts in oil, drained and 2 tablespoons oil
reserved
3 tablespoons lemon juice
1 pound closed mushrooms, very finely sliced
4 tablespoons chopped cilantro

Beat together oil and lemon juice. Put mushrooms onto a large plate.
Pour over oil and lemon mixture. Season to taste. Let stand at room
temperature for about 1 hour, turning occasionally, until softened. Blot
artichokes with paper towels. Put mushrooms and marinade into a
serving bowl with artichokes. Add cilantro and toss to combine.
4 servings

CHICKEN AND MANGO SALAD

1 pound arugula or mixed salad leaves, torn into pieces
4 cups cold cooked chicken, cubed
1 large ripe mango, pitted, peeled, and diced
2 tablespoons lime juice

Put salad leaves into a serving bowl. Add chicken and mango. Sprinkle over lime juice. Season well. Toss to combine.

4 servings

TUNA AND CORN PASTA SALAD

$^1/_2$ pound fusilli (twists)
10 ounce can water-packed tuna, drained and flaked
11 ounce can Mexican-style corn, drained
3 tablespoons bottled fat-free dressing or Fruity Dressing (see page 287)

Cook pasta in boiling salted water according to the package instructions, until just tender. Drain and leave to cool. Put pasta into a serving bowl. Add tuna and corn. Season to taste. Pour over dressing and toss to combine. Cover and chill for 30 minutes before serving.

4 servings

SHRIMP, SPINACH, AND AVOCADO SALAD

1 pound young leaf spinach
1 pound peeled cooked shrimp
2 ripe avocados
2 tablespoons lime juice

Tear spinach leaves into bite-size pieces and put into a serving bowl. Add shrimp. Halve, pit, and peel avocados (see page 15). Dice flesh and add to bowl. Sprinkle over lime juice. Season well. Toss to combine.

4 servings

NUTRITIONAL KNOW-HOW

Oily fish, such as sardines, mackerel, herring, salmon, and tuna, are rich in omega-3 fatty acids—unsaturated fats widely believed to help protect against heart and circulatory problems. Mackerel and herring also offer an excellent source of vitamin D.

LOW-FAT, NO-FAT DRESSINGS

FRUITY

2 tablespoons lemon juice
2 tablespoons unsweetened apple juice
1 tablespoon olive oil
1 clove garlic, minced

Put ingredients into a screw-top jar. Season to taste. Replace lid and shake until blended.

4 servings

SPICY

4 tablespoons orange juice
1 tablespoon honey
1 tablespoon red wine vinegar
$1/2$ teaspoon allspice

Put ingredients into a screw-top jar. Season to taste. Replace lid and shake until blended.

4 servings

SWEET AND SOUR

1 tablespoon honey
1 teaspoon whole-grain mustard
$1/4$ cup unsweetened apple juce

Blend together honey and mustard in a small bowl. Gradually beat in apple juice. Season to taste.

4 servings

CREAMY

3 tablespoons reduced-calorie mayonnaise
2 tablespoons low-fat or nonfat plain yogurt
1 teaspoon Dijon mustard
1 tablespoon lemon juice

Beat together mayonnaise, yogurt, and mustard. Beat in lemon juice. Season to taste.

4 servings

TANGY

$^1/_4$ cup lime juice
1 tablespoon unsweetened pineapple juice
2 teaspoons red wine vinegar
$^1/_2$ inch piece finely grated fresh gingerroot

Put ingredients into a screw-top jar. Season to taste. Replace lid and shake until blended.

4 servings

COOK'S KNOW-HOW

Store-bought fat-free dressings are convenient to use for salads but some are rather glutinous and artificial-tasting. When time allows, use these dressings instead. Otherwise, use a squeezing of lemon or lime juice, or try balsamic vinegar or a flavored wine vinegar (see pages 104-5).

GUILT-FREE DESSERTS

SPICED BANANAS

2 bananas
2 tablespoons freshly squeezed orange juice
1 tablespoon clear honey
1 teaspoon allspice

Peel and slice bananas in half lengthwise. Put into a shallow ovenproof dish. Blend together orange juice, honey, and allspice. Pour over bananas. Cover and bake in a preheated oven, 350°F, for 20-25 minutes, until bananas are slightly softened.

2 servings

SUMMER BERRIES WITH ORANGE SAUCE

finely grated zest and juice of 1 orange
8 ounce carton low-fat or nonfat vanilla yogurt
$^3/_4$ pound mixed berries (raspberries, strawberries, blackberries, blueberries)

Blend orange zest and juice with yogurt. Cover and chill in the refrigerator for 30 minutes. Put berries into serving dishes. Top with orange sauce.

2 servings

MARSHALLOW AND FRUIT KABOBS

$^1/_2$ pineapple, peeled, sliced, and cored
1 small melon, halved and deseeded
1 papaya, halved and deseeded
8 marshmallows

Cut fruit into chunks. Thread alternately onto wooden skewers, previously soaked in water for 30 minutes, with 2 marshmallows on each. Broil under medium heat, turning frequently, until marshallows are just browned.

4 servings

GRAPE AND YOGURT LAYERED DESSERT

2 egg whites
1^1/$_4$ cups low-fat or nonfat apricot yogurt
^{1}/$_4$ pound seedless black grapes, halved
^{1}/$_4$ pound seedless green grapes, halved

Beat egg whites in a bowl until stiff. Put yogurt into a separate bowl and fold in egg whites. In tall glasses, layer yogurt mixture and grapes, finishing with a layer of yogurt. Decorate with a few grape halves.

4 servings

APRICOT SWIRL

^{1}/$_2$ pound ready-to-eat dried apricots
2 teaspoons sugar
juice of 1 large orange
1^1/$_4$ cups low-fat or nonfat plain yogurt

Put apricots, sugar, and orange juice in a pan. Bring to a boil, stirring. Reduce heat to low, cover, and simmer for about 10 minutes. Leave to cool. Put into a food processor or blender and whizz until smooth. Swirl with yogurt into glass serving dishes.

4 servings

NUTRITIONAL KNOW-HOW
Dried fruits offer a good source of fiber and nutrients, including iron and potassium. They are great for providing a healthy energy boost.

DESSERTS

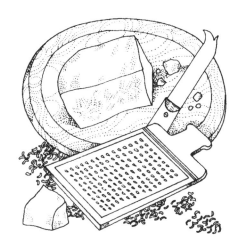

PASTRIES, PIES, AND BAKES

MILLE FEUILLES SLICES

$^1/_2$ pound puff pastry dough, defrosted if frozen
heavy or whipping cream
confectioner's sugar
jam

Roll pastry dough into a rectangle about $^1/_2$ thick. Cut into fingers.
Transfer to a cookie sheet. Bake in the center of a preheated oven, 475°F,
for about 13-15 minutes, until firm and pale brown in color. Cool on a
wire rack. Lightly whip cream. Fold in a little sugar, to sweeten. Sandwich
fingers together with jam and cream. Blend a little water with
confectioner's sugar, until mixture coats back of a spoon. Cover tops of
slices with frosting. Leave to set.
Makes 3–4

JAM PUFFS

$^1/_2$ pound puff pastry dough, defrosted if frozen
jam
1 egg white, for brushing
superfine sugar, for sprinkling

Roll out pastry dough until wafer-thin. Cut into large squares. Put a
little jam on one half of each square, dividing it diagonally. Fold over the
plain dough so that it nearly meets edges on the other side. Turn in the
edges so that the join is just away from the edge of the now triangular
shape. Transfer puffs to cookie sheets, turning them to keep joins on
underside. Brush with egg white and dust liberally with sugar. Bake near
the top of a preheated oven, 475°F, for 10-12 minutes, until puffed and
golden brown.
Makes 6

APPLE TURNOVERS

$^1/_2$ pound shortcrust pastry dough (store-bought or use Short Crust
recipe on page 294, made with 2 cups flour, $1^1/_2$ cups fat)
flour or semolina, for dusting
$^3/_4$ pound peeled and very thinly sliced apples
brown sugar

Roll out pastry dough thinly. Cut into large rounds. Transfer to a
cookie sheet. Dust dough with a little flour or semolina, to prevent fruit
making it soggy. Cover half of each dough round with apple slices.
Sprinkle with a little sugar. Dampen dough edges. Fold over plain dough
halves to enclose filling. Press edges together to seal. Bake in the center of
a preheated oven, 425°F, for about 25 minutes. Sprinkle with sugar before
serving.

Makes 6

CHOCOLATE PEACH PUFFS

3 ounces semisweet chocolate, broken into pieces
4 small ripe peaches or nectarines, halved and pitted (see page 306)
$^3/_4$ pound puff pastry dough, defrosted if frozen
confectioner's sugar, for dusting

Grease and lightly dampen a cookie sheet. Melt chocolate in a
heatproof bowl over a pan of simmering water. Slice fruit very thinly.
Roll out pastry dough thinly on a lightly floured surface. Cut out four 5
inch rounds using a small bowl or saucer as a guide. Transfer dough
rounds to cookie sheet. Spoon melted chocolate onto dough, spreading
to within 1 inch of edges. Arrange fruit slices in an overlapping circle
over chocolate. Make small flutes around edges of dough with the back
of a knife. Bake in a preheated oven, 400°F, for 15 minutes. Dust pastries
with confectioner's sugar. Broil for 1-2 minutes, until lightly caramelized.
Leave to cool slightly before serving.

4 servings

APRICOT CRUMBLE

1$^1/_4$ pounds skinned, pitted, and sliced apricots (see page 306)
about $^1/_3$ cup packed brown sugar, plus extra for cooking apricots
1 cup all-purpose or self-rising flour
4 tablespoons/$^1/_2$ stick/$^1/_4$ cup butter or margarine

Put apricots in an ovenproof dish with about 3 tablespoons water and sugar to taste. Cook in the center of a preheated oven, 350°F, for 10-15 minutes, until tender. Sift flour into a bowl. Cut in butter or margarine until fine crumbs form. Stir in sugar. Sprinkle over fruit. Bake in the center of the oven for 25-30 minutes, until topping is crisp and golden brown. Serve hot.

4 servings

PIE SHELLS

SHORT CRUST

1$^1/_2$ cups all-purpose flour
6 tablespoons/$^3/_4$ stick chilled butter, margarine, or shortening, or a mixture, diced

Sift flour into a bowl with a little salt. Cut in fat until fine crumbs form. Stir in ice water, a little at a time, with a knife, until it begins to bind. Form into a ball. Roll out on a lightly floured surface. Use to line a greased 9 inch pie plate, or tart or quiche pan. To "bake blind," lightly prick bottom of shell with a fork. Put in a sheet of aluminum foil. Top with beans or rice. Bake in the center of a preheated oven 375-400°F, for 15-20 minutes, until dough is just set. To finish cooking, remove foil and bake for 5-10 minutes more, until golden brown. Also use in place of store-bought shortcrust pastry dough for other recipes in the book.

Makes enough to line a 9 inch pie plate, or tart or quiche pan

SWEET CRUST

1¹/₂ cups all-purpose flour
¹/₄ cup superfine sugar
6 tablespoons/³/₄ stick chilled butter, diced
1 egg yolk

Sift flour into a bowl with a little salt. Stir in sugar. Cut in fat until fine crumbs form. Stir in egg yolk and ice water, a little at a time, with a knife, until crumbs begin to bind. Form into a ball. Roll out on a lightly floured surface. Use and bake as Short Crust pastry shell (see opposite).
Makes enough to line a 9 inch pie plate, or tart or quiche pan

CRUNCHY CEREAL CRUST

1¹/₄ cups quick-cooking rolled oats
¹/₄ cup sugar
2 tablespoons finely chopped nuts
4 tablespoons/¹/₂ stick/¹/₄ cup butter

Combine oats, sugar, and nuts with a little salt in a bowl. Mix well. Stir in melted butter. Sprinkle with water. Stir until well blended. Spread over bottom and sides of an 8 inch pie plate, or tart or quiche pan. Press down firmly with the back of a spoon. Bake in a preheated oven, 375°F, for 15-20 minutes, until crisp and golden brown.
Makes enough to line an 8 inch pie plate, or tart or quiche pan

GRAHAM CRACKER CRUST

6 tablespoons/³/₄ stick butter
1 tablespoon golden syrup or corn syrup
2 cups graham cracker crumbs

Melt butter with syrup in a pan over low heat. Remove from heat and stir in crumbs. Line bottom and sides of an 8-9 inch pie plate, or tart or quiche pan with mixture. Press down firmly with the back of a spoon. Cover and chill until firm. It does not require baking. For a variation, use gingersnap crumbs in place of graham cracker crumbs.

Makes enough to line a 8-9 inch pie plate, or tart or quiche pan

PIE FILLINGS
SYRUP PIE

Use Short Crust pie shell (see page 294)

grated zest of $1/2$ lemon and 1 tablespoon lemon juice
4 tablespoons golden syrup or corn syrup
crushed cornflakes
light cream, to serve

Combine lemon zest and juice with syrup. Spread over bottom of pie shell after first stage of "baking blind" (see page 294). Sprinkle with crushed cornflakes. Reduce oven to 350°F and bake for 15-20 minutes more, until dough is crisp. Serve with cream poured over.

6 servings

PEACH AND MASCARPONE PIE

Use Sweet Crust pie shell (see page 295)

1 cup mascarpone cheese
$1^1/_4$ pounds peaches, skinned, pitted, and sliced (see page 306)
3 tablespoons packed dark brown sugar
toasted coconut chips or dry unsweetened shredded coconut

Put cooled fully baked pie shell onto a cookie sheet. Spoon mascarpone into pie shell. Arrange peach slices on top. Sprinkle with sugar. Broil under high heat briefly until sugar caramelizes. Sprinkle with coconut and serve immediately. 6 servings

APPLE AND GINGER PIE

Use Sweet Crust or Graham Crust pie shell made with gingersnaps
(see page 295)

1^1/$_4$ cups sweet apple purée
^{3}/$_4$ cup heavy cream, whipped
2 tablespoons chopped preserved ginger with a little syrup from jar
confectioner's sugar

Fold apple purée into whipped cream with ginger and syrup. Spoon
into pie shell. Sift with sugar.

6 servings

CHERRY AND ALMOND PIE

Use Crunchy Cereal Crust pie shell made with chopped almonds
(see page 295)

15 ounce can bing cherries, drained and syrup reserved
2 level teaspoons cornstarch
2 tablespoons redcurrant jelly
^{3}/$_4$ cup slivered almonds, toasted

Arrange cherries in pie shell. Blend cornstarch with 1^1/$_4$ cups reserved
syrup. Heat in a small pan with redcurrant jelly over low heat, stirring,
until mixture thickens and clears. Leave to cool slightly, then spoon over
fruit. Scatter over almonds. Leave to cool and set before serving.

6 servings

GRAPE MERINGUE PIE

Use Graham Cracker Crust pie shell (see page 295)

4 level tablespoons strained apricot jam
about $^1/_2$ pound seedless green grapes
10-12 mini meringues (store-bought or use recipe on page 309)
cream, to serve

Heat jam with 3 tablespoons water in a small pan over low heat, until it forms a smooth glaze. Arrange grapes in center of pie shell. Brush with warm glaze. Leave to cool. Arrange meringues in a ring around grapes. Serve with cream.

6 servings

COOK'S KNOW-HOW
Use the pie shells on pages 294-5 for filling with other varieties of fresh, canned, or lightly cooked fruits, or use canned pie fillings.

PLUM BETTY

8 tablespoons/1 stick/$^1/_2$ cup butter or margarine
8 small slices whole-wheat bread
2 pounds ripe red plums, halved and pitted
$^1/_4$ cup demerara sugar or packed light brown sugar

Grease a large, shallow ovenproof dish with a little of the butter or margarine. Melt remainder in a pan. Cut bread to fit sides and bottom of dish, reserving remaining bread and trimmings. Dip bread pieces, one by one, into melted butter or margarine and line dish. Put plums into dish. Grate remaining bread and trimmings into fairly coarse crumbs. Toss in remaining melted butter or margarine. Stir in sugar. Spread bread crumb mixture over plums. Cover with greased waxed paper. Bake in a preheated oven, 400°F, for 40 minutes. Remove paper and cook for 20 minutes more, until crisp and golden brown. Serve warm or cold with cream.

6 servings

APPLE BROWN BETTY

1^1/$_4$ pounds peeled sliced apples
brown sugar
2 teaspoons apple pie spice
6 slices white bread, crusts removed, spread with butter or margarine

Cook apples and sugar to taste in a pan with very little water over low heat until soft. Sprinkle with spice. Sprinkle bottom of an ovenproof dish with sugar. Cut bread into fingers. Put half, buttered side down, in dish. Cover with apple mixture, then remaining bread fingers. Sprinkle lightly with sugar. Bake in the center of a preheated oven, 400°F, for 10-15 minutes, then lower heat to 325°F and cook for 25-30 minutes, until crisp and golden brown.
4-6 servings

GINGER PEARS

4 ripe, firm pears
ginger ale, ginger beer, or root beer

Peel and halve pears. Put into an ovenproof casserole dish. Cover with ginger ale, ginger beer, or root beer. Bake in the bottom of a preheated oven, 325-350°F, for about 1 hour. Serve hot or allow to cool, refrigerate, and serve chilled.
4 servings

BAKED PEACHES WITH ALMONDS AND HONEY

4 large ripe peaches, halved
and pitted
4 tablespoons/^{1}/$_2$ stick/
^{1}/$_4$ cup butter
^{1}/$_2$ cup slivered almonds
4 tablespoons clear honey

Grease a shallow ovenproof dish, large enough to take peach halves. Arrange peaches in dish, skin side down. Dot with butter. Sprinkle with almonds and dizzle with honey. Bake at the top of a preheated oven, 400°F, for 10-15 minutes, until almonds are lightly browned. Serve with juices drizzled over.

4 servings

BAKED RUM BANANAS

6 bananas
$1/4$ cup packed dark brown sugar
1 tablespoon, $1/8$ stick butter
3 tablespoons dark rum

Peel bananas and slice slantwise. Put into an ovenproof dish, sprinkling a little sugar between layers. Beat butter with remaining sugar and rum. Spread on top of bananas. Bake in a preheated oven, 400°F, for 20-30 minutes. Serve hot, with scoops of vanilla ice cream, if you like.

4-6 servings

BAKED APPLES

4 medium-large tart apples

Remove cores from apples with an apple corer or pointed knife. Using a sharp knife, make a circular cut around waist of each apple, to prevent skin from bursting. Arrange apples in a greased, shallow ovenproof dish. Fill centers with one of fillings below. Pour $1^1/4$ cups water into dish. Bake in the center of a preheated oven, 375°F, for 50 minutes-1 hour, basting from time to time with juices, until tender.

GINGER AND APRICOT

3 tablespoons apricot jam
2 tablespoons chopped preserved ginger
1$^{1}/_{2}$ tablespoons butter

Combine jam and ginger. Spoon into apple centers. Top each with a little butter. Serve with cream flavored with a little syrup from preserved ginger, if you like.

GRANOLA AND HONEY

3 tablespoons crunchy granola
3 tablespoons clear honey
1$^{1}/_{2}$ tablespoons butter

Combine granola and honey. Spoon into apple centers. Top each with a little butter.

COCONUT FUDGE

2 tablespoons/$^{1}/_{4}$ stick butter
1-2 tablespoons light brown sugar
3 tablespoons shredded dry unsweetened coconut

Combine ingredients and spoon into apple centers.

ORANGE

2 oranges
3 tablespoons orange marmalade
1 tablespoon butter

Finely grate zest of oranges. Squeeze juice from 1 orange. Blend 2-3 tablespoons orange juice with marmalade and orange zest. Spoon into apple centers. Top each with a little butter. While apples are cooking, remove pith from zested orange. Segment fruit (see page 35). Remove apples a few minutes before serving. Spoon a few orange segments on top. Return to oven to finish cooking.

MAPLE SYRUP AND MACAROON

4 tablespoons macaroon crumbs (store-bought or see pages 325–6)
4 tablespoons maple syrup
$1^1/_2$ tablespoons butter

Combine macaroon crumbs with syrup. Spoon into apple centers. Top each with a little butter.

4 servings

FRUIT FAVORITES

MELON AND RASPBERRIES IN SAUTERNES

1 small ripe cantaloupe melon
$1^1/_4$ cups raspberries
$^1/_2$ bottle Sauternes

Working over a bowl to catch juice, halve and deseed melon. Scoop out flesh with a melon baller, or dice flesh. Divide melon and raspberries equally among 4 glass dishes. Pour over any melon juice. Cover and chill in the refrigerator for at least 2 hours. Just before serving, pour some of chilled Sauternes into each dish to almost cover fruit. Serve at once.

4 servings

SUMMER FRUIT COMPOTE

4 cups mixed blackcurrants and blackberries
scant $^1/_2$ cup superfine sugar
1$^1/_2$ cups raspberries
whipped cream, to serve

Put blackcurrants and blackberries into a heavy-bottomed pan with sugar over low heat. Cook, stirring occasionally, for 10 minutes, until tender. Remove pan from heat. Add raspberries and leave to cool. Spoon fruit into individual serving bowls. Serve with whipped cream.   6 servings

MARSHMALLOW-TOPPED FRUIT

3 ounces marshmallows
$^2/_3$ cup evaporated milk
few drops vanilla extract
fresh fruit, sliced, or canned

Cut marshmallows into quarters with kitchen scissors. Put all ingredients into a heatproof bowl over a pan of simmering water, until warm and marshmallows have almost dissolved. Serve spooned over fruit.
4 servings

CARAMELIZED ORANGES WITH PINEAPPLE

4 oranges
$^3/_4$ cup sugar
1 small pineapple

Remove zest from 2 oranges. Slice into very fine strips. Put zest into a pan of boiling water. Simmer for 2 minutes. Remove and drain well. Put sugar and $^1/_2$ cup water into a pan over low heat. Stir constantly until sugar dissolves. Boil syrup until it turns golden brown. Be careful not to let it over-cook and become too dark. Remove from heat. Remove pith and peel from oranges. Cut each orange into 6 or 7 slices. Peel, core, and slice pineapple. Make alternate layers of orange and pineapple in a heatproof dish. Sprinkle with orange zest. Pour over hot caramel.

4 servings

SPICED CARAMEL ORANGES WITH APRICOTS

4 large oranges
$^1/_3$ cup dried ready-to-eat apricots, chopped
$1^1/_4$ cups sugar
1 teaspoon ground cinnamon

Peel zest of two of the oranges very thinly with a vegetable peeler. Slice thinly into matchstick strips. Simmer strips in a small pan with apricots and enough water to cover for 10 minutes, until zest is very tender. Drain and set aside. Working over a bowl to catch juice, remove all pith and peel from all oranges. Slice oranges into rounds. Put sugar into a pan with $^2/_3$ cup water and cinnamon. Bring to a boil, stirring constantly. Boil rapidly, without stirring, until syrup turns golden brown. Remove from heat. Add $^1/_4$ cup cold water and collected orange juice. Return to heat and stir until caramel dissolves. Arrange orange slices in a shallow serving dish. Scatter over apricots and orange rind. Pour caramel over oranges. Chill well before serving.

4 servings

CRISPY-TOPPED BANANA RICE

14 ounce can creamed rice
2 bananas, peeled and sliced
brown sugar

Heat through rice in a pan or in a microwave oven. Put into a flameproof dish. Top with banana. Cover with a layer of brown sugar. Broil under low heat until sugar caramelizes.

4 servings

BANANAS IN COCONUT MILK

1 large or 2 small bananas
1 cup canned coconut milk
3 tablespoons light brown or demerara sugar

Peel banana(s) and halve lengthwise. Cut each half into 4 pieces. Put coconut milk, ¹/₃ cup water, and sugar into a pan. Simmer, stirring occasionally, for about 6 minutes. Add banana and cook for 4 minutes until heated through. Serve hot.   2 servings

PINEAPPLE WITH RUMBLED MASCARPONE

1 pineapple, peeled, sliced, and cored
¹/₃ cup mascarpone cheese
2 tablespoons rum
2 tablespoons light brown sugar

Heat a griddle pan over high heat and cook pineapple for 2 minutes on each side. Alternatively, broil under high heat. Combine mascarpone, rum, and sugar. Serve pineapple with mascarpone mixture spooned over.
4 servings

PANETTONE WITH PEACHES AND CREAM

4 peaches, halved and pitted (see page 306)
4 slices panettone
ground cinnamon, for dusting
¹/₄ cup thick or whipped cream

Heat a griddle pan or nonstick skillet over medium heat. Cook peaches on each side for about 5 minutes, until slightly charred. Toast panettone slices for 1-2 minutes on each side, until golden. Arrange peaches on panettone and dust with cinnamon. Spoon over cream.
4 servings

PEACHES BRÛLÉE

6 peaches, skinned (see below)
2 tablespoons Cointreau or other orange liqueur
1¹/₄ cups heavy cream, whipped
¹/₂ cup packed light brown sugar

Halve and pit peaches. Arrange cut sides down in a shallow ovenproof dish. Pour over liqueur. Spread cream over peaches to cover them completely. Sprinkle with sugar. Broil under high under for 3 minutes, until sugar has caramelized. Leave to cool. Chill well in the refrigerator before serving.

6 servings

COOK'S KNOW-HOW
Peaches and apricots can be skinned in the same way as tomatoes. Put into a heatproof bowl. Pour over boiling water and leave for about a minute. Rinse in cold running water. Peel away skin.

GRIDDLED FIGS WITH YOGURT AND HONEY

8 ripe figs
¹/₄ cup thick plain yogurt
2 tablespoons clear honey

Heat a griddle pan until hot. Cook figs for 8 minutes, turning occasionally, until charred on the outside. Alternatively, broil under high heat. Cut in half and arrange on 4 individual plates. Serve with a spoonful of yogurt, drizzled with honey.

4 servings

PEARS IN CHOCOLATE SAUCE

14 ounce can pear halves or quarters in natural juice or syrup, to taste
¹/₄ pound semisweet chocolate

1 tablespoon/$^1/_8$ stick butter
$^1/_2$ cup slivered almonds, toasted

Drain pears, reserving juice or syrup. Divide between 4 individual glass dishes. Spoon over a little juice or syrup. Break chocolate into pieces. Melt with butter and 2-3 tablespoons water in a heatproof bowl over a pan of simmering water. Spoon hot sauce over pears. Sprinkle with toasted almonds and serve immediately.

4 servings

GRAPE BRÛLÉE

1 pound seedless grapes
$1^1/_4$ cups sour cream
$^1/_2$ cup packed light brown sugar

Put grapes into a shallow flameproof dish. Spread sour cream over top to cover completely. Sprinkle with enough sugar to make an $^1/_8$ inch layer. Cover and chill in the refrigerator for an hour or so. Broil under high heat until sugar is caramelized. Serve immediately or chill until required.

4-6 servings

SUMMER PUDDING

about 4 cups mixed currants and berries (blackcurrants, blackberries, blueberries)
$^1/_4$ cup superfine sugar
$1^2/_3$ cups raspberries
8 slices white bread, crusts removed

Put mixed currants and berries into a heavy-bottomed pan with sugar over low heat. Cook, stirring occasionally, for 10-15 minutes, until tender. Add raspberries and leave to cool. Strain fruit, reserving juice. Cut 3 circles of bread the same diameter as a $3^1/_2$ cup bowl. Shape remaining bread to fit around sides of bowl. Soak all bread in the reserved juice. Line bottom of bowl with one of circles, then arrange shaped bread around sides. Pour in half the fruit. Put another circle of bread on top. Cover with remaining fruit. Top with remaining bread circle. Cover with a saucer small enough to fit inside bowl. Put a 1 pound weight on top. Chill in refrigerator overnight. Turn onto a serving plate. Pour over any remaining fruit juice. Best served with whipped cream.

8 servings

MANGO WITH THAI STICKY RICE

$2^1/_4$ cups glutinous rice, soaked overnight
$^2/_3$ cup sugar
$1^1/_4$ cups canned coconut milk
2 ripe mangos

Drain and rince rice well. Cook in a steamer for about 30 minutes. Give rice a good shake halfway through steaming to ensure it is evenly cooked. While rice is steaming, combine sugar and coconut milk in a large bowl. Stir well. When rice is cooked, add to coconut mixture. Stir for 2-3 minutes to achieve a creamy consistency. Cover with a lid and leave at room temperature for 30 minutes. Pit, peel, and slice mangos. Arrange in a dish around rice.

4 servings

DESSERT CLASSICS

CARAMEL-TOPPED RICE PUDDING

2 tablespoons short-grain rice
1-2 tablespoons sugar
$2^1/_2$ cups milk
light brown sugar

Put rice into an ovenproof dish. Add the 1-2 tablespoons sugar to taste and milk. Stir to combine. Bake in the bottom of a preheated oven, 325°F, for 1 hour. Remove from oven. Top with a layer of brown sugar. Reduce oven to 275°F and cook for 20-25 minutes more, to allow topping to caramelize, or broil under high heat until sugar caramelizes.

2-3 servings

CLASSIC CHOCOLATE MOUSSE

9 ounces semisweet chocolate
6 small eggs, separated
1 tablespoon brandy or dark rum

Melt chocolate in a heatproof bowl over a pan of simmering water. Remove chocolate from heat. Beat in 5 egg yolks (use remaining egg yolk for another recipe), then brandy or rum. Beat egg whites in a separate bowl until stiff. Fold lightly into chocolate mixture. Pour into a bowl or spoon into individual dishes. Cover and chill in the refrigerator for at least 2 hours before serving.

4 servings

MINI COFFEE MERINGUES

3 egg whites
$^3/_4$ cup superfine sugar
1 tablespoon instant coffee powder
$^2/_3$ cup heavy cream

Beat egg whites until stiff but not dry. Gradually beat in sugar and coffee powder, until stiff and glossy. Spoon or pipe small mounds of meringue onto cookie sheets lined with baking parchment. Bake in a preheated oven, 225°F, for 2-2$^1/_2$ hours, until meringues are crisp and dry. Leave to cool. Whip cream until it just holds its shape. Sandwich pairs of meringues together with cream.

Makes 20

ZABAGLIONE

4 egg yolks
$^{1}/_{4}$ cup sugar
7 tablespoons sweet Marsala
lady fingers, to serve

Put egg yolks, sugar, and 1 tablespoon warm water in a heatproof bowl over a pan of simmering water. Beat with a balloon or rotary whisk (not an electric beater) until pale in color and frothy. Beat in Marsala a little at a time. Continue beating over heat for 5-10 minutes, until mixture increases in volume, becomes thick and foamy, and holds its shape in a spoon. Remove from heat immediately and spoon into tall wine glasses. Serve immediately with lady fingers.

3-4 servings

CRÈME BRÛLÉE

$1^{1}/_{4}$ cups heavy cream
12 drops vanilla extract
2 egg yolks
$^{1}/_{2}$ cup superfine sugar

Put cream and vanilla extract into a small pan over very low heat. Beat egg yolks with 2 tablespoons of the sugar in a heatproof bowl. Stir in cream. Stand bowl over a pan of simmering water. Stir constantly until mixture thickens slightly. Pour into 4 ramekin dishes. Bake in a preheated oven, 325°F, for 8 minutes. Cool slightly, then refrigerate until thoroughly chilled, preferably overnight. Sprinkle evenly with remaining sugar. Broil under high heat until sugar has caramelized. Cool, then chill for 2 hours before serving.

4 servings

ICED DESSERTS

COFFEE ICE CREAM

3 eggs
scant $^1/_2$ cup superfine sugar
$1^1/_4$ cups light cream
3 tablespoons instant coffee powder
$1^1/_4$ cups heavy cream

Beat eggs and sugar together in a bowl until smooth. Bring light cream and coffee just to a boil in a small pan. Stir into egg mixture. Transfer to top of a double boiler, or to a heatproof bowl over a pan of gently simmering water. Cook gently, stirring continuously, until custard is thick enough to coat the back of a spoon. Strain into a bowl. Leave to cool, stirring occasionally to prevent a skin forming. Whip heavy cream until soft peaks form. Fold into cold custard. Pour into a rigid container, cover, and freeze for 2-3 minutes, until half frozen. Remove from freezer and stir well. Return to container and freeze until solid. Transfer ice cream to refrigerator about 20 minutes before serving, to soften.

6-8 servings

PINEAPPLE ICE CREAM

1 large pineapple
3 egg whites
scant $^1/_2$ cup superfine sugar
$1^1/_2$ cups heavy cream, whipped

Cut pineapple in half lengthwise. Scrape out flesh and juice into a bowl, discarding hard core. Transfer to a food processor or blender and purée. Beat egg whites until stiff. Gradually add sugar, beating continuously. Fold in cream and pineapple. Pour into a rigid, freezerproof container. Cover and freeze for 1 hour. Remove from freezer and stir well. Return to freezer and freeze until solid. Transfer to refrigerator about 20 minutes before serving, to soften.   6-8 servings

MARSHMALLOW AND PINEAPPLE ICE CREAM

$^1/_4$ pound marshmallows
$^2/_3$ cup milk
8 ounce can crushed pineapple in natural juice, drained
$^2/_3$ cup heavy cream, whipped

Chop marshallows. Melt three-quarters with milk in a pan over low heat. Pour into a bowl and leave to cool. Add remaining marshmallows and pineapple. Fold in whipped cream. Pour into a rigid, freezerproof container. Cover and freeze until firm.

4 servings

RICOTTA AND RUM BOMBE

5 egg yolks
$^1/_2$ cup superfine sugar
5 tablespoons rum
2 cups fresh ricotta cheese, strained

Line a 5-cup freezerproof mold with aluminum foil. Put eggs and sugar into a bowl. Beat with an electric blender or beater until light and fluffy. Fold in rum until well blended. Fold in ricotta a little at a time. Spoon mixture into mold and smooth surface. Cover with foil. Freeze until solid. Unmold onto a serving plate.

4-6 servings

BLOOD ORANGE GRANITA

2 pounds blood oranges
generous 1 cup sugar

Using a sharp knife, cut off top and bottom of oranges. Cut away white pith and peel. Working over a bowl to catch juice, cut out segments (see page 35). Squeeze any remaining juice from oranges. Strain juice into a pan, add sugar, and heat until dissolved. Put orange flesh into a food processor or blender. Whizz until smooth. Mix in juice. Pour into ice cube trays and freeze. To serve, chill serving dishes for a few minutes in freezer. Remove granita ice cubes from freezer. Whizz in food processor or blender for 30 seconds. Transfer to chilled dishes.

4 servings

RASPBERRY SHERBET

3 cups raspberries
$1/2$ cup sugar
2 egg whites

Rub raspberries through a nylon strainer to remove pips. Put sugar and $1^1/_4$ cups water into a pan over low heat. Stir until sugar dissolves. Boil briskly, without stirring, for 8 minutes, until a syrup has formed. Leave to cool. Stir syrup into raspberry purée. Pour into a shallow, rigid, freezerproof container. Freeze for 1 hour, until just smooth. Beat egg whites in a bowl until stiff. Fold into raspberry mixture. Return mixture to container. Cover, seal, and freeze. Transfer sherbet to refrigerator 10–15 minutes before serving, to soften

4-6 servings

MANGO AND PASSIONFRUIT SHERBET

2 ripe mangos
4 passion fruits
1 tablespoon lemon juice
scant $1/2$ cup superfine sugar

Slice mangos either side of narrow stone. Peel flesh. Cut any flesh from stones. Halve passionfruit and scoop out flesh. Put mango and passionfruit flesh into a food processor or blender. Whizz to a purée. Alternatively, rub through a strainer. Put lemon juice, sugar, and $2/3$ cup water into a pan. Heat just until sugar dissolves. Stir into fruit purée. Leave to cool. Turn fruit purée into a rigid, freezerproof container. Cover, seal, and freeze until firm, stirring once or twice during freezing. Transfer sherbet to refrigerator 15 minutes before serving, to soften.

4 servings

STRAWBERRY ICE

2¹/₂ cups strawberries, hulled
scant 1 cup superfine sugar
1 tablespoon lemon juice
1 egg white

Put strawberries, sugar, and lemon juice into a food processor or blender. Blend to a purée. Beat egg white in a bowl until stiff. Fold into purée. Pour into a shallow freezer tray or rigid freezerproof container. Freeze until firm. An hour before serving, transfer to refrigerator, to soften a little. Scoop into glass dishes to serve.

4 servings

PEACH WATER ICE

¹/₂ cup sugar
4 large peaches
juice of 1 lemon

Put sugar with ²/₃ cup water into a small pan over low heat. When sugar has completely dissolved, boil rapidly for 5 minutes. Leave until completely cold. Skin and pit peaches (see page 306). Without delay, purée flesh in a food processor or blender, or press through a nylon strainer. Mix with lemon juice to prevent discoloration. Stir in cold syrup. Pour into a shallow freezer tray or rigid freezerproof container. Freeze until firm. An hour before before serving, transfer to refrigerator, to soften a little. Scoop into glass dishes to serve.

4 servings

COFFEE WATER ICE

2$^1/_2$ cups finely ground Continental roast coffee, plus extra to decorate
6 tablespoons sugar
whipped cream, to serve

Put coffee and sugar into a warmed earthenware pitcher or heatproof bowl. Pour over 4$^1/_4$ cups boiling water. Leave to infuse for 20-30 minutes. Leave to cool. When cold, strain through a filter paper. Pour into a shallow freezer tray or rigid freezerproof container. Freeze, without stirring, until frozen to a granular but solid mush. Serve in tall glasses, with a spoon, topped with a whirl of whipped cream and sprinkling of ground coffee.
4-6 servings

CHILLED DESSERTS
RHUBARB FOOL

1 pound rhubarb, coarsely chopped
$^1/_2$ cup packed light brown sugar
grated zest of 1 small orange
about 1 cup heavy cream

Put rhubarb into a pan with very little water, sugar, and orange zest over low heat. Simmer until tender. Drain and leave to cool. Whip cream until it just holds its shape. Fold into rhubarb. Spoon into glass dishes.
4 servings

CHILLED RASPBERRY FOOL

1$^2/_3$ cups raspberries
$^1/_4$ cup superfine sugar
grated zest and juice of $^1/_2$ orange
1 cup heavy or whipping cream

Reserve 4 raspberries. Put remainder into a food processor or blender with sugar and orange zest and juice. Purée until smooth. Rub raspberry purée through a nylon strainer to remove pips. Put cream into a large bowl. Whip until thick. Fold raspberry purée lightly but thoroughly into cream. Spoon fool into 4 stemmed glasses. Chill for 3-4 hours. Decorate with reserved raspberries before serving.

4 servings

COOK'S KNOW-HOW
If you don't have any superfine sugar, grind ordinary white sugar in a coffee grinder to make it finer.

STRAWBERRY AND ORANGE CRUSH

1²/₃ cups strawberries, hulled
2 tablespoons superfine sugar
1-2 tablespoons Cointreau or other orange liqueur
1 cup heavy or whipping cream

Reserve 4-6 strawberries for decoration. Put remainder into a food processor or blender with sugar. Briefly process to combine. Put liqueur and cream into a bowl. Whip until stiff. Fold strawberry mixture into cream. Spoon into individual glass dishes. Slice reserved strawberries and use to decorate. Chill for at least 30 minutes before serving.

4 servings

IRISH WHISKEY SYLLABUB

grated zest and juice of 1 large lemon
6 tablespoons clear honey
¹/₂ cup Irish whiskey
1¹/₄ cups heavy cream, chilled

Put lemon zest and juice, honey, and whiskey into a large bowl. Let stand as long as possible for flavors to develop. Gradually beat in cream until mixture begins to thicken. Spoon into wine glasses. Chill until required. If left for several hours, the syllabub will separate into a thick cream on top and clear liquid at the bottom.

4-6 servings

COFFEE CHESTNUT WHIP

15 ounce can unsweetened chestnut purée

2 teaspoons instant coffee

$^1/_2$ cup superfine sugar

$^2/_3$ cup heavy or whipping cream

Mash chestnut purée until softened in a bowl. Dissolve instant coffee in $^1/_4$ cup boiling water. Beat into chestnust purée with sugar. Whip cream until soft peaks form. Fold lightly into chestnut mixture. Spoon into four tall glasses. Chill for 30 minutes before serving.

4 servings

DATE AND NUT HONEYED YOGURT

5 tablespoons clear honey

2 tablespoons chopped fresh dates

$^2/_3$ cup thick plain yogurt

2 tablespoons chopped pistachio nuts or almonds

Spoon 2 tablespoons honey into bottom of two straight-sided glasses. Sprinkle dates on top. Spoon over yogurt. Sprinkle with nuts and drizzle over remaining honey. Chill for 30 mintues before serving.

2 servings

CHERRY CHOCOLATE POTS

15 ounce can pitted bing cherries, drained

$^1/_4$ pound semisweet chocolate, plus extra to decorate

4 eggs, separated

2 tablespoons/^{1}/$_4$ stick butter

Divide cherries between six small, deep dishes. Break chocolate into pieces. Melt in a heatproof bowl over a pan of simmering water. Remove chocolate from heat. Beat in egg yolks and butter. Beat egg whites in a separate bowl until stiff. Fold lightly into chocolate mixture. Spoon into dishes. Chill in the refrigerator for at least 2 hours. Shave an extra piece of chocolate with a vegetable peeler. Decorate pots with shavings and serve.

6 servings

GINGER ORANGE TRIFLE

6 oranges
1 pound ginger cake
2^1/$_2$ cups heavy or whipping cream, whipped

Remove peel and pith from 3 of the oranges. Slice flesh very thinly. Remove any pips. Line sides of a glass bowl or dish with orange slices. Slice ginger cake. Squeeze juice from 2 of the remaining oranges. Sprinkle over cake. Arrange cake on top of orange slices. Top with cream. Remove peel and pith from remaining orange. Cut into segments with a serrated knife. Use to decorate top of trifle. Cover and chill for at least 1 hour.

4 servings

ICED CHOCOLATE MOUSSE WITH WHIPPED CREAM

4 eggs, separated
^{1}/$_2$ cup superfine sugar
^{1}/$_4$ pound semisweet chocolate, broken into pieces
1^1/$_4$ cups heavy cream

Put egg yolks and sugar into a bowl. Beat with a hand-held beater, until mixture is thick and fluffy. Melt chocolate with 3 tablespoons water in a heatproof bowl over a pan of gently simmering water. Remove from heat and cool slightly. Beat chocolate into egg yolk mixture. Whip cream until soft peaks form. Carefully fold into chocolate mixture. Beat egg whites in a bowl until stiff. Carefully fold 1 tablespoon into mousse, then fold in remainder. Pour mixture into 8 individual dishes. Chill.

8 servings

MANDARIN CREAMS

2 x 11 ounce cans mandarin orange segments
2 x $^1/_4$ ounce envelopes gelatin
$^2/_3$ cup sour cream
$^2/_3$ cup plain yogurt

Drain juice from mandarins into a measuring cup. Make up to $1^1/_4$ cups with cold water. Reserve a few segments for decoration. Roughly chop remainder. Put gelatin into a small heatproof bowl with half the measured juice. Stand in a pan with water to come halfway up sides of bowl. Leave, stirring occasionally, until gelatin dissolves. Add remaining juice. Leave in a cool place until just beginning to set. Fold in chopped fruit, sour cream, and yogurt. Spoon into individual serving dishes. Refrigerate until set. Decorate with reserved segments before serving.

6-8 servings

ORANGE CREAM CRUNCH

3 tablespoons medium oatmeal
6 tablespoons clear honey
grated zest and juice of 1 orange, plus slices for decorating
$1^1/_4$ cups heavy or whipping cream

Spread oatmeal evenly on a cookie sheet. Broil under medium heat for 2-3 minutes, until golden brown. Leave to cool. Put remaining ingredients into a bowl. Lightly whip for 3-5 minutes with a hand-held electric beater. Stir in toasted oatmeal. Decorate with orange slices. Refrigerate until required.   4 servings

YOGURT LAYERED CRUNCH

$^2/_3$ cup fruit yogurt
$^1/_4$ cup low-fat soft cheese, ricotta, or mascarpone cheese
2 tablespoons heavy cream
$^2/_3$ cup graham cracker or cookie crumbs

Combine yogurt and cheese in a bowl. Whip cream lightly with a fork
to thicken. Fold into yogurt mixture. Spoon into individual tall glasses
layered with graham cracker or cookie crumbs.

2 servings

CHOCOLATE LAYERED CRUNCH

2 cups whole-wheat bread crumbs
$^2/_3$ cup packed light brown sugar
6 tablespoons drinking chocolate powder
1 cup whipping cream

Combine bread crumbs, sugar, and chocolate. Mix well. Lightly whip
cream. Arrange layers of cream and bread crumb mixture in tall glasses.
Finish with a bread crumb layer, topped with a spoonful of cream. Chill
for 1 hour before serving.

6 servings

PINEAPPLE GINGER CHANTILLY

2 x 8 ounce cans crushed pineapple
$1^1/_4$ cups heavy cream
$^1/_4$ cup confectioner's sugar
8 ounce package gingersnaps

Drain pineapple. Whip cream until thick. Fold in pineapple and sugar.
Reserve 2-3 gingersnaps. Sandwich remaining cookies, one on top of the
other, with half the cream. Carefully put the roll on its side. Wrap in

waxed paper or aluminum foil. Refrigerate for at least 2-3 hours or overnight. To serve, put roll on a serving plate. Cover with remaining cream. Crush reserved gingersnaps. Sprinkle over cream. Serve sliced obliquely for a decorative effect.

6-8 servings

PINEAPPLE AND AMARETTI ROLL

1 large ripe pineapple
2 cups heavy cream
1¼ cups amaretti crumbs
2 tablespoons Kirsch

Remove and halve green top of pineapple. Reserve best half for decoration. Cut away skin from pineapple, removing "eyes" with the point of a knife. Slice, then cut each slice in half. Dry on paper towels. Remove cores. Lightly whip cream, reserving one third. Stir amaretti crumbs into remaining cream. Sandwich half-slices of pineapple together with cream mixture, to form a half roll on a serving plate. Stir Kirsch into reserved cream. Cover pineapple completely. Mark cream to look like pineapple skin, if you like. Replace green top. Chill until required.

8 servings

COOKIES AND CANDY

COOKIE CLASSICS

SHORTBREAD FINGERS

16 tablespoons/2 sticks/1 cup butter
$^1/_2$ cup superfine sugar, plus extra for sprinkling
scant $^1/_2$ cup cornstarch
$2^1/_2$ cups all-purpose flour

Beat butter and sugar together in a bowl until light and fluffy. Sift in 2 flours and mix well to combine. Press mixture into a rectangular baking pan about 12 x 8 inches. Mark with tines of a fork. Bake in a preheated oven, 275°F, for 30 minutes. Reduce temperature to 250°F and cook for 1-1$^1/_2$ hours more. Remove from oven. Cut into 32 fingers. Sprinkle with sugar. Leave to cool slightly in pan before transferring to a wire rack to cool completely.
Makes 32

MELTING MOMENTS

6 tablespoons/$^3/_4$ stick butter
$^3/_4$ cup confectioner's sugar
$^1/_4$ cup all-purpose flour
$^3/_4$ cup cornstarch

Beat butter and sugar together in a bowl until very soft and light. Sift flour and cornstarch together. Work into butter and sugar mixture. Put into a pastry bag fitted with a large rose tip. Pipe into neat shapes onto greased cookie sheets. Bake in the center of a preheated oven, 350-375°F, for 15 minutes. Remove and leave to cool on cookie sheets. To make Chocolate Melting Moments, use $^1/_4$ cup cocoa powder in place of flour.
Makes about 18

COCONUT MACAROONS

2 medium egg whites
$^5/_8$-$^3/_4$ cup superfine sugar
about scant 2 cups dry unsweetened shredded coconut
5-6 glacé cherries

Beat egg whites in a bowl until frothy but not stiff. Add sugar. Stir in coconut steadily (you may need less, depending on size of egg whites). The mixture should just roll into balls—about 10-12. Transfer to lightly greased cookie sheets. Allow room for mixture to flatten out during cooking. Press half a glacé cherry on top of each cookie. Bake in center of a preheated oven, 350-375°F, for 18-20 minutes. Remove from cookie sheets when nearly cold.
Makes 10-12

OATMEAL MACAROONS

2 medium egg whites
$^5/_8$-$^3/_4$ cup superfine sugar
about 1$^3/_4$ cups rolled oats
5-6 glacé cherries

Make in the same way as Coconut Macaroons (see above), but using rolled oats in place of coconut.
Makes 10-12

ALMOND MACAROONS

2 medium egg whites
$^5/_8$-$^3/_4$ cup superfine sugar
1$^1/_2$ cups ground almonds, plus 10-12 blanched almond halves
almond essence

Make in the same as Coconut Macaroons (see page 325), but using ground almonds in place of coconut, adding a few drops almond essence to mixture, and topping with almond halves in place of glacé cherries.
Makes 10-12

VIENNESE WHIRLS

6 tablespoons/^{3}/$_4$ stick butter
^{1}/$_4$ cup confectioner's sugar, plus extra for dusting
^{3}/$_4$ cup all-purpose flour
about 10 glacé cherries, halved

Beat butter and sugar together in a bowl until light and fluffy. Sift flour with a little salt into a separate bowl. Gradually add to butter mixture, beating well after each addition, until mixture is smooth. Spoon dough into a pastry bag fitted with a 1 inch star tip. Pipe stars about 1^1/$_4$ inches in diameter onto cookie sheets. Decorate with glacé cherry halves. Bake in a preheated oven, 400-425°F, for 8-10 minutes. Leave to cool on sheets before removing. Dust with confectioner's sugar.
Makes about 20

CHOCOLATE CHIP COOKIES

8 tablespoons/1 stick/^{1}/$_2$ cup butter, softened
^{1}/$_4$ cup superfine sugar
1 cup all-purpose flour
^{1}/$_3$ cup chocolate chips

Beat butter and sugar together in a bowl until light and fluffy. Add chocolate, then stir in flour. Put about 16 spoonfuls of mixture onto greased cookie sheets, leaving space for cookies to spread. Bake in a preheated oven, 375°F, for 15-20 minutes. Allow to cool on sheets.
Makes about 16

PEANUT COOKIES

8 tablespoons/1 stick/$^1/_2$ cup soft margarine
$^1/_2$ cup superfine sugar
$1^1/_4$ cups self-rising flour
$^1/_3$ cup chopped peanuts

Beat margarine and sugar together in a bowl until light and fluffy. Sift in flour and stir in nuts. Blend to form a dough. Put $1^1/_2$ inch balls of dough onto greased baking sheets. Bake in a preheated oven, 350°F, for 15–20 minutes. Leave to cool on sheets.
Makes about 20

ALMOND COOKIES

12 tablespoons/$1^1/_2$ sticks/$^3/_4$ cup butter
$^1/_2$ cup packed light brown sugar
2 cups all-purpose flour
$^1/_2$ cup finely chopped almonds

Beat butter and sugar together until light and fluffy. Sift in flour with a little salt and stir in almonds. Blend to form a dough. Form into a 10 inch long roll on a lightly floured surface. Wrap dough in aluminum foil and chill for a few minutes. Cut roll into $^1/_4$ inch thick slices. Transfer to greased cookie sheets, spacing a little apart. Bake in a preheated oven, 325°F, for 15–20 minutes. Leave to cool on sheets.
Makes about 40

QUICK PECAN COOKIES

8 tablespoons/1 stick/$^1/_2$ cup butter or margarine
$^1/_4$ cup superfine sugar
1 cup all-purpose flour
$^1/_2$ cup chopped pecan nuts

Beat butter or margarine and sugar together in a bowl until light and fluffy. Stir in flour and nuts. Put small teaspoonfuls of dough onto greased cookie sheets, leaving space in between for cookies to spread. Bake for 15–20 minutes. Leave to cool on sheets.

Makes about 18

GINGER DROP COOKIES

8 tablespoons/1 stick/$^1/_2$ cup butter or margarine
$^1/_2$ cup superfine sugar
2 teaspoons ground ginger
1 cup self-rising flour

Beat butter or margarine and sugar together until soft but not light. Stir in ginger, then sift in flour. Blend to make a stiff dough. Form into about 25 balls. Transfer to greased cookie sheets, leaving space in between for cookies to spread. Bake in a preheated oven, 250°F, for 30–40 minutes. Leave to cool on sheets.

Makes about 25

MORE COOKIES
ORANGE COOKIES

2 cups all-purpose flour
10 tablespoons/$^5/_8$ cup butter or margarine
$^1/_2$–$^3/_4$ cup superfine sugar
very finely grated zest of 1–2 oranges

Sift flour into a bowl. Cut in butter or margarine until fine crumbs form. Add half the sugar and orange zest. Knead firmly and work in remaining sugar. The dough should not need any liquid, but if necessary, add a few drops orange juice. Put dough onto a very lightly floured surface. Form into a long 2–2$^1/_2$ inch diameter roll. Wrap in aluminum foil and chill for a few minutes. Cut into thin slices with a sharp knife.

Put onto ungreased cookie sheets (they should not spread). Prick lightly with a fork. Bake in the center of a preheated oven, 325-350°F, for 10-12 minutes. Cool on cookie sheets.
Makes 14-18

OATMEAL COOKIES

2 cups self-rising flour
1¹/₃ cups medium oatmeal
10 tablespoons/⁵/₈ cup butter or margarine
2 tablespoons golden syrup or corn syrup

Sift flour into a bowl with a little salt. Stir in oatmeal. Cut in butter or margarine. Dissolve syrup in a small pan with 2 tablespoons hot water. Add to mixture and knead well. Gradually add another 2 tablespoons hot water, or as much as is required to create a firm rolling consistency. Roll out on a lightly floured surface to about ¹/₄ inch thick. Cut into small or large rounds. Mark into 4 triangles. Transfer to lightly greased cookie sheets. Bake in center of a preheated oven, 325-350°F, for about 15 minutes. Cool on sheets, then lift off carefully.
Makes 20-24

CHOCOLATE STARS

scant 1 cup all-purpose flour
1 heaped tablespoon cocoa powder
6 tablespoons/³/₄ stick butter or margarine
about 2 tablespoons golden syrup or corn syrup

Sift flour and cocoa powder together into a bowl. Beat butter or margarine together with syrup until soft and light. Work in flour mixture. Put into a pastry bag with a large rose tip. Pipe large stars onto greased cookie sheets. Bake in the center of a preheated oven, 325°F, for about 15 minutes, until firm. Cool on sheets.
Makes 20-24

DATE AND LEMON FINGERS

2^1/$_4$ cups cookie crumbs
finely grated zest of 1 lemon, plus about 1 tablespoon lemon juice
1^1/$_4$ cups pitted dates, chopped
up to ^{2}/$_3$ cup sweetened condensed milk

Put cookie crumbs into a bowl. Add lemon zest and juice and dates.
Mix well. Add enough condensed milk to bind. Lightly grease an 8 inch
tart or shallow cake pan. Turn mixture into pan and smooth flat. Cover
and refrigerate overnight. Cut into small wedges or fingers.

Makes 16 small wedges or fingers

GRANOLA AND CHOCOLATE ORANGE FINGERS

^{1}/$_4$ pound semisweet, or bitter or unsweetened chocolate
^{1}/$_2$ pound fruit and nut granola
finely grated zest of 1 orange, plus 2 tablespoons orange juice
up to ^{2}/$_3$ cup sweetened condensed milk

Break chocolate into pieces and melt in a heatproof bowl over
simmering water. Put granola into a separate bowl. Stir in orange zest and
juice, then chocolate. Mix well. Add enough condensed milk to bind.
Turn mixture into a lightly greased tart or shallow cake pan and smooth
flat. Cover and refrigerate overnight. Cut into small wedges or fingers.

Makes 16 small wedges or fingers

BROWN SUGAR COOKIES

12 tablespoons/1^1/$_2$ sticks/^{3}/$_4$ cup butter
^{1}/$_2$ cup packed light brown sugar
2 cups all-purpose flour

Beat butter and sugar together in a bowl until light. Beat in flour and
blend until smooth. Form into a roll on a lightly floured surface. Wrap in

aluminum foil and chill for a few minutes, until firm. Cut into $^1/_4$ inch slices. Transfer to greased cookie sheets. Bake in a preheated oven, 350°F, for about 20 minutes. Leave to cool on sheets.

Makes about 18

BUTTER COOKIES

2 cups all-purpose flour
10 tablespoons/$^5/_8$ cup butter
generous 1 cup superfine sugar
1 egg yolk

Sift flour into a bowl. Cut in butter until fine crumbs form. Stir in sugar with a little salt. Work in egg yolk until a stiff dough forms. Roll out on a lightly floured surface about $^1/_4$ inch thick. Cut into rounds with a pastry cutter. Transfer to greased cookie sheets. Prick lightly with a fork. Bake in a preheated oven, 375°F, for about 35 minutes. Leave to cool on sheets.

Makes about 18

COCONUT AND GINGER DELIGHTS

$2^2/_3$ cups dry unsweetened shredded coconut
$^2/_3$ cup sweetened condensed milk
$^1/_4$ cup candied ginger, chopped

Beat coconut into condensed milk in a bowl a little at a time until well blended. Form into about 26 balls. Transfer to greased baking sheets. Decorate with candied ginger. Bake in a preheated oven, 400°F, for 10-15 minutes. Leave to cool on sheets.

Makes about 26

COCONUT DROPS

2 egg whites
$^1/_2$ cup sugar
$2^2/_3$ cups dry unsweetened shredded coconut

Beat egg whites in a bowl until stiff. Add sugar and coconut. Beat until well blended. Line baking sheets with greased baking parchment. Put teaspoonfuls of dough onto paper. Bake in a preheated oven, 350°F, for 15–20 minutes. Leave to cool on sheets.

Makes about 28

ALMOND AND COCONUT FINGERS

$2^1/_4$ cups amaretti or macaroon crumbs
$^2/_3$ cup dry unsweetened shredded coconut
8 tablespoons/1 stick/$^1/_2$ cup butter or margarine
$^7/_8$ cup condensed milk

Mix together cookie crumbs and coconut in a bowl. Melt butter or margarine and add to bowl with condensed milk. Mix together until well blended. Press mixture into a jelly roll pan. Cover and refrigerate for several hours or overnight. Cut into fingers.

Makes 24

COOK'S KNOW-HOW
When completely cold, store cookies in an airtight container. Do not store in the same container as cakes, since they will cause the cookies to soften.

CANDY FAVORITES

PEANUT FONDANTS

$2^2/_3$ cups confectioner's sugar
pinch cream of tartar
$^1/_4$ cup chopped unsalted peanuts
1 egg white

Sift sugar and cream of tartar into a large bowl. Add peanuts. Gradually add egg white, drawing mixture together with a spatula. Knead into a smooth ball. Form small pieces into miniature rolls. Put into candy paper shells. Leave to set.

Makes about 36

PEPPERMINT AND VANILLA FONDANTS

$1^3/_4$ cups confectioner's sugar
2 tablespoons condensed milk
peppermint or vanilla essence
grated chocolate or chopped pistachio nuts

Sift sugar into a bowl. Blend in milk until smooth and creamy. Flavor with a few drops of peppermint or vanilla essence. Roll into balls and coat with grated chocolate or chopped pistachios. Press into candy molds and leave to set. Remove and serve.

Makes about 25

ALMOND DATES

1 box dates
blanched almonds
$^1/_2$ pound marzipan
superfine sugar

Split dates open and remove pits. Wrap an almond for each date in a small piece of marzipan. Form into a roll and fill date cavity. Mark marzipan with a criss-cross pattern. Roll filled dates in sugar. Put into paper candy shells.

COCONUT ICE

2$^2/_3$ cups confectioner's sugar, plus extra for dusting
4 tablespoons condensed milk
2 cups dry unsweetened shredded coconut
1 drop red food coloring

Put sugar into a bowl. Blend in milk. Stir in coconut and divide in half. Tint one half pale pink with food coloring. Shape both portions of mixture into identically sized bars. Press firmly together. Dust a plate with sugar. Put coconut ice on plate and leave until firm.

PECAN PRALINE

2 cups packed light brown sugar
$^1/_2$ cup milk
4 tablespoons/$^1/_2$ stick/$^1/_4$ cup butter
1 cup chopped pecan nuts

Put all the ingredients into a heavy-bottomed pan over low heat, until sugar and butter have melted. Bring to a boil and cook to "soft ball stage"—a teaspoon of mixture dropped in cold water should form a soft ball. Remove from heat. Stir until mixture thickens and becomes creamy. Put spoonfuls onto aluminum foil or waxed paper. Leave to cool.
Makes about 20

CREAM CANDY

1$\frac{1}{2}$ cups milk
2 teaspoons Angostura bitters
4$\frac{1}{4}$ cups sugar
8 tablespoons/1 stick/$\frac{1}{2}$ cup butter

Put milk, bitters, and sugar into a pan over low heat, until sugar dissolves. Add butter. Bring to a boil. Continue boiling to 255°F or "hard ball stage"—a teaspoon of mixture dropped in cold water should form a fairly hard ball. Stir to prevent burning. Remove from heat. Beat until mixture thickens and becomes creamy. Very quickly spread into a well-greased baking pan. Mark into squares. Leave to cool. Cut into squares when cold and set.

Makes about 40 squares

TREACLE TOFFEE

8 tablespoons/1 stick/$\frac{1}{2}$ cup butter
$\frac{1}{3}$ cup black treacle
$\frac{3}{4}$ cup packed light brown sugar
pinch cream of tartar

Put butter, treacle, and sugar with 2$\frac{1}{2}$ tablespoons water in a pan over low heat, until butter has melted and sugar dissolved. Add cream of tartar. Boil to 260°F. Pour into a greased 6 inch square pan. When starting to set, mark into squares with a greased knife. Leave until cold. Break up into 1 inch squares.

Makes 36 squares

FUDGE

2 cups and 2 tablespoons sugar
$\frac{2}{3}$ cup evaporated milk

4 tablespoon/$^1/_2$ stick/$^1/_4$ cup butter

Put all ingredients into a large pan with $^2/_3$ cup water over low heat, until sugar dissolves. Bring to a boil. Boil to 240°F or "soft ball stage"—a teaspoon of mixture dropped in cold water should form a soft ball. Remove from heat. Add flavoring. Beat until mixture thickens and becomes creamy. Pour into a greased 6 inch square pan. Leave to set. Cut into squares when cold.

Makes 36

VANILLA FLAVOR

Add $^1/_2$ teaspoon vanilla essence.

COFFEE FLAVOR

Add 2 teaspoons coffee essence.

CHOCOLATE FLAVOR

Use $^1/_4$ pound semisweet chocolate and an extra 4 tablespoons/$^1/_2$ stick/$^1/_4$ cup butter in place of water.

MENUS

EVERYDAY EATING

COMFORT COOKING FOR 4

LIGHT MEAL

Chorizo and Bean Soup, page 54
Sesame Seed Slices, page 59

MAIN MEAL

Creamy Fish Bake, page 174
Mashed Potatoes with Cilantro, page 113

Maple Syrup and Macaroon Baked Apple, page 302

LIGHT MEAL

Baked Potatoes with Ham, Cheese, and Corn Filling, page 28
Spiced Cole Slaw, page 89

MAIN MEAL

Crispy-baked Chicken, page 185
Scalloped Potatoes with Onions, page 111
Glazed Baby Carrots, page 106

Marshmallow-topped Fruit, page 303

LIGHT MEAL

Pepperoni and Mushroom Omelet, page 17
mixed leaf salad
crusty bread

MAIN MEAL

Seafood Pilau, page 130
Tomato and Cilantro Salad, page 91

Pears in Chocolate Sauce, page 306

LIGHT MEAL

Chunky Pan-fried Sandwich, page 32
tomato quarters

MAIN MEAL

Pork and Apple Packages, page 240
Bubble and Squeak, page 26

Apricot Crumble, page 294

LIGHT MEAL

Eggplant and Mozzarella Filled Tortillas, page 30
green salad

MAIN MEAL

Pappardelle with Pesto and Potatoes, page 118
Zucchini with Oregano, page 106

Orange Cream Crunch, page 319

HEALTHY EATING DAYS FOR 4

BREAKFAST

Sunshine Cocktail, page 14

LUNCH

Baked Potatoes with Tuna and Bean Filling, page 28
mixed salad

MAIN MEAL

Lamb with Zucchini, page 280
Artichoke and Bell Pepper Stir-fry, page 110

Apricot Swirl, page 290

BREAKFAST

Spiced Dried Fruit Cup, served with low-fat or nonfat plain yogurt,
page 15

LUNCH

Zucchini and Pimiento Chilled Soup, page 52
crusty whole-wheat bread

MAIN MEAL

Shrimp and Cilantro Couscous 131
mixed leaf salad

Marshmallow and Fruit Kabobs, page 289

BREAKFAST

Cranberry and Blueberry Smoothie (double quantity), made with low-fat plain yogurt, page 223

LUNCH

Bean Pâté, page 275
Crudités and Pita Chips, pages 44–5

MAIN MEAL

Steamed Chicken with Bok Choy, page 281
Potato and Avocado Purée, page 112

Grape and Yogurt Layered Dessert, page 290

HEALTHY EATING DAYS FOR 2

BREAKFAST

Minted Strawberries with Avocado, page 14

LUNCH

Swiss Cheese and Apple Cocktail, made with low-fat or nonfat plain yogurt, page 50

MAIN MEAL

Chili Seafood Pasta (half quantity), page 283
mixed salad

Spiced Bananas, page 289

BREAKFAST

Mango and Melon Melange, page 15

LUNCH

Turkey and Apple Cole Slaw, page 285
crusty whole-wheat bread

MAIN MEAL

Salmon and Sweet Potato Patties, page 277
lightly cooked broccoli flowerets

Summer Berries with Orange Sauce, page 289

BREAKFAST

Spiced Peach and Almond Smoothie, made with low-fat plain yogurt, page 223

LUNCH

Tuna Terrine (half quantity), page 274
sliced tomatoes
whole-wheat toast

MAIN MEAL

Pork Chops with Tomatoes and Oregano, page 282
lightly cooked green beans or fava beans

Griddled Figs with Yogurt and Honey, made with low-fat or nonfat plain yogurt, page 306

FAST FOOD FOR 4

LIGHT MEAL

Potato, Cheddar, and Pimiento Wrap, page 65
crisp salad

MAIN MEAL

Pea and Mint Soup, page 274

Spaghetti with Cherry Tomatoes and Cilantro, page 264
mixed leaf salad with Parmesan shavings

Panettone with Peaches and Cream, page 305

LIGHT MEAL

Hot Salsa Shrimp Filled Tortillas, page 30
green salad

MAIN MEAL

Chicken Liver Pâté, page 43

Honeyed Pork Chops, page 243
Parsnip and Carrot Sour Cream Mash, page 115

Pineapple with Rumbled Mascarpone, page 305

LIGHT MEAL

Smoked Chicken and Arugula Salad, page 93
crusty bread

MAIN MEAL

Asparagus Soup, page 55

Trout with Almonds, page 163
Mashed Potatoes with Pesto and Parmesan, page 113
lightly cooked leeks

Crispy-topped Banana Rice, page 304

FAST FOOD FOR 2

LIGHT MEAL

Asparagus with Eggs and Parmesan, page 267

MAIN MEAL

Crabmeat with Ginger Soup, page 56

Steak with Smoked Oysters, page 236
Griddled Warm New Potatoes (half quantity), page 112
lightly cooked green beans

Date and Nut Honeyed Yogurt, page 317

LIGHT MEAL

Salami Stack, page 31

MAIN MEAL

Egg and Shrimp Mayonnaise, page 49
Chicken and Rice, page 184; cooked frozen peas

Bananas in Coconut Milk, page 305

LIGHT MEAL

Fresh Herb Omelet, page 17
mixed salad

MAIN MEAL

Broiled Haloumi Cheese and Beefsteak Tomatoes, page 51

Broiled Salmon with Spiced Sour Cream, page 167
boiled new potatoes
lightly cooked broccoli flowerets or snowpeas

Yogurt Layered Crunch, page 320

FOOD FOR TWO

WEEKEND BRUNCHES

Scrambled Eggs with Smoked Salmon, page 20
Shrimp and Chili Soufflé Omelet, page 18
Potato and Bacon Patties, page 24
Corned Beef Hash, page 25
Egg-fried Swiss Cheese Sandwich, page 32

SWEET TREATS

Chocolate Crispies, page 74
Mille Feuilles Slices, page 292
Strawberry, Vanilla, and Mint Shake, page 222
Banana, Chocolate, and Peanut Butter Smoothie, page 225
Chocolate Truffles, page 158

ROMANTIC DINING

Crabmeat and Papaya Cocktail, page 49

Steaks with Blue Cheese, page 235
boiled new potatoes or Griddled Warm New Potatoes (half quantity),
page 112
lightly cooked spinach

Baked Rum Bananas (half quantity), page 300

Timbales of Smoked Salmon, page 161

Creamed Chicken with Zucchini, page 189
Mashed Potatoes with Cheddar and Scallions (half quantity), page 114

Chocolate Peach Puffs (half quantity), page 293

Quick Gazpacho, page 53

Haddock with Sour Cream and Mushrooms, page 170
New Potatoes with Lemon and Thyme (half quantity), page 112

Caramel-topped Rice Pudding, page 308

EASY ENTERTAINING

SUMMER LUNCH FOR 8

Figs with Parma Ham (double quantity), page 34

Fish Steaks with Ginger (double quantity), page 177
Shrimp Couscous Salad, page 98

Roasted Asparagus with Cilantro and Lime, page 36

Summer Pudding, page 307

Indian Tea Punch, page 213

BARBECUE FOR 6

Spiced Skewered Shrimp, page 81
pita bread brushed with Garlic or Chili Oil, page 102, cooked on
barbecue rack until puffed up

Skewered Lamb Koftas, page 75
Tomato and Cilantro Salsa, page 84
Sweet Potato and Mushroom Kabobs, page 82

Peaches with Gingersnaps, page 83

SUMMER LUNCHES FOR 4

Avocado-stuffed Tomatoes, page 254

Asparagus Omelet page 16
Mixed Leaf Salad with Pecan Cheese Balls, page 92

Mango and Passionfruit Sherbet, page 313

Shrimp and Avocado Cocktail, page 49

Warm Duck and Orange Salad, page 93
Potato Salad, page 88

Chilled Raspberry Fool, page 315

Fava Bean and Mint Dip 38
Crudités and Pita Fingers, pages 44–5

Broiled Salmon Steaks with Cucumber and Chive Sauce, page 164
New Potatoes with Lemon and Thyme, page 112

Strawberry and Orange Crush, page 316

FORMAL DINNERS FOR 4

Proscuitto and Melon, page 34

Griddled Lobster Tails with Oregano Butter, page 160
Fennel Baked with Cream and Parmesan, page 107
boiled new potatoes with mint

Spiced Caramel Oranges with Apricots, page 304

Bell Pepper and Tuna Rolls, page 37

Veal with Cream Sauce, page 232
Peperonata, page 108
Roast Potatoes with Rosemary and Garlic, page 111

Melon and Raspberries in Sauternes, page 302

Pear and Blue Cheese Salad, page 36

Tagliatelle Verde with Snowpeas and Lemon, page 263
Beets with Parmesan, page 258

Coffee Chestnut Whip, page 317

Liver Pâté, page 42

Crispy Roast Duck with Orange, page 199
Potatoes and Spinach with Ginger, page 108

Crème Brûlée, page 310

Pan-fried Scallops with Bacon, page 46

Mustard Beef, page 242
Scalloped Potatoes with Onions, page 111

Ricotta and Rum Bombe, page 312

French Onion Soup, page 57
Swiss Cheese Toasts, page 60

Spinach Tart, page 268
Charbroiled Bell Peppers, page 36

Caramelized Oranges with Pineapple, page 303

CASUAL BRUNCH FOR 6

Proscuitto and Mozzarella Slices, page 22

Spanish Tortilla, page 20
Mushroom and Sour Cream Filled Tortillas, page 29
Chicken and Charbroiled Bell Pepper Filled Tortillas, page 29
mixed leaf salad

Grape Meringue Pie, page 298

Orchard Punch, page 212

MAKE-AHEAD LUNCH FOR 8

Cucumber and Strawberry Salad (double quantity), page 34

Coronation Chicken (double quantity), page 185
Spiced Fruit and Nut Rice Salad (combine cooked rice, fruits, and nuts; cover and refrigerate until required; bring to room temperature and toss with melted cumin butter before serving), page 97
Tabbouleh, page 99

Pineapple and Amaretti Roll, page 321

INFORMAL VEGETARIAN DINNER FOR 8

Crispy Potato Skins page 26
Spicy Sweet Potato Wedges, page 26
Avocado and Chili Dip and Cilantro and Yogurt Dip, page 27

Eggplant, Tomato, and Mozzarella Mountains (double quantity), page 259
Pasta Salad with Asparagus and Pine Nuts, page 265
Zucchini and Cherry Tomato Pasta Salad, page 96

Pineapple Ice Cream 311
gingersnaps or Ginger Drop Cookies, page 328

CELEBRATION DINNER FOR 8

Baked Scallops with Butter and Breadcrumbs (double quantity), page 46

Beef Olives (double quantity; cook in bottom of oven at 350°F for scallops), page 234
Parsnip and Potato Mash with Roasted Garlic (cook garlic in top of

oven for about 1 hour 15 minutes, until soft), page 114
Honey-glazed Turnips, page 106
lightly cooked green beans

Iced Chocolate Mousse with Whipped Cream, page 318

FINGER BUFFET FOR 18-20

Curried Nuts, page 152
Spicy-glazed Cashews, page 153

Spicy Sausage Rolls, page 138
Phyllo Pastry Parcels with Ricotta and Spinach and Feta and Mint,
page 140

Filled Cherry Tomatoes, page 142
Walnut and Gorgonzola Chicory, page 142
10 Tricolore Toothpick Kabobs, page 148
10 Chevre and Black Olive Toothpick Kabobs, page 149
10 Melon and Parma Ham Toothpick Kabobs, page 149

Sesame Chicken Skewers (double quantity), page 144
Shrimp Saté (double quantity), page 145
Beef Saté (double quantity), page 146
Ginger and Chili Dip, page 146
Peanut and Chili Dip, page 147

Mango and Pineapple with Chocolate Sauce (double quantity; serve
sauce warm), page 73
Coconut Rum Rockies, page 157
Chocolate Truffles, page 158

Kir Punch, page 215

INDEX

e

f

ham and pineapple 64

peanut butter and banana 65

pesto, cheddar, and pimiento 65

salmon and cream cheese 65

tuna and bell pepper 64

NOTES & RECIPES

NOTES & RECIPES

NOTES & RECIPES

NOTES & RECIPES

NOTES & RECIPES